Reminiscences of

Admiral Arleigh Burke, USN
Retired

Volume II
Special Series on Selected Subjects

Oral History Office
U. S. Naval Institute
Annapolis, Maryland

Preface

This is volume II in the special series of taped interviews with Admiral Arleigh Burke at his home in Bethesda, Maryland, during 1979. They cover his duty on the General Board (April 1947-July 1948); his service on the Korean Armistice Delegation during the early months of its existence (July-December 1951) while fighting continued; and his pathfinding efforts as head of Op-30 - the Strategic Plans Division of the Navy.

One can say, in retrospect, that the prodigious contributions of Admiral Burke to the navy and the country are illustrated in part by his tours of duty on the General Board and in Op.30. These two assignments would seem to forecast the nature and direction of his actions when later he served as Chief of Naval Operations. Apparently Burke was put on the General Board to provide youthful vigor to its deliberations. The reader will see what he was able to accomplish in one short year. The Board was asked to make a study of the naval shore establishment. Burke's global vision saw in this a need to establish plans and policy for years ahead. The study grew to include the military and all pertinent governmental agencies. Op-30 provided an even greater canvas for the master planner. We see him there, surrounded by a Blue Ribbon staff, coping with a plethora of subjects that indeed embraced the entire world. (The Admiral told me one time that his role as a 'trouble-shooter' in the navy began with his assignment as Chief of Staff to Admiral Mitscher in World War II and continued through the years. "I got pretty good at it," he said with a puckish grin.)

Admiral Burke has made corrections to the original transcript. It has been re-typed and an index added. Several selected papers are included in an appendix.

John T. Mason, Jr.
Director of Oral History

March 1980

ADMIRAL ARLEIGH BURKE, U. S. NAVY (Ret)

Arleigh Burke was born far from the sea in Boulder, Colorado on October 19, 1901. On June 7, 1923 he was graduated from the U. S. Naval Academy, commissioned Ensign in the United States Navy, and married to Miss Roberta Gorsuch of Washington, D.C.

Throughout his professional career, Arleigh Burke had prepared himself for combat with the enemy having served in battleships, destroyers, and having received the degree of Master of Science in Engineering at the University of Michigan. Then, when World War II came, he found himself, to his great disappointment, in a shore billet at the Naval Gun Factory in Washington, D.C. After persistent effort on his part, he received orders to the South Pacific where, under Admiral Halsey, he successively commanded Destroyer Division 43, Destroyer Division 44, Destroyer Squadron 12, and Destroyer Squadron 23. This latter Squadron, known as the "Little Beavers" covered the initial landings in Bougainville in November 1943 and fought in 22 separate engagements during the next four months. During this time the "Little Beavers" were credited with destroying one Japanese cruiser, nine destroyers, one submarine, several smaller ships, and approximately 30 aircraft. Because he pushed his destroyers just under boiler-bursting speed, he became known as "31-knot Burke".

From Destroyer Command in the South Pacific he reported in March of 1944 as Chief of Staff to Commander, Fast Carrier Task Force 58, Admiral Marc Mitscher. While serving with this famed carrier force, Arleigh Burke was promoted to Commodore and participated in all its naval engagements until June 1945 shortly before the surrender of Japan. He flew many combat missions. He was aboard both BUNKER HILL and ENTERPRISE when they were hit by Japanese suicide planes during the Okinawa campaign.

At the outbreak of the Korean war, Admiral Forrest Sherman, then CNO, ordered Admiral Burke to duty as Deputy Chief of Staff to Commander Naval Forces, Far East. From there he assumed command of Cruiser Division FIVE, and in July 1951 he was made a member of United Nations Truce Delegation to negotiate with the Communists for a military armistice in Korea. After six months in the truce tents he returned to the Office of Chief of Naval Operations where he served as Director of Strategic Plans Division until 1954.

In April 1954 he took command of Cruiser Division SIX, and in January 1955 assumed command of Destroyer Force Atlantic Fleet in which capacity he served until he became Chief of Naval Operations in August 1955.

Admiral Burke has received numerous combat awards during his forty-two years in the Navy including the Distinguished Service Medal, the Navy Cross, the Legion of Merit and the Purple Heart. But none are more cherished than two awards which came early in his career. In 1928 while serving aboard USS PROCYON he was commended for the "rescue of shipwrecked and seafaring men", and in 1939 while serving in his first command, USS MUGFORD, he was commended

ADMIRAL ARLEIGH BURKE, USN (Ret.)

when his destroyer won the fleet gunnery trophy with the highest score that had been achieved in many years. His ship also stood third in engineering competition and high in communication competition.

On August 1, 1961, after serving as CNO and naval member of the JCS longer than any other officer, Admiral Burke retired from the Navy. His active duty covered a span of 42 years.

Since his retirement he has been active in many public service activities and has been on the Board of Directors of numerous corporations.

Admiral and Mrs. Burke now reside at 8624 Fenway Drive, Bethesda, Maryland 20034.

List of Citations which have been awarded

ADMIRAL ARLEIGH A BURKE, U.S. NAVY (RET.)

For his service in Destroyer Squadron 23 Admiral Burke was awarded the Distinguished Service Medal, the Navy Cross, the Legion of Merit, and is entitled to the Ribbon for, and a facsimile of, the Presidential Unit Citation awarded Destroyer Squadron 23. The citations follow, in part:

Distinguished Service Medal: "For exceptionally meritorious service to the Government of the United States in a duty of great responsibility as Commanding Officer of a Destroyer Division and subsequently a Destroyer Squadron operating against the enemy Japanese forces in the South Pacific Area from early February to December 1, 1943. Throughout this period, Captain Burke led his forces in many offensive operations.....His indomitable fighting spirit and great personal courage contributed directly to the success of our forces in that area and were in keeping with the highest traditions of the United States Naval Service."

Navy Cross: "For extraordinary heroism and distinguished service...as the Commander of a destroyer squadron operating in the Northern Solomon Islands area during the period from midnight October 30 to noon November 2, 1943. (His) squadron, as a part of a task force, participated in the first bombardment of the Buka-Bonins area and also in the first daylight bombardment of the Shortland area....During the night of November 1-2, a heavier gunned Japanese naval force was met and decisively defeated with the loss to the enemy of one cruiser and four destroyers sunk, and an additional two cruisers and two destroyers damaged. The action contributed much to the success of our operations at Empress Augusta Bay. Thereafter, a heavy air attack by sixty-seven enemy dive bombers was fought off with a total of seventeen enemy planes being destroyed..."

Legion of Merit (with Combat "V") "For exceptionally meritorious conduct... as Commander Destroyer Squadron Twenty-three, in action against the enemy Japanese forces northwest of the Bismarck Archipelago, at Kavieng, New Ireland, and the Duke of York Island, February 17 to 23, 1944... (He) expertly directed his squadron in destroying two Japanese naval auxiliary vessels, one large cargo ship, a mine layer, four barges and inflicting severe damage on enemy shore installations and subsequently effected a skillful withdrawal without damage to his vessels..."

Presidential Unit Citation to Destroyer Squadron 23: "For extraordinary heroism in action against enemy Japanese forces during the Solomon Islands campaign, from November 1, 1943 to February 23, 1944....Destroyer Squadron Twenty-three operated in daring defiance of repeated attacks by hostile air groups, closing the enemy's strongly fortified shores to carry out sustained bombardments against Japanese coastal defenses and render effective cover and fire support for the major invasion operations in this area...The brilliant and heroic record achieved by Destroyer Squadron Twenty-three is a distinctive tribute to the valiant fighting spirit of the individual units in this indomitable combat group of each skilled and courageous ship's company...."

Citations awarded Admiral Arleigh A. Burke, USN (Ret.)

As Chief of Staff, Commander Fast Carrier Task Force, Pacific (Task Force 38), Admiral Burke was awarded a Gold Star in lieu of the Second Distinguished Service Medal, the Silver Star Medal, a Gold Star in lieu of the Second Legion of Merit, and a Letter of Commendation, with authorization to wear the Commendation Ribbon. The Citations follow in part:

Gold Star in lieu of Second Distinguished Service Medal: "For....outstanding service....as Chief of Staff to Commander First Carrier Task Force, Pacific during action against enemy Japanese Forces in the Pacific War area from December 15, 1944 to May 15, 1945...Commodore Burke was in large measure responsible for the efficient control under combat conditions of the tactical disposition, the operation, the security and the explosive offensive power of his task force in its bold and determined execution of measures designed to force the capitulation of the Japanese Empire...throughout the seizure of bases at Iwo Jima and Okinawa, including two carrier strikes on Tokyo, a carrier strike on the Kure Naval Base, and an engagement with the Japanese Fleet on April 7, in which several hostile men-o-war were destroyed by our aircraft...."

Silver Star Medal: "For conspicuous gallantry and intrepidity as Chief of Staff to Commander FIRST Carrier Task Force in action against enemy Japanese forces in the Pacific War area, May 11, 1945. When the flagship on which he was embarked was hit by two enemy suicide dive bombers, Commodore Burke proceeded to a compartment in which personnel were trapped by fire and heavy smoke, and succeeded in evacuating all hands. When the flagship to which he had removed his staff was in turn hit by a suicide plane on May 14, he again arranged for the transfer of his command to a new ship. In spite of all difficulties he maintained tactical control of the Task Force throughout, thereby contributing materially to the success of the operations...."

Gold Star in lieu of the Second Legion of Merit: "For exceptionally meritorious conduct...as Chief of Staff to Commander, Carrier Task Force, Pacific Fleet, from March 27 to October 30, 1944....(He) planned and executed a long series of successful offensive operations in support of the reduction of the other perimeter of Japanese defenses in New Guinea, the Carolines, the Marianas, Halmahera and the Philippine Islands. Largely as a result of Commodore Burke's superb professional skill, tireless energy and coolness of decision throughout these operations and during repeated air attacks carried out in strength against heavily fortified strongholds in enemy-controlled waters, the Pacific Fleet has been brought within range of the Japanese Empire itself to continue our relentless drive against the enemy."

Letter of Commendation: "For distinguishing himself in action with the enemy while serving as Chief of Staff to Commander First Carrier Task Force, Pacific on 11 May 1945. When the ship in which he was embarked was hit by two enemy aircraft...with utter disregard for his personal safety, (he) efficiently organized the evacuation of endangered personnel. His courage together with his prompt and efficient action was responsible for saving these men..."

Citations awarded Admiral Arleigh A. Burke, USN (Ret.)   Page 3

Admiral Burke is also entitled to the Presidential Unit Citation to the USS BUNKER HILL, the Presidential Unit Citation to the USS LEXINGTON, and the Navy Unit Commendation to the USS ENTERPRISE. These vessels were, at various times during his period of service, flagships of the Fast Carrier Task Forces in the Pacific.

From September 1950 until May 1951 he served as Deputy Chief of Staff to Commander, U. S. Naval Forces, Far East, and for "exceptionally meritorious conduct (in that capacity) from 3 September 1950 to 1 January 1951..." he was awarded a Gold Star in lieu of The Third Legion of Merit. The citation further states: "Bringing a sound knowledge of Naval Administration and professional skill to his assigned task, Rear Admiral Burke reorganized the rapidly expanded staff to meet its ever increasing responsibilities and, through his unusually fine conception of the essentials of modern warfare, materially improved the mutual functioning of the Operations, Plans and Intelligence Sections of the Staff.... (and) contributed immeasurably to the success of Naval Operations in the Korean theater..."

While serving as Commander Cruiser Division Five from May to September 1951, and also as a Member of the Military Armistice Commission in Korea, Admiral Burke was awarded an Oak Leaf Cluster in lieu of the Fourth Legion of Merit, by the Army (Headquarters U. S. Army Forces, Far East) by General Order #5. as follows: "For exceptionally meritorious conduct in the performance of outstanding services as a delegate with the United Nations Command delegation, United Nations Command (Advance) in Korea, from 9 July to 5 December 1951. Admiral Burke's keen discernment and decisive judgment were of inestimable value in countering enemy intransigence, misrepresentation and evasion with reasoned negotiation, demonstrable truth and conciliatory measures. As advisor to the Chief Delegate on all phases of the Armistice Conferences, he proffered timely recommendations for solutions of the varied intricate problems encountered. Through skillful assessment of enemy capabilities, dispositions and vulnerable abilities and brilliant guidance of supporting staff officers (he) significantly furthered progression toward success of the United Nation's first armed bid for World Peace.."

In addition to the Navy Cross, the Distinguished Service Medal with Gold Star, the Legion of Merit with two Gold Stars and Oak Leaf Cluster (Army), the Silver Star Medal, the Commendation Ribbon, the Purple Heart Medal (for wounds received while serving on board USS CONWAY during July 1943), the Presidential Unit Citation Ribbon with three stars, and the Navy Unit Commendation Ribbon. Admiral Burke has the American Defense Service Medal, Fleet Clasp; the Asiatic-Pacific Campaign Medal with two silver stars and two bronze stars (Twelve engagements); the American Campaign Medal; World War II Victory Medal: Navy Occupation Service Medal, Europe Clasp; the National Defense Service Medal; and the Philippine Liberation Ribbon, Korean Service Medal, and United Nations Service Medal. He also has been awarded the Ul Chi Medal and the Presidential Unit Citation from Republic of Korea.

Prior to his retirement Admiral Burke was awarded the Third Distinguished Service Medal by the President, John F. Kennedy, in a ceremony in the White House Rose Garden.

ADMIRAL ARLEIGH A. BURKE, U. S. NAVY (RET.)
CHRONOLOGICAL TRANSCRIPT OF NAVAL SERVICE

Jun 1923 - Apr 1928 USS ARIZONA
Apr 1928 - Jun 1928 USS PROCYON
Jun 1928 - Sep 1928 Fleet Base Force
Sep 1928 - May 1929 USS PROCYON
Jun 1929 - Sep 1930 U.S. Naval Academy Postgraduate School, Annapolis, Md.
                      (under instruction)
Sep 1930 - Jun 1931 University of Michigan, Ann Arbor, Michigan (under instruction)
Jun 1931 - May 1932 Navy Yard, Washington, D.C. (under instruction)
Jun 1932 - Apr 1933 USS CHESTER
Apr 1933 - Sep 1934 Base Force, U. S. Fleet
Sep 1934 - Apr 1935 Staff, Base Force, U. S. Fleet
May 1935 - Jun 1937 Bureau of Ordnance, Navy Department, Washington, D. C.
Jun 1937 - Jun 1939 USS CRAVEN (DD-382) (Executive Officer)
Jun 1939 - Jul 1940 USS MUGFORD (Commanding Officer)
Aug 1940 - Jan 1943 Navy Yard, Washington, D. C.
Feb 1943 - May 1943 Destroyer Division 43 (CO)
May 1943 - Aug 1943 Destroyer Division 44 (CO)
Aug 1943 - Oct 1943 Destroyer Squadron 12 (CO)
Oct 1943 - Mar 1944 Destroyer Squadron 23 (CO)
Mar 1944 - Jul 1945 Staff, FIRST Carrier Task Force, Pacific (Chief of Staff)
Jul 1945 - Oct 1945 Headquarters, Commander in Chief, U. S. Fleet (Head of Special
                      Defense Section)
Oct 1945 - Feb 1946 Bureau of Ordnance, Navy Department, Washington, D. C.
Mar 1946 - Sep 1946 Staff, EIGHTH Fleet (Chief of Staff and Aide)
Sep 1946 - Mar 1947 Staff, U. S. Atlantic Fleet (Chief of Staff and Aide)
Apr 1947 - Jul 1948 Navy Department, Washington, D. C. (Member of General Board)
Jul 1948 - Dec 1948 USS HUNTINGTON (CL-107) (CO)
Dec 1948 - Jan 1950 Office of Chief of Naval Operations, Navy Department,
                      Washington, D. C.
Jan 1950 - Aug 1950 Department of Defense, Research and Development Board,
                      Washington, D. C. (Navy Secretary, R&D Board)
Sep 1950 - May 1951 Naval Forces, Far East (Deputy Chief of Staff)
May 1951 - Dec 1951 Cruiser Division 5 (CO, also Delegate, Military Armistice
                      to arrange Armistice between U. N. Forces and Communist
                      Forces in Korea)
Dec 1951 - Mar 1954 Office of CNO, Navy Department, Washington, D. C. (Director
                      Strategic Plans Division)
Mar 1954 - Jan 1955 Cruiser Division 6 (CO)
Jan 1955 - Jun 1955 Destroyer Force, U. S. Atlantic Fleet, (CO)
Aug 1955 - Aug 1961 Chief of Naval Operations, Navy Department, Washington, D. C.
Aug 1961 - present Retired

DECLARATION OF TRUST

The undersigned does hereby appoint and designate as his (her) Trustee herein, the Secretary-Treasurer and Publisher of the United States Naval Institute to perform and discharge the following duties, powers, and privileges in connection with the possession and use of a certain taped interview between the undersigned and the Oral History Department of the United States Naval Institute.

1. Classification of Transcript.

   ( )a. If classified OPEN, the transcript(s) may be read or the recording(s) audited by the qualified personnel upon presentation of proper credentials, as determined by the Secretary-Treasurer of the U.S. Naval Institute.

   (X)b. If classified PERMISSION REQUIRED TO CITE OR QUOTE, the user will be required to obtain permission in writing from the interviewee prior to quoting or citing from either the transcript(s) or the recording(s).

   ( )c. If classified PERMISSION REQUIRED, permission must be obtained in writing from the interviewee before the transcribed interview(s) can be examined or the tape recording(s) audited.

   ( )d. If classified CLOSED, the transcribed interview(s) and the tape recording(s) will be sealed until a time specified by the interviewee. This may be until the death of the interviewee or for any specified number of years.

2. It is expressly understood that in giving this authorization, I am in no way precluded from placing such restrictions as I may desire upon use of the interview at any time during my lifetime, nor does this authorization in any way affect my rights to the copyright of my literary expressions that may be contained in the interview.

Witness my hand and seal this 21st day of April 19 79

Arleigh Burke

I hereby accept and consent to the foregoing Declaration of Trust and the powers therein conferred upon me as Trustee:

R E Bowler Jr
4/24/79

Burke #7 - 1

Interview No. 7 with Admiral Arleigh Burke, U.S. Navy (Retired)

Place: His residence in Bethesda, Maryland

Date: Thursday morning, 3 May 1979

By: John T. Mason, Jr.

Q: Sir, today we're going to talk largely about the period when you served on the General Board, which was from March 1947 to July 1948. However, before you begin a discussion of the things that occurred during that period, I think you have something more general to say.

Adm. B.: Yes, I do.

In going over my files on the General Board, on which I spent about two days, I realized more than I had in going over the other files, that my files are very incomplete. Since I do not usually go into other files because there isn't time to do that, the incompleteness of my files leaves a lot of data that are available in the regular files or are available some place else, that I don't have.

Q: I think the informed historian who's working in an area is perfectly well aware of this fact.

Adm. B.: I'm not so sure, from reading their output. There's so much information in the world that historians don't always really dig into things. I find in my own letters, for example, in this business here with the General Board episode that there are a lot of things I didn't mention, or I mentioned them in regard to an official report which I had before me when I wrote that letter and which I do not now have. For example, I saw a lot of references to a paper on the Middle East that I wrote, but I haven't seen that Middle East paper because it was an official paper and it's in the general archives, I suppose. That's probably the most important paper I had during my tour on the General Board.

I did want to put that warning in because this current research makes me realize more than ever before that what I'm talking about I really know just superficially now. It's a long time ago. I go over my notes and they bring back some memories but not the reasons, nor the struggle that we went through to develop some of the papers.

Q: Yes, but what you are contributing will prove to be very useful to men who are working on particular subjects and who will go elsewhere for documents that pertain.

Adm. B.: I know you think so for we've had this discussion before! I'm not so sure, but if it helps it's all right.

Q: Tell me how you happened to go to the General Board. Ordinarily, I think, the General Board membership was comprised of men who were quite senior in rank and in age, and here you were a young, vigorous captain being assigned to the General Board. How did this happen?

Adm. B.: I wondered about that when I first went down to the archives last week. I wondered how in the world did I get there. I had forgotten and I didn't find the answer in those files on the General Board. I found it in the files of the time I was still on Admiral Mitscher's staff.

In that file, I found a letter from Admiral Towers, who was at that time CinCPac. He had written a letter to Admiral Mitscher which arrived in January. Admiral Mitscher at that time was in the hospital.

Q: This was shortly before he died.

Adm. B.: Shortly before he died. He was in the hospital and the doctor had told me that he was not to be disturbed with any papers and Mrs. Mitscher had asked me to open his mail and handle it. So I did and among them I found this letter from Admiral Towers, who apparently had written to Admiral Mitscher before and asked him if Admiral Mitscher would release me to go to the General Board, which Admiral Towers expected to be ordered to head. He wanted to reinvigorate the board and make it more purposeful than it had been immediately after the war. The General Board had been a very powerful and important influence before the war. During the war, of course, it wasn't, and he wanted to revitalize it. That's what the CNO had asked him to do, either Admiral King or Admiral Nimitz.

This letter to Admiral Mitscher referred to previous correspondence and said that he knew that Admiral Mitscher wanted me to stay with him, but that he thought Admiral Mitscher should consider (since I'd been with him a long time) Admiral Towers's needs, and he hoped that he would release me sometime in the coming spring. He'd like to have me report by March, I think it was, anyway in the spring of 1947.

Well, the letter was very embarrassing for me to answer, but I did write to Admiral Towers and told him that I was embarrassed and flattered by the kind remarks about Burke he made, and that Admiral Mitscher was in the hospital. I was opening his mail and that although I didn't think that Admiral Mitscher would return to full active duty, as long as he needed me I was going to stay with him. When Admiral Mitscher did not need me any more, I'd be happy to go to the General Board if he wanted me to. But I wouldn't leave as long as I could help Admiral Mitscher in any way.

Well, of course, Admiral Mitscher died very shortly thereafter. That letter of Admiral Towers's was dated 17 January, I see. At that time Admiral Mitscher was so ill that I couldn't take decisions to him, so I reported it to the CNO orally, and to Admiral Gatch, who was the next senior in the Atlantic Fleet and was Acting CinCLant. Admiral Gatch requested that the CinCLant Admin remain in <u>Pocono</u> and we on Admiral Mitscher's staff would run the administration. Admiral Gatch said he hoped there'd be very few things on which he would have to make a decision. There were very few things. Most of our work was routine at that time.

After Admiral Mitscher died there was a long time when we didn't know who was to become CinCLant or what was going to be done. Finally, Admiral Blandy was ordered to CinCLant, and in March I took Pocono down to Trinidad where Admiral Blandy was in Missouri, or would be in Missouri in the latter part of March. Rear Admiral Johnson was his chief of staff. We arrived in Trinidad early in March, I think the 3rd or 4th of March, and I went over to see Admiral Blandy and arrange for the turnover of the command with Admiral Johnson. He had just arrived, too. They were having a lot of important social functions, including a reception for the governor general of Trinidad. Also Admiral Blandy wanted me to survey the United States Naval Base with him.

I'm bringing this social matter up because it had one minor effect on me.

John Shaw was the governor general of Trinidad, but I think the acting governor was Dos Santos and because Pocono had a barge and I was unattached, Admiral Blandy asked me if I would escort some important official and his wife to the reception. I was to meet them in the barge and take them to Missouri for this big reception and dinner. I said yes. The reason that he asked me to do that was that the wife, who was a young woman, probably about forty, had rheumatoid arthritis so badly that even her hands were completely crippled. She smoked a lot of cigarettes but she couldn't pick up a cigarette. I was to help her get up the accommodation ladder, that was the big impediment, to get her into the boat and out to the ship and up the ladder. She wanted to go to the party. Well, she weighed about 140 pounds, I remember, and I had a great deal of difficulty getting her up the ladder, but she was a staunch person and she walked up slowly, pain or no pain. Finally, we got her there and I escorted her around. After the party we got her back into the barge without much difficulty. Unfortunately, the tide had run out. We were at low tide and when we came in alongside the pier, the pier was up four or five feet above the barge, and I didn't know how in the world to get her out. I got her up on the steps of the barge, of course the barge was rolling a little bit, and she couldn't hold onto things, and her husband had to hold her in place. I got on the pier and then reached down to pick her up. I had to squat, and I put my arms under her arms, locked my hands behind her back, and lifted her from the barge. Well, 140 pounds of dead weight —

Q: Dead weight at that point and that angle.

Adm. B.: Yes, and my back snapped. But I got her topside all right and got her over into her car. They shoved off and I collapsed on the dock.

Q: The pain was so bad?

Adm. B.: Well, I just couldn't move. I just fell. So the barge crew bundled me into the boat and took me back to Pocono, and the doctor said, "Hell, you just pulled your back out, that's all. You've pulled a lot of ligaments and you're in a bad way. Take it easy."

I said, "What are you going to do for it?"

"I'm not going to do a damned thing. It's just a question of time now. I can't do very much."

And I said, "What am I going to do?"

He said, "You'll feel better in time. Get a night's sleep and you'll feel better in the morning. It will come back, but just don't strain yourself any more."

That ended all of my parties and going around, but we turned the data over to Admiral Blandy. He relieved, took command, and then we sailed <u>Pocono</u> to San Juan, where I was to be detached. I spent most of that time in my bunk, but in San Juan I was feeling a little better and the staff gave me a party. I remember this party in the officers' club in San Juan, and after a drink or so my back didn't feel quite so badly. I was on crutches and they helped me get back and forth.

The secretary of the navy had come down, Mr. Sullivan, in his plane. He saw me, or I saw him, and he offered to give me a ride back in his plane. He was going back directly to Washington, so that was wonderful for me. I came back with him. He tried to teach me gin rummy and took all my money, but I got back in mid-March with orders to report the 1st of April. I had a little leave. Of course, I went home and went to bed, and then went out to the hospital. They said the same thing the doctor aboard ship had said, there wasn't much they could do. They gave me a few exercises and said it would take time, nothing was broken, I'd just torn all my ligaments - a lot of ligaments.

About the time that I got orders to the General Board, the Naval Engineering Society had invited me to give a speech - that is, the American Society of Naval Engineers - on the 18th of April.

Q: In Washington?

Adm. B.: In Washington, at the Statler Hotel, and it was a big speech. I'd written the speech out, and I told the doctor about it and said I had to make that speech. He said, "Well, you can't do it," and I said:

"There must be some way that you can help me - put an injection in my back or some place to ease the pain while I make the speech."

He said, yes, he could do that but he said it would be like Cinderella because pain is nature's way of making sure you didn't jar things loose again. He said:

"If I take the pain away, you're going to make it worse. But I'll do that. I'll hire a room in the Statler and you and I will go down in that room. You'll go to your affair just at the time of dinner, you can't go ahead of time. I'll take you down." And so he did, and he gave me a shot of something into my back in two or three places and it felt pretty good. He put me in my seat at the table and I felt fine by that time, but he said, "This is going to wear off in about an hour and a half, and when it wears off you're going to be in real pain. The chances are it's going to be really bad, but I'll be here and I'll take you back to the hospital."

Q: He put a ceiling on the time you could speak, didn't he?

Adm. B.: That is right and that's why he did this injection just before the dinner. He said, "Don't eat anything, don't drink anything, and don't move. Be very, very careful."

So I got up and made the speech after dinner and I felt pretty good. An hour and a half went by and nothing much happened. I thought, well, I ought to have at least a drink and a sandwich, so I got a drink and a sandwich, and the doctor came around and said, "How do you feel?" I said, "I feel fine."

Do you know, that pain never came back!

Q: It never came back at all?

Adm. B.: Well, I had a weak back. I had to take exercises for years for a bad back, but at that time everything fell back into place apparently. It was a little painful, but not bad. I could walk around, so I reported in and went down to duty. I've always wondered exactly what happened. I never did know it.

Q: Nor did the doctor?

Adm. B.: Nor did the doctor.

Admiral Towers arrived about the time I did, and the problem that had just been assigned to the General Board by Vice Admiral McMorris, who was a wonderful man, was a survey of the shore establishment. When I arrived, they were just starting it, and I sat in on a couple of conferences mostly on the Bureau of Supplies and Accounts, to see how the Board handled a problem, and I was given the problem of the Bureau of Engineering and the marines. When we started on this study, the basic problem was to determine what is the shore establishment for. Well, it's to support the fleet. So the basic idea was to cut everything out, reduce it, because all the shore establishment, as everything else in the navy, had grown tremendously during the war. It grew to meet wartime needs, and there were a lot of installations kept on that really weren't performing a very useful service now.

Q: That's the sort of thing you discovered when you were with the Atlantic Fleet.

Adm. B.: Exactly the same thing. So basically we had to know what was the size of the fleet, what was the composition of the fleet. Where would the fleet likely operate, in peace and in war? What were the war plans and were they up to date? That's where we had to start, because we had to know what the shore establishment should do and to know that we had to know what kind of an outfit the shore establishment was to do it for, and where the depots and facilities should be located. Then, we had to examine all the other service facilities like schools and so forth which indirectly supplied the fleet. In addition to that, we had to take into consideration the mobilization requirements. In other words, how should the shore establishment be built so that it could mobilize fast and take care of an expanded fleet in time of war as well as remain efficient in its peacetime support of the fleet. That meant tables of usage, a survey of geographic locations, and a lot of other things. We got that finished by and by.

Q: It took you quite a long time, didn't it?

Adm. B.: Oh, yes, it took a long time, and it was difficult.

Q: As I recall, Mr. McNeil, the comptroller, added a new element. He was concerned about reactions on Capitol Hill.

Adm. B.: Yes, he emphasized that because a reduction in the shore establishment always has political connotations, because every congressman and senator is all for reduction, but only reductions in other people's areas, not in their own. So it had to be backed with facts and supported by real hard data and even with that data we would not be able to do exactly what should have been done, because of political -

Q: Perhaps at this point it would be well for me to ask another question. A detailed study like this with all its ramifications required a lot of concentration and a lot of effort. Was the General Board, the composition of the General Board, up to such a study?

Adm. B.: No, neither was anybody else. There was no single organization, particularly a small one, that was fully competent to make that study, just as there isn't now. But what it can do is make an initial study and then from the reactions of that study, you can arrive at pretty good conclusions. I mean it takes playback from the people who are concerned, that is, the shipyards and other shore facilities themselves and the people in the area and the fleet.

All that the General Board could do was to start it and recommend. This is because it was an advisory committee. It was not responsible for the action taken. But to do that there had to be a small group of very knowledgeable men and that's what Admiral Towers had decided to create.

Q: You mean he tried to make the membership knowledgeable?

Adm. B.: Yes. He and Admiral McMorris. The previous members of the General Board had been older people, Admirals just about to retire, some of them active and very good, but all of them looking forward to retirement, and the problems that were presented to the General Board were short-range problems. They weren't major long term problems. So Admiral Towers had asked for the people he wanted, who he thought would help. Among the younger people was a Colonel Pate, who later became commandant of the Marine Corps, myself, and I think Savvy Hoffman, and some junior rear admirals, and we had Admiral McMorris, who was a very fine, knowledgeable man. Squidge Lee, a commander then, became the Board secretary.

Q: What sort of a staff did you have to implement all this?

Adm. B.: Very little staff, and that was good, because as soon as you get a big organization to study important problems it is done by an inexperienced staff of beautiful writers who produce volumes and volumes of paper but don't arrive at the guts of the problem. Any similarity with the present White House staff and this description is purely coincidental. A very small staff who have to do most of their own work only take on the important things. They soon have to separate the important matter from the unimportant matter and they have to arrive at fundamentals. This is the advantage of a very small staff in any organization.

One of the situations that is very bad now is that there are tremendous numbers of studies made by tremendous staffs that cost large amounts of money, but they can't be read. The action officers are very few in any organization, and any paper has to be short enough and concise enough so - or abstracted in such a manner that one man can absorb it and make the decision. This is what happens to the president. He's snowed with data, a lot of it erroneous. He doesn't know what data are right and which are wrong. He can't have the experience to have the judgment for making his own decisions on all problems and so he's got a tremendous staff that snow him under with paper, I think. It looks that way.

This was a big advantage of the General Board. Of course, an advisory group in any organization is very apt to be bypassed. Its recommendations do not have to be accepted.

then the man who makes that decision should be and sometimes is, criticized for not doing what it was suggested that he do. An advisory board is never any good if its advice isn't usually accepted. It can't always be accepted, but it's got to be good enough so that its advice is accepted usually, and it can't be bypassed just to get the kind of advice that the head man wants.

Q: In this instance, you apparently had a very potent chairman who had influence in the navy, as a whole, so that must have been helpful?

Adm. B.: Yes, it was. He was good and Admiral McMorris was good, Towers was good, but the influence of any advisory board is, correctly, dependent upon the quality of the work that the advisory board does, but primarily it's dependent upon whether the action people, the management, really wants to accept advice. Do they really want advice, or is it just a procedural matter for them?

Q: In your time on the Board, if you reflect on it, was the feeling prevalent that you were able to make a real contribution in this area or in other areas that you alluded to?

Adm. B.: When I first went on there, of course, the General Board had not been very influential for a long time because of the war. Naturally, it shouldn't have been. And so most people felt it couldn't contribute anything.

Q: You mean most of the people who served on it felt that?

Adm. B.: No, most of the people in the management of the navy. There are a lot of people in management in most civilian organizations and military organizations who don't want any advice outside of their own shop. They feel that an advisory group doesn't really have all the knowledge and certainly not the responsibility for carrying out the project and so an advisory group can be pretty free with its advice.

Q: They're out of the mainstream, so to speak?

Adm. B.: They're out of the mainstream, and there's some truth to that and sometimes the advice is not sound. But an advisory board can be helpful. I'm on quite a few advisory groups now. Take a completely different one, the Citadel, for example. I'm not on that board of advisors now but the Citadel have an advisory group that really has had great influence on the Citadel. They tackle important problems, they give their advice to the university, and the university quite frequently follows it or, if they do not follow it, they come back and report why it was not feasible or desirable to accept that particular report, which they sometimes do.

Q: But that's somewhat different, is it not, because it's in the academic area?

Adm. B.: No, academic institutions are not exactly the same as businesses or military organizations, but there are many similar characteristics. Academic groups sometimes try to postulate that academic institutions are unique to themselves and that there is some mystic about them that only an academician understands, but sometimes they lose their students, they lose the function of their organization, they get sidetracked lots of times. Then they find that organization, procedures and competent people working to accomplish stated and understood objectives are important.

Q: And they need finances the way anything else does.

Adm. B.: They certainly do need finances and lots of them these days - well, take right now, the colleges are competing for students and lowering their standards to get tuition. If they don't get a certain number of students there's a certain number of professors who aren't going to be there next year. So if they can get a student who pays his bills and helps the university, they may lower their standards to do it. That's why the education in some universities is not worth a damn. A lad graduates and he suddenly finds out that he hasn't learned anything real that will help him get a job or keep one. This is the crisis that the educational institutions are in now and that's not going to be cured quickly. Advisory groups to these universities might have helped, but really an advisory group is just that, an advisory group. It isn't an action group.

This was debated thoroughly in the General Board. What can we do? This survey of the shore establishment was going to hurt lots of people. I mean lots of people were going to be disrupted because the shore establishment had to be reduced, and nobody wants to be reduced or phased out. It had to be done very carefully, but it had to be done, so it took a lot of study and it stirred things up in the navy. The General Board was stirring things up because we asked a lot of questions. For example, in my particular bailiwick, the Bureau of Ships, the question of closing shipyards came up naturally. Did we need that many shipyards? Not in peacetime. Would we need them in war? Maybe not. Well, which shipyards should be closed, which shipyards do the best work at cheapest cost, which are quality yards? Which are in the best locations - had the most expertise in various special skills? There are hundreds of things that enter into such a decision, but politically, it became obvious that the navy could not close shipyards then. Congress wouldn't let us, but we still recommended some of them be closed for that would be best for the United States in the long run.

Q: You were going into a time of unemployment, were you not? And some economic depression in the country?

Adm. B.: Right, and it was a very difficult decision for navy management to make.

This study, of course, had all sorts of ramifications, but all of them went back to fundamentals. What is the United States going to try to do in the future? What are the policies of the United States? What international support does the United States have? What's the economic situation apt to be in the United States, the political situation, which way will we probably go? There was no such policy, there wasn't any.

Q: Was that a surprise?

Adm. B.: No, it wasn't a surprise that there was no overall policy, but it was a surprise that there were no elements of that policy either. Our form of government prohibits the making of long-range policy - it doesn't prohibit it, that's not true, what happens is a new administration comes in and wants to make its own mark and so it changes a lot of actions, things are being done wrong they say, that their predecessors have started. New administration means different decisions, different most everything.

Q: Not likely to get as much political credit!

Adm. B.: They don't, but the British form of government hasn't actually worked any better, although they do (or at least did) follow long-range policies, and for a hundred years or so they followed them very carefully. The shadow government system contributed to the basic policy of the British government, but now they don't follow their old rules, and no other nation has real long-term policies because they don't want to put themselves into a rigid position to meet events that they don't know anything about, future events, and may not be able to even influence.

We had other problems that were submitted to us -

Q: Would you follow that trend of thought now? Did this force you into the future study of what's going to happen in ten years?

Adm. B.: No. This was the genesis of seeing the need for such a study. There should have been some basic policy, not necessarily for ten years, but for three, four, or five years, that the United States is going to try to accomplish certain objectives, not rigid, but a general idea, so that all people in government could be working toward a common goal, or at least many of them would be working toward a common goal, and stop the business of various elements of government being adversaries to each other, tearing down some other part of the government. Of course, some of it needs to be torn down but it should be done carefully and with thought behind it. We hadn't reached it then, but we have now reached the stage where we're tearing down things just to get the money for another element.

Q: Working at cross purposes?

Adm. B.: Yes.

Q: The reason I asked that question was because I am aware of the fact that the next year the board did undertake this ten-year study, and I just wondered if the two were directly related.

Adm. B.: Yes, they were somewhat related for that final study came about because of the lack of basic information on the survey of the shore establishment.

Q: Did Admiral Towers realize this when the study was begun?

Adm. B.: No, and very few of the Board really wanted to start such a massive project that had so much chance of failure. I developed a little paper, I think – I can't now find the original – suggesting that it be discussed as some way of developing a policy for the government – some way for the government to develop a policy for itself. They said, well, that's not our business, our business is the navy. I said, "Yes, but we can't go very far unless we know the government intends to try to do – we can't make very definite recommendations – unless we know what the rest of the government is going to do. We can't make recommendations about the size of the navy, if we don't know about the economy of the country and what future administrations are apt to do with our resources."

We have limited resources in many areas and what we can do is going to be dependent upon the availability of those resources.

They weren't very enthusiastic about that because it was not our billet. I kept hammering every once in a while, making myself obnoxious, and they did what's always done, and they elected me mess treasurer!

Q: Of course!

Adm. B.: If you complain about the food, you're elected mess treasurer, so I got elected mess treasurer and they said if I wanted to do this I'd have to give them more than just a general idea, give some examples, "You're the honcho, you run it."

Well, I had a staff of Burke, but I did start on it at that time. As I went through this survey of the shore establishment I wrote notes to myself as to what data we needed that we didn't have, that wasn't available, and by the time we got through with that I had written a pretty good bunch of notes. I probably couldn't read them all then either, my handwriting is illegible.

Q: I'd like to make one observation and ask a question at this point about this.

You were pointing up and realizing the complexity of modern society which is a product of World War II, really, the interdependence of nations and all that. The question I'd like to pose is would this have been a legitimate problem to arise prior to World War II? Would you have been raising these questions prior to World War II, or was this the result of World War II experience?

Adm. B.: It was a result of World War II experience primarily. I would not have done that before because the world was pretty stable before, and many policies, although they weren't written, were generated and followed without a great deal of change.

Q: They had continuity?

Adm. B.: They had continuity, and also because President Roosevelt served so long as president, he had the same administration, and this, of course, changed slowly. So I don't think it would have developed then. Also, President Roosevelt had another characteristic. He kept things pretty close to his chest and there were a lot of things that he told one group and didn't tell another group. In other words, he played one group against another, as politicians, I suppose, always do, and he was very successful at it. But still, even so, his policies were pretty consistent and pretty effective, whether you like them or not! He was effective in it. He did what he proposed to do.

But the world after the war had collapsed, just like our services collapsed after World War II. We demobilized, we had no combat capability at all for a while, so had the civilian element collapsed. Our previous standards, previous goals, were changing. They were changing fast and nobody knew what was happening. Nations were falling and rapidly changing governments. The whole world was in chaos, not violent chaos, just uncertainty. The United States was the only country that could set a policy because everything depended upon the U.S. policy. So, as a leader of the world, we had to know, I thought, where the hell we were going, and we didn't seem to know. We didn't seem to have a world that we were aiming for as a nation. Some individuals did but not as a nation.

There were a lot of other arguments -

Q: Well, now, this effort on the part of the General Board, wrestling with such a major expansive topic, took you outside the confines of the navy itself, did it not?

Adm. B.: Yes, but this didn't happen in the first year on the board. This grew. Every time I said, "Look, what we really ought to have is to know what the other services are doing." And they said, OK, "you find out." We're six or seven or eight men. We can't change all of these things. You couldn't possibly do it. We didn't have the staff, we didn't have the background, there was no way we could do that. I told them yes, there is, and they said "Show us." So I kept getting more and more projects, my own individual projects.

There was one other point that came up there. Do you remember Sterling Cole?

Q: Yes, Sterling Cole of New York.

Adm. B.: Yes. He was a wonderful man and a very capable congressman. Well, within the services, there was a fight between the army air corps and the army. The army air corps wanted to separate itself from control of the Army. At the same time, there were a lot of people in the army who thought that this separation was inevitable eventually if something wasn't done and that the way to save the army and keep the army in control was to unify everything, with army influence on the top. This was just starting and there were a lot of papers being proposed on ways to do this.

The secretary of the navy, who was Mr. Forrestal at that time - and most naval officers thought there was great need for cooperation between the services. We'd all seen that, all of us who'd been in the war. There was a great need to know more about the other services, and there was a particularly great need for the other services to know more about the navy because they didn't know a damned thing about it. Cooperation, the ability to work with one another easily, even equipment, which we had fairly well coordinated before the war, but even equipment, we could coordinate better.

Well, Mr. Forrestal put out a memorandum, which I haven't seen for years, but he put out some sort of a memorandum which said that naval officers would - he gave his opinion on this, which was fairly favorable towards unification - that naval officers shouldn't imply or guess - naval officers shouldn't oppose this from a parochial point of view.

Q: It was more than an implication, I think!

Adm. B.: Well, I think he said so but I'm not really sure because I don't have the memorandum. I haven't seen it recently.

Anyway, Mr. Cole got hold of this and he wrote to Mr. Forrestal and asked him just what he meant. There was a lot of correspondence between Mr. Cole and Mr. Forrestal, and Mr. Forrestal gradually said that a naval officer could say what he thought before Congress, he's not muzzled –

Q: And Cole asked that he issue an AlNav?

Adm. B.: Yes, telling them that they could. Forrestal started by saying, of course, every naval officer knows that, and Cole said, "I don't think they do."

That problem was so extensive that it influenced and affected every other problem. I mean the conversation always turned to that during the discussion of any problem.

Q: As I recall, Admiral Blandy introduced something, he made a request that you study the feelings of the flyers who wanted to go over into the air business.

Adm. B.: Yes, he did, and so did a lot of other people. That was a time when a lot of naval aviators felt that if a separate air force was created they wanted to go into it, join the air force. As it turned out, they did this because they didn't know very much about what was being proposed. They just thought that an organization devoted entirely to aviation would be a very fine organization and they'd like to belong to it. There were quite a few, but they hadn't really studied the problem.

We got into this, all right, we discussed it. I don't think we ever wrote a paper on it, but –

Q: It was perfectly natural that you'd get involved in that, too, then. And something else that you added in a memo I found, you said that the pay for naval officers was insufficient, so this was another thing thrown into the hopper and that had direct bearing, didn't it?

Adm. B.: Yes. Well, this problem within the navy of what to do with aviators, what would our aviators do, what would the navy do, if we had a separate air force and no aviation at all within the navy itself, how would we operate - that was, of course, the most important problem. As a matter of fact, I think I did do a paper on that, on what the navy could do in the future if it had to rely upon a sister service for support from the air. I'm sure I wrote a rough draft, whether I ever finished it or not I don't know, but it turned out that the navy would be hopeless, wouldn't be able to operate, to function, without its own inherent aviation, because you couldn't call upon another service who had control of aviation soon enough, you couldn't plan for every contingency. Not every contingency that actually did occur would you know about in advance, so you couldn't change things very fast if you had to deal with another organization. So the navy just couldn't function in war.

Q: You knew from firsthand this problem!

Adm. B.: Right, but still we had to examine it. From the way we operated that was necessarily true, but maybe the navy could be operated some other way. If we were to have carriers in the U.S. arsenal, who manned the carriers, sailors or aviators? You always got back to the thing that you had to have both aviators in carriers and sailors had to be able to both fly and operate ships.

As a result of this problem, though, it became so serious that that's the time that Mr. Forrestal had a conference of all the naval aviators, all the senior aviators, from all over the world.

Q: To which Mitscher took you?

Adm. B.: Yes, to which Admiral Mitscher made me go. No, I guess it wasn't that time -

Q: No, it was prior.

Adm. B.: Prior to that time.

I see that Mr. Cole and I had correspondence about this time, too.

Q: Cole did not get a straightforward answer from Forrestal?

Adm. B.: He got a straightforward answer, but there were holes in it! He didn't get a satisfactory answer, and he kept heckling Forrestal, and Forrestal gradually changed his position. Of course, eventually, Forrestal shifted over completely to the other side, but when he was secretary of the navy he was all for careful consideration of unification, and he should have been. I mean that was not a bad position for him to take. He got misled because he didn't understand that things were going to turn out the way they did turn out, where it was a question of battling for control instead of battling for the best organization. He didn't realize at first that the unification proposals were frequently a ploy to get control of all the armed services.

Q: How did it happen that Sterling Cole wrote you on the General Board and sent you copies of Forrestal's letters, of the correspondence he had with Forrestal, and then asked you for an opinion of two bills that were in the House?

Adm. B.: I don't know how that happened. It probably was because I had to testify before his committee. He was on the navy committee.

Q: The Naval Affairs Committee?

Adm. B.: Yes, and probably because I testified up there, but I'm not sure.

Q: You took advantage of what was implied by Forrestal when you replied to Cole on June 6th, because you were fairly frank in what you said.

Adm. B.: Yes, and I'm sure that I sent Mr. Forrestal a copy of that letter. This is another thing. Mr. Forrestal was a great man. You could disagree with him, he didn't like it - nobody does, I guess - but you could disagree with him. But nobody likes to be undercut and this is a great danger in government services. There are too many people who do undercut, and they sometimes don't even know they're doing it. But you've got to lay it on the line with the man with whom you disagree.

Q: Would you let me ask one more question in this area before I let you go on to something else?

In your efforts to deal with this tremendous problem, tremendous subject and study, you naturally did reach out beyond the navy, you had to, to the other services. Did you find in those efforts any fertile soil, so to speak? Did you find that the State Department, for instance, was also thinking in terms of a need for some overall plan of government and policy?

Adm. B.: Yes. The other services were, and they gave some very good answers. They helped.

Q: They were thinking about this, then?

Adm. B.: Yes. They weren't thinking about exactly the same problem. They thought such a study wouldn't do any good, but they gave us good answers to our questions. There was not any overwhelming desire for them to do a similar study, although later on, after we submitted the study, they changed somewhat. Initially, when we started these studies there weren't very many people in the navy who were enthusiastic either - and we didn't go to the other services right away. The initial reaction when you propose a massive project is don't brush it off on me. They don't want anything to do with it because - it's a natural reaction and it's probably a good one.

Q: What I'm trying to underscore, I suppose, is the feeling

that there wasn't a great deal of this in the other services and that you were kind of a catalyst or you were kind of a bit of yeast that was generating interest.

Adm. B.: It did, it generated interest, but the place that it finally generated interest was with Mr. Forrestal himself over in SecDef.

Q: Did you have a chance to talk to Mr. Forrestal about this particular area?

Adm. B.: Yes, but not much. The secretary is a very busy man, and if you speak for ten minutes that's a pretty good long time, but you can't get much across in ten minutes on a philosophical basis. Forrestal was very friendly and I could go and see him whenever I wanted to see him. He would talk to me, but you can't take a busy man's time.

Q: Did you see him at all outside of his office?

Adm. B.: Not very often.

Q: In his home, for instance?

Adm. B.: No. His home life was very sad.

Q: He was a great poker player, however.

Adm. B.: Yes, he was a great poker player and I'm not because before I left home my father was a good poker player and when I was a kid about 15 he got a deck of cards, laid some hands out, and said, "What would you do with this?"

After he got through, he said, "Son, you stay away from all cards. You don't have any card sense whatever. Don't ever gamble with cards."

Q: So you took that advice!

Adm. B.: I got to be a pretty good bridge player once, but never poker.

No, I didn't see Mr. Forrestal very often. When he played poker like Truman and other people, or Eisenhower and his bridge, it's complete relaxation. I'm sure - I don't know this because I've never been in any offices like that, but I'm sure that it's a chance to unwind a little bit.

I did go to his home a couple of times. I don't remember just when. But not very often. He worked late at night. He got there pretty early in the morning, and usually the best time to see him was around 7:30 or eight o'clock in the morning. That's when I went to see him. I dealt quite frequently with his aides because you can't bypass aides. There's nothing worse than a fellow bypassing the aides of a senior official, and the reason is that the aides wonder what the hell is happening. They aren't in it, but they ought to be in it because they can help - so I usually went through the aides.

Q: And the aides were pretty bright young men, too!

Adm. B.: Oh, they're always bright, or they used to be! They were in those days.

Q: Was Herb Riley there at that time?

Adm. B.: Yes, Herb Riley, Charlie Buchanan, Smedberg. They were all wonderful people.

These big problems weren't the only ones that the General Board had. I found in my files a paper that I wrote on line officers versus specialists. That's an old problem. It's a problem right now, a very big problem right now.

Q: In the modern navy.

Adm. B.: In the modern navy it's a terrific problem. My thesis was "What is a navy for? A navy is to fight. Who fights? Line officers." OK, that is really the definition of a line officer, a combat officer, and so what does he have to know? Well, he has to have a hell of a lot of knowledge of people, of equipment, of tactics, strategy, everything. He has to have a vast knowledge, technical knowledge. So he has to have education. Line officers could also become specialists in a limited sense. In other words, like most of us were in those days, I had a specialty, in ordnance and, within ordnance, I was an explosives man. I stuck with my specialty for quite a few years and I knew it pretty well, but never at the expense of my line duties.

Q: It was always on the periphery, wasn't it?

Adm. B.: Always on the periphery and always as a side issue that would help in my line duties but not replace them.

So, how many specialists do you need, how many people

do you need who are designated specialists, who are, say, ordnance engineers? Well, you don't need very many because they can't fight. They aren't trained that way and, after a while, they are incapable of it because they haven't the proper knowledge.

Q: And there's the other factor that they're discriminated against in terms of advancement, aren't they?

Adm. B.: Not any more, they aren't.

Q: But they were then?

Adm. B.: They were then, and they should be. I at one time seriously considered becoming an EDO, when I was around commander, captain. I guess right after the war. Oh, I don't know, maybe before. But I seriously considered becoming an EDO because I liked research, I liked to work with material, I liked to be able to see things get completed and stay in one place for a long time. I had a good wife, I liked to see her once in a while, too. There were a lot of reasons. Whitey McClaren, who was probably one of the most brilliant men in my class, did become an EDO. He did it with the clear knowledge that he would remain a captain for ever and ever. That was not a penalty. That was the most senior rank that a specialist could have, and should have, because he was also an adviser and it didn't really make any difference what his rank was. He became a specialist because he liked that kind of work more than he liked line work.

Burke #7 - 34

Q: But there are very few men who would do it in that way?

Adm. B.: No, there were a lot of them who would have done it then but there were very few openings. Now, it's completely different, but then that was accepted. Take the corps of mathematicians, for example, the people who taught at the Naval Academy. They expected to stay there and teach and become great mathematicians, and they did.

Whitey did this, he became an EDO, and I think he retired as a captain, as he expected to, and he's quite happy about that. So did others. The exceptions were in engineering, construction. There were a few people who became flag officers in their own specialty, only rear admirals, though. The chief of the bureau was their top job, their big job, and there might be a chief and there might be an assistant chief who were flag officers, but that was all. The people of my class who became EDOs did that expecting to eventually become captains, but the captain part didn't make much difference. They liked that kind of work.

Q: It does make a difference in terms of pay, however?

Adm. B.: Yes, but the pay is not so damned important.

Q: Well, with families to support, it is a factor.

Adm. B.: The navy doesn't make families, the navy doesn't make children. Men make children, and if you make too many you're making problems for yourself, and if you're careless you make problems for yourself. But there is a reasonable amount of pay. The pay of a naval officer is important, but it's not paramount, it shouldn't be, like it is now. Pay is not the main reason for becoming a naval officer, although you wouldn't think so from reading periodicals.

To bring up that point, though, what is important to a naval officer is his self-respect and the respect of other people for his profession and for him within the profession. That is important, and we lost some of that some place in the last 30 years.

I'm embarrassed at the moment - to get on a completely different subject - I get social security. Both my wife and I are about seventy-eight. Neither one of us would take social security when we were sixty-five we wouldn't take it, but when you reach seventy-two, you get it anyway, so I did. But it's wrong. Every time I see a raise in social security it gripes me because I didn't come into the navy to get social security and I've got enough without it. It helps. I mean the money is useful as hell.

Q: And it's tax-free!

Adm. B.: It's tax-free, but it gripes me just the same. So it isn't money. When you try to buy a combat man, which you can do, you've got a mercenary force. That's what it is. It has a limited amount of loyalty. There are mercenaries in Rhodesia. They aren't there primarily for the money in that, even.

Q: No.

Adm. B.: As I read in the <u>Wall Street Journal</u> or some place.

Q: Well, to go back to your paper on the line officer versus the specialist, you were outlining the position you took at that time.

Adm. B.: Yes. I thought that all line officers should have a specialty - no, not all of them, but most line officers, should become specialists early in their career in a technical part of their profession, electrical engineering, or shipbuilding, not shipbuilding, but communications, intelligence, ordnance, every technical line. Then along about the time he's a commander or a captain, he should branch out and since he would have kept his line proficiency all the time through those years, at that time he should get rid of his specialty, get out of it, and become solely a general line officer.

Q: I suppose that was possible at that time with a specialty because things didn't move as rapidly as they do now, but to be removed from your specialty for a year or two at sea and then come back, you've lost a lot of territory.

Adm. B.: That is right, so what is a specialist for? A line officer, I mean, a specialty in the line. It's not to be able to design equipment, from scratch, it's not to be able to come up with an innovative process that's brand new, that changes the whole concept. Some of them did, but not very many. What it does do is to give the line officer knowledge enough so that he knows what has happened while he is at sea, he can look back and find out what has happened, if he wants. True enough, he can't catch up. He can't go deeply into research, he can't get into the details of engineering, or of any line, particularly as he gets a little older, as he gets a little more senior, rather. So he is there as an interface between a man who is a general line officer, and not intimately familiar with the details of explosives, for example, and the explosives research people, the production people, who are not familiar with naval operations. He's a man who's in between. He knows the language of both, he can understand both of them. To that extent, line officers should specialize, but when they become solely specialists, which a great number of people are now, then they build things, particularly if they get into control of the situation, without knowledge of the operational requirements. They think they have all the data but they don't know. They're not responsible for future operations, they're not responsible for the money or the numbers of weapons. We're in one hell of a mess now because we've got weapon systems that are so expensive, so complex, that they can't be used. They can't be purchased, we can't get enough. They're wonderful when they work and they are good but they don't _always_ work. It's a push-button business that's wonderful if it works, but you've got to have reliability - a lot of other factors that only the operators are really concerned about - not that the specialists aren't cognizant of them, but the operators are the ones who are going to be responsible for the damned systems in combat and they are the ones who are going to think supposing it doesn't work, supposing something goes wrong, what do I do?

Q: Yes.

Adm. B.: While the specialist is back on the beach and he can correct it for the next time in his tests.

Q: In effect, are you not equating the line officer who has a knowledge in these various areas with the general practitioner among doctors?

Adm. B.: Yes, and this, too, has become overspecialized, perhaps. I don't know about the doctors, but I go in for a hip operation and I can have cancer but the doctor has very little chance of finding it because he's only interested in orthopedics! Fortunately, they make you go through a general physical examination for just that reason.

We're in a bad way now because we've got too many specialists and too few line officers. We don't have a single organization - or, within our organization, we don't have anybody who's responsible for weapon systems. No way. This is why we don't have weapons at sea. They're all in research laboratories. Nobody fights, for God's sake get some guns and weapons on these ships or something. But they haven't done it because there's nobody <u>responsible</u> now for weapons systems.

Another thing that we had was <u>Navy Regulations</u>.

Q: Oh, yes.

Adm. B.: That was another problem, to revise Navy Regulations.

Q: Who instigated a study of this sort?

Adm. B.: The secretary of the navy usually. The General Board was adviser to both the CNO and the secretary of the navy. Either one of them could ask the General Board to attack a problem, to advise them on a problem, and it was probably the secretary who probably got a lot of letters from various people saying that Navy Regulations were written just like they were in 1817, the world has changed now, it's altogether different, and why do we have to abide by this silly old thing. We want to see it changed. It's in stilted language, modern language is different, and why don't you bring it up to date. It's just like the Bible or anything else. The secretary said he didn't know how to do that, so he dumped it on the General Board. It was a good thing to study. They have to be revised periodically, but it's a question of what should be changed and what shouldn't, and it takes a lot of searching to go back and find out what should be done. Nearly everything in a regulation, anybody's regulations, is caused by casualties some time or other. All safety precautions are caused by something that happened in the past.

Q: Some specific.

Adm. B.: Something specific like there might be a nice new regulation here on the operation of nuclear-power plants because of the Three Mile incident. That's what <u>Navy Regulations</u> were. It takes a lot of work. A thing like that is not to revise the whole book but to find out what is causing people trouble and revise those portions of it, because <u>Navy Regulations</u> should be revised every two or three years.

Q: Be selective about it?

Adm. B.: Yes, you can't revise it for all time.

This brings up another point. A lot of people want to solve the problem and put it on the shelf, completely solved, and very few problems are amenable to that sort of thing, that sort of solution. A technical problem, even, doesn't work that way. What is the best technical arrangement now will not be, probably, five years from now. Americans particularly have a way of saying, "Well, we've done that now. We don't have to ever tackle that problem again." But it always comes back and so what has to be done with problems is to find a way to live with them, the best way to live with them, but you're going to have to review them periodically and the important problems quite frequently. That's what's happening in energy, has been happening in energy for a long, long time.

Q: I guess it's only in the area of philosophy that you can arrive at a truth and have it as a permanent bit of knowledge?

Adm. B.: At least for two weeks! Even then, did you read Reston's article - who was it who wrote the article in the <u>Wall Street Journal</u> this morning on the advantages of aging? He'd just reached sixty-five.

Q: No, that's Vermont Royster.

Adm. B.: Yes. He was quoting a great many Greek and Roman philosophers and he doubted if they knew what they were talking about.

Q: I think he made one point. The fact that these men who talked about the joys of old age didn't actually live to find out whether they were joyful or not!

Adm. B.: True.

Q: There was another question that you investigated and I don't know whether it was related to the larger problems or not, the Taylor Model Basin?

Adm. B.: Yes. We didn't have a proper model basin and there weren't very many in the United States or in the world, so we wanted to build a model basin - we wanted a model basin that would last for some time. So we commented on the design of the David Taylor Model Basin in Carderock. That was an interesting project.

Q: You did that yourself, didn't you? Did you dig into it yourself?

Adm. B.: Yes, I dug into it, but I don't know whether I did it by myself or not. I may have. They did that sometimes.

Q: What were your findings?

Adm. B.: I haven't any idea now, except that it was a good thing because it's still there. I think the object was to see if we had room enough for facilities for the foreseeable future, because we knew that speed was going to increase, or I thought the speed of ships was going to increase, so we needed a model basin that would handle high-speed elements like hydrofoils. That was the days before surface-effects ships, but still something like that was bound to come along. I didn't find that report.

I've got here a flock of notes on Admiral Blandy's suggestion on morale and efficiency in the navy.

Q: Yes. Would you talk about that? That came in in 1947, did it, that request?

Adm. B.: I don't know when it came in, 1 August 1947, I think, on morale and efficiency, and that was caused by the conditions I have discussed before, the too-rapid demobilization, the postwar letdown, the unsettled international situation, we had too many ships in commission, too few men to man them, overworked men, non-scheduled operations. A man can't make personal plans because he's always upset by official changes of orders. Lack of trained people, particularly, the need for schools, the need for a training base. Most of our old-timers who were trained got out at the end of the war, and we couldn't keep up with the training. We didn't have people to do the training. We'd lost them.

Q: Blandy was facing the same problems that Ingram had faced when he was there.

Adm. B.: Yes, and Admiral Mitscher faced, all of them had faced, and they're facing the same thing now. Now they've got tremendous training establishments ashore, so maybe now - I say this without knowing anything about it - maybe they're top-heavy with instructors who should be operators. Maybe it's top-heavy. The balance of these things always shifts back and forth. You always have to examine such things and nobody wants to examine it because if you've got a good training school going and you're training, say, electronics men and you need four hundred per unit time, you set up a school to train four hundred per unit time and you start those four hundred per unit time coming out, pretty soon you don't need four hundred per unit time because something changes, you've filled up the gap, and then you've got a school with a certain number of instructors all going nicely, it's running very smoothly, except you don't need the product, so much product, any more. What do you do? You cut it down. When you cut it down, the school's going to hell. The efficiency's all shot, because you're taking good people out and making them operators, and this is no way. But still you can't keep turning out surplus people. So you've got to cut it.

This is a lack of realization, of people not wanting to believe or not really believing, what's true, what's going to happen. We don't want to believe what's going to happen in our economy at the moment.

Q: You can't avoid the human factor, can you?

Adm. B.: No, you can't, so you have to make tough, hard decisions and make them after you've analyzed as much as you can within the time that you've got, make them as right as you can, but then you have to stand by them and force the decision on people that hurt people. Because it does hurt people. You can't do anything productive without adversely affecting some people. You can't even give people money without affecting other people who have to provide that money or not distributing it to suit everybody.

Q: Well, in answering the request of Admiral Blandy, was the board able to be helpful to him?

Adm. B.: Not to him, but to the problem we were because many of us had faced the same problem that he had. For example, Admiral Mitscher had cut out a lot of ships of the Atlantic Fleet.

Q: And a lot of shore establishments?

Adm. B.: And a lot of shore establishments, and Admiral Blandy had to continue that process, but it's a problem that, with the lack of trained men, can't be cured overnight. The big objective is not to have to fight when you're in a situation like that, and fortunately we didn't. The navy was aware of the problem and aware of the cures and eventually we pulled out of that predicament.

I see a roster here of the General Board.

Q: When you were serving with it?

Adm. B.: When I first came on, yes. Hedding was on the board, too.

Q: Yes, he was the man you succeeded with Admiral Mitscher.

Adm. B.: Yes, but he soon left the General Board. He was there temporarily. Savvy Hoffman was the other one.

Q: Wasn't Freddie Boone on there also?

Adm. B.: Yes, he was one of the rear admirals. Boone, who was an aviator, Momsen was a submariner —

Q: Swede Momsen?

Adm. B.: Swede Momsen was a submariner.

Q: Bellinger was on there, wasn't he?

Adm. B.: Bellinger was there in the beginning, but he left very soon.

Q: He was retiring, I would think.

Adm. B.: I don't know whether he retired or whether he went to get the Sixth Fleet, but he left in May or June.

I wrote to an awful lot of people about our studies, among them was Speed Edwards, in my class, who was an EDO. I just saw him yesterday. As a matter of fact, he gave a big luncheon for the class and reminded me of these papers. He and his staff must have devoted several hundreds of hours of work preparing answers to these questions we had raised, I had raised, on what to do with BuShips, and what BuShips should do.

Q: As a whole, BuShips was not very happy, however, was it?

Adm. B.: No, nobody's ever happy to change their organization when advised. They gripe, and I would, too, but I'd do what they did also. I would examine it and say, "Well, perhaps the scoundrel has got something. This one might be all right. We have to do something and this is probably the best thing we could do." And they would eventually come to accept it without enthusiasm, but they'd do it right. They would see that. Not everybody, but you take a man like Admral Cochran, the Chief of BuShips, he would do that, he would accept it and carry it through as the best thing to do. But nobody ever likes to have change in their outfit suggested from the outside.

BuShips submitted a lot of data, too, and organizations within BuShips submitted a lot of data. So it ended up that we had a fairly good survey of the shore establishment. I knew about BuShips in detail -

Burke #7 - 47

Q: On the whole, did you get the cooperation of the various elements of the navy that you were studying?

Adm. B.: No, not always, but Speed Edwards, for example - he and his staff read those letters very carefully. And they submitted long letters in reply that had good solutions, not necessarily solutions, but good data which took a long time to get and collate.

Another fellow we had -

Q: Let me ask first, since you were talking about BuShips as one of your immediate responsibilities, you said the other was the marine corps. Did you get cooperation there? You haven't said anything about that.

Adm. B.: I did, but when Randy Pate came to the General Board he took over the marines study, so all I had to do was start that and then Randy took it over.

Q: It was logical that he should.

Adm. B.: Yes, it was a good division.

One interesting little problem here was in reference to the proper speed for merchant ships. There was a growing demand at that time for high-speed merchant ships.

Q: When you talk about high-speed merchantmen, what do you mean? How many knots?

Adm. B.: Eighteen to twenty-two knots. Merchantmen before World War II made around 10 knots.

Q: Yes, 6 and 8, too.

Adm. B.: Yes, and they were profitable then. The cost of increased speed didn't offset the advantages of speed, but as labor charges went up, as the cost of material shipped went up, and the shipping charges went up, then the time in transit became more and more important, and turn-around time became more important. So they wanted higher-speed ships - and ships that could be loaded and unloaded quickly. Also, they were able to make engines and propellers and forms of ships that would give higher-speed ships without adding greatly to the cost of new ships.

Q: I suppose refrigeration also introduced another element?

Adm. B.: Yes. Refrigeration took a big jump during the war because our navy started the really big refrigerating units. They weren't in existence before the war. Small refrigerating units in ordinary supply ships, but -

Q: Well, that had its bearing on speed, too?

Adm. B.: Yes.

We came to the conclusion that the shipbuilders were right in their estimates and that Admiral Cochran was right, that the most economical way of transporting goods would be to put increased speed in ships, make ships larger and with fast unloading facilities.

Q: Did this particular study lead you to a broader study of

the relationship with the merchant marine, to the navy?

Adm. B.: No, not that study. That had always been a problem. Most naval officers when I was a kid realized that the merchant marine was an integral part of our maritime strength and the navy was greatly dependent on the merchant marine. In the olden days, of course, they were practically interchangeable, but as the maritime unions became more powerful they separated themselves from the navy. They took steps to separate themselves, small steps, and the navy became less interested because they couldn't be depended upon, the ships couldn't be depended upon as navy ships could be. Then, the owners had to make money in order to stay in existence –

Q: To pay the wages!

Adm. B.: To pay the wages, and they couldn't make money, so they eventually disintegrated, and that's one big reason we have very little merchant marine now. But the need is still there, the need for a strong merchant marine and for very close cooperation with the navy and the navy's very close cooperation with them. That also is true with the fishing industry.

The factor that got me interested in the necessity for all maritime affairs to be closely coordinated, not necessarily through a super agency but through cooperation, was a study of the Soviet system of using all their maritime capabilities. The Soviets did a very good job and they still do a very good job on coordinating their maritime activities.

The cooperation between their merchant marine and their navy is very great, and I imagine there's a great swapping of men and material.

Q: It's almost the same, isn't it, the same service?

Adm. B.: Yes, as far as intelligence gathering and non-combat activities, in lots of ways it is. I think the intelligence services probably are just as active in the fishing and merchant marine fleets as they are in their navy, maybe more so.

Q: Doesn't it spring, though, from the political setup, the fact that one's duty is to the state and individualism doesn't count?

Adm. B.: Yes, probably. They can enforce mutual support and we could not.

Our great trouble now is not only in the large number of dissident groups, not always actually dissident necessarily, but self-serving groups who work for the good of their own group and nobody else's, and who don't want to cooperate with anybody unless they themselves get a payoff from it. This is true in every walk of life now and this is why we have so many divisive and adversary elements.

Q: Going back to the merchant marine again, what is your prognosis for a merchant marine in this country related to the navy and available to the navy in time of war?

Adm. B.: I don't think there'd be a chance that an adequate merchant marine could be available to the navy during a war. Cooperation will be hard to come by. First, there won't be very much merchant marine. Most of our merchant marine is now under foreign flags. A lot of those ships will come back but not their crews who are foreigners. They'll turn the ships over all right but it may be too late.

The big trouble is that most of our own goods that we manufacture are shipped in foreign-flag ships. I think we carry only 5 per cent of our own products that we ship overseas. This is a pitiful small percentage of our great trade to carry in our own bottoms. The percentage of imports into the United States carried in United States bottoms is probably less than 5 per cent. We are the only great nation who carries such a very small portion of its imports and exports in its own flag ships.

The problem has been recognized for the last 50 years I know. There have been interminable discussions and reports and suggestions but the amount of goods carried in U.S. ships has gone down year by year. Much of the discussion is about who is to blame for this sad condition. Shippers, the people who have to pay the freight, can't be expected to ship in U.S. ships when they can get much lower rates from foreign ships. The differential between the rates of U.S. ships and foreign ships is too great for any shipper who ships very much to absorb. A little bit they could but if they try to absorb too much the cost of the material they ship will go up so much they can't sell it.

What are the reasons why U.S. ship freight rates are higher than the rates of their competition? High wages is part of it. Productivity, high costs of building ships in the United States, governmental over regulations, less aggressive or skillful shipping firms management, foreign subsidies of their shipping - all these are part of the problem and it will take more than to cure just one of these factors to have U.S. shipping be able to compete with foreign firms. We are simply not competitive and the same impotency is becoming evident in other U.S. industries too. We simply have to work harder or we will not only have no shipping but we will have too little of much else. Inflation is made worse by the same factors that cause us to be unable to compete in world markets. We are in for real trouble unless we snap out of it. The old maxim applies - the lead dog stumbles, the lead dog dies. We are now the lead dog among nations and if we stumble too much the other nations will not be averse to giving us a little push downward - unless that would be contrary to their own interests.

But now to get back to the merchant marine. So we lose a tremendous economic advantage and the tremendous advantage of experience in cooperation between a viable merchant marine and the navy, which the Soviets have and which we used to have and now don't have. This is not just intelligence. We do use a few merchant ships to refuel sometimes. We can use them for re-supply, but the navy doesn't like to do that because they feel that they wouldn't be able to depend on the merchantmen in time of trouble.

In the Solomons, for example, I got very irate with merchantmen because they worked five days a week, they got extra pay when they reached the war zone, they got extra pay for many other things too. A seaman in the merchant marine got a tremendous salary, probably more than I got as a captain, but I remember one time when I was the senior officer in a harbor in the Solomons, there were maybe a dozen merchantmen in there, and Washing Machine Charlie came over and dropped one bomb, which he did every night, he dropped it on the beach or some place at random -

Q: Just an annoyance!

Adm. B.: Just an annoyance, just to let you know that he was around. Well, the next morning bright and early a couple of captains came over to have me sign a statement that they were under attack. I said, "Hell, you weren't under attack. We didn't even man our batteries. We didn't shoot at anything. Washing Machine Charlie comes in here every night." And they said they thought I ought to sign it because they'd heard a bomb. I wouldn't sign it and they were griped as hell.

Sometimes we'd have to get ammunition in a hurry. Mostly the ships that came up with ammunition were navy ships, ammunition ships, but once in a while a merchant ship would have a cargo of ammunition. Would they help? Not a damned bit. If you had to load up on ammunition to get out of there to do some fighting at night, to get a loadful of ammunition, they wouldn't help do it.

Q: It was after hours.

Adm. B.: Or even during hours, they were not going to help you at all. Yet they wouldn't let you touch their hatch covers or operate their winches and they wouldn't man them themselves. They were very strict on union rules. Well, that left a big sour memory. Now, not all of them were that way, I'm sure.

Q: Can you see the possibility of a relaxation in these labor rules in wartime?

Adm. B.: No, not until we're hurt. What'll happen is that we'll get hurt, we'll have to do something, we'll do it, and then it will get all right, but it may not be soon enough to be effective. This is true of a lot of things.

I notice here that in the middle of August of '48 I started getting interested in this general problem, I mean really interested.

Q: You mean the big problem?

Adm. B.: The big problem, yes - overall governmental policy and strategy.

Q: The interelationship of planning and policy?

Adm. B.: Yes, the international problem, so I joined the Brookings Institution, which Dr. Pavlovsky headed, a wonderful old man. He wasn't so old, but I thought he was then.

And Bucky Harris, a marine, was connected with Brookings,

and so I did a lot with him. I joined the atomic-warfare people, I mean their organization, to get their publications and things. And I got hold of Gallery -

Q: Dan, you mean?

Adm. B.: Dan Gallery, because he was a guided-missile man at that time, and Dr. Henry Porter, whom I had known when I was in the Bureau of Ordnance, in guided missiles.

That's when I started asking about the international situation. What the devil is the international situation - what are other nations doing about nuclear weapons, missiles, and other weapons systems?

We also had Panama Canal problems. That was a problem that was given to the General Board.

Q: The Panama Canal?

Adm. B.: Yes, not whether we should turn it over to anybody or not, but whether we should try to expand, to widen, the Panama Canal, whether we should build another canal in Nicaragua or some place else. That was just a general study and we did that.

Q: What was the result of the study?

Adm. B.: I think it was that we should add a third set of locks, bigger locks, but keep the old locks. The question, if I remember rightly, was that the Gatun Lake did not hold enough water to operate the big locks all the time. In other words, there would have to be operating instructions not to run the water down and use the present locks as much as possible for ships that could go through and use the big locks only sparingly, not to use them for smaller ships that could go through at a slightly delayed time, depending on water supply.

We had a pay problem, too, there.

Q: You say you joined the Brookings Institute. What did you acquire through this contact?

Adm. B.: I went there I think once a week. I've forgotten now, but probably Friday.

Q: For lectures?

Adm. B.: For lectures, and I met their people in discussion periods. These were discussion periods, whenever they had them, and I think it was Friday afternoon. I would go there and listen to their discussions and participate in them. I found a card that I had from Brookings Institution that made me a member of the club or whatever it was that got me a discount on their books and things.

Q: And, of course, it involved association, I suppose, even in a social sense with some of these people who were specialists?

Adm. B.: Yes, I got so I knew quite a few of them there. During that time, too, I see I had to make some speeches at various places. One of them in Raleigh.

I also wrote an estate-management folder.

Q: Estate-management?

Adm. B.: Yes, and the reason for that was that when Admiral Mitscher died, Mrs. Mitscher didn't know where any of his papers were. She didn't know anything about Admiral Mitscher's affairs, not a damned thing. It was sad. It was very sad. I asked quite a few officers what they did. Well, a lot of them didn't do anything. Their papers were in the same sort of a mess. So I wrote to several insurance companies, particularly Northwestern Mutual Life Insurance Company, who replied and gave me a lot of data. Then I sent them a rough draft and they gave me a lot of suggestions. So I wrote a pamphlet, a little bit of a pamphlet, maybe half a dozen pages, about what a man should do - not what a man should do, but a pamphlet that a man could fill in so that his wife would have all of the dope on his estate and references as to who she should call, what she should do, when he died. This was a pretty good little thing.

Q: Was this to be distributed throughout the navy?

Adm. B.: Well, I turned it over to the Navy Mutual Aid and they distributed it to all the people who belonged to Navy Mutual Aid. Then I gave it to the insurance companies and they used parts of it. Hancock and Northwestern Mutual Life used it for a while, and then they improved on it. So did Navy Mutual Aid.

Q: And that was purely on your own initiative?

Adm. B.: Yes, but the interesting part of this - I can't find that pamphlet now, I don't know where it is. It must be down in my files some place, but I don't have it here. I didn't find it in this group of files.

Benny Katz, who's retired now, but he was a destroyer skipper in the Solomons with me, has recently written several books, elementary pamphlets, on this same subject, not just on what happens when a man dies but also on the running of a small business, small estates, and so forth. So that started that. Anyway, Mutual Aid does that now.

Q: I'd like to ask about a memo you wrote on 14 August 1947 to Admiral Towers, in which you asked that the General Board members be briefed by Admiral Parsons on atomic energy and the navy. Do you recall that and the results of it?

Adm. B.: Oh, yes. Was that atomic energy or atomic weapons?

Q: Atomic energy and the navy, that's the way it was worded.

Adm. B.: This came about because Deke and I were very good friends and a lot of things were happening in the nuclear field that we ordinary line officers didn't know anything about, neither did anybody else. I mean there were possibilities, and Deke knew most about the possibilities so we should pick his brains - get his ideas. So Admiral Towers did ask Deke to come over and brief us on the possibilities of nuclear power and the possibilities of new nuclear weapons

This was a forerunner of trying to get - well, this is where I got the basic data that I needed later on for Polaris, for example.

Q: Oh, I see.

Adm. B.: For atomic weapons, for Polaris. Nuclear weapons at that time were exploded by two different systems. One was the Fatman. Fatman exploded a sphere of explosive around the nuclear core which squeezed the nuclear core until there was pressure enough to make the core become critical and explode and the other, the gun type, fired a nuclear core into another nuclear assembly so that it became critical.

Anyway, the design, the research, had gone along so that it was possible to make nuclear weapons much smaller and much more powerful. They kept getting bigger and bigger and bigger. Where was it going to end, what was the future of this thing? And what about power, could it be controlled? Of course, they were working on nuclear power all the time. Could they ever make a nuclear-power plant small enough to put into an aircraft, for example? We actually did a lot of research on aircraft nuclear-power plants at one time.

Q: In connection with that request that you made through Admiral Towers to Parsons, you also had another request that the General Board have a briefing on the United Nations. What provoked that?

Adm. B.: Bucky Harris had been in the UN. He spoke French

very well, had gone through the Ecole de Guerre, had served with the French army for a year before we entered the war, and was then assigned to the United Nations. I had quite a bit of correspondence with him and discussion with him whenever he came to Washington on the United Nations and international affairs. What other nations did was going to affect the United States, so, having started on nuclear matters, I thought what else should we know? Well, you can't get everything, but the United Nations was one of the factors that might become influential - international affairs, future international relations, and the prospect of what nations would do that would affect the United States - might affect the United States.

Then there were other subjects, too, that I remember. Missiles, weapon systems, features of ships, all the possibilities of the future that would affect the navy. You can't have lectures on all those things to very few men. There wasn't very much time and there weren't very many people. You could study these things until hell freezes over and nothing comes out, so we had to produce a paper. Somehow, there had to be some sort of a result. It was obvious that none of us were going to stay there for very long. I actually did stay there for a little over a year, but two years is about the maximum, and so if we were going to get anything out by that group it had to come out fairly soon. So I think I submitted a list of subjects and possible briefers to the General Board and probably unofficially to Admirals McMorris and Towers on how we could be briefed. It was good background information, anyway, even if they couldn't use it. This brings up a subject.

I used to go over and see Admiral Towers in the evening quite frequently. He lived in what is now Quarters A in the old hospital complex That was the first time I ever tangled with a martini that I couldn't handle. He liked martinis and he had them in old fashioned glasses and I'm sure they were 90 per cent straight gin, 5 per cent water, and a couple of drops of vermouth.

Q: Did he have the habit of making them beforehand, too?

Adm. B.: Yes, they were cold. They tasted very nice and they were wonderful, but I drank one of those one time and I came out reeling, and I said never again would I do that. Well, I did do it again when I was CNO and went over to see President Eisenhower, because he did the same thing, only they were old fashioneds. I never learned.

Anyway, these briefings did some good. About that time, I notice in this General Board file, that this was the place that a question arose on a *Life* article called Bull's Run. Did you see that? Did you notice that?

Q: No.

Adm. B.: Well, this was an article criticizing Admiral Halsey and creating the impression that Admiral Halsey and Admiral Oldendorf and Admiral Kinkaid were at loggerheads, and perhaps others, Sprague. It looked as if _Life_ wanted to develop another Sampson-Schley controversy. I wrote to _Life_ on Bull's Run and got letters back from Oldendorf, Kinkaid, and Halsey, all of whom agreed with my letter and there was no controversy. Nothing more appeared in _Life_ and I got a letter from _Life_ that defended what they had done as being the truth and said that Admiral Halsey was the only one who had attacked the other people. Of course, Admiral Halsey hadn't written that article. He'd approved it, though. It was ghost-written.

Q: I have a notation on Oldendorf's letter to you dated 5 December 1947.

Adm. B.: Well, that's what that was about. I think there was another letter but there may have been just this one.

At this same time, when we were getting briefed, one of the things that we had found during World War II was that we ran out of certain materials, minerals particularly.

Q: Raw materials?

Adm. B.: Raw materials, chrome, molybdenum, rubber, and so they stockpiled many of these scarce minerals. We went to great efforts to get natural rubber, for example. This was before synthetic rubber had really been made good enough to be a good substitute for natural rubber. I started to check on raw materials and I found a tremendous list of things and a lot of work that had been done on the shortage of raw materials in the United States by one of the temporary civilian organizations, wartime organizations, I've forgotten which. There was an indication that if we had a war, no matter who our allies were, we were going to be hard put to it to get some of the raw materials in sufficient quantity during war, so they decided to stockpile. They had stockpiled during World War II, but there was need for a peacetime stockpile.

Along with that, oil was a material that we had to have in war. Although we could produce all the oil we needed in war at that time ourselves, sooner or later, we were going to run short of oil. That became evident then, and so I subscribed to the World Oil Atlas and Oil Weekly at that time. That's when I first got interested in energy.

I also have here a note that I couldn't find anything on one of the most interesting problems that we had, and that was approval of the WAVES's uniforms. I don't have any reference to it in my files and I know we had a lot -

Q: Was the General Board asked to approve their uniforms?

Adm. B.: We were asked to advise on the type of uniforms, particularly dress uniforms. Mainbocher, as you know, designed the uniforms and they sent a group of models down. They were all beautiful girls.

Q: That must have been a pleasant sight!

Adm. B.: It was very pleasant. They wanted to know how much, how deeply, we wanted to go into this. Well, of course, we wanted to know what the story was. I remember the whole board was sitting there for the first session and they were going to show the different kinds of possible dress uniforms. They started off with lingerie, and the briefing stopped right there. Admiral McMorris said, "Now, there'll be none of this. This is just a peep show! We don't give a damn what the girls wear in lingerie, we just want the finished product, a dressed girl."

All these models were beautiful, streamlined model types and that was no good. We wanted ordinary, nice-looking, dumpy women that we've got in the WAVES to model them. That took a couple of weeks until they built some uniforms and they got some regular WAVES to model them. Still good looking girls though - but better fed than models. At that time, we approved finally, or recommended approval, for the dress uniforms that the WAVES now have.

So one of the things that the General Board had on its permanent agenda was the recommendation of the uniform boards. It all passed through there, but there's no record of that in my files.

Q: There's another item I wanted to ask you about, and that's all I saw was a notation, a copy of your letter, thanking Admiral Holloway, who was then superintendent of the Naval Academy, for sending data on the academy which you said would be presented to the General Board. What was the background of that?

Adm. B.: This was the question of motivation, the motivation of midshipmen, the same thing that bothers me very much right now about midshipmen. Not their education, not their basic knowledge. Although I think midshipmen may not get enough engineering, not enough technical knowledge, and too much knowledge that they're not going to be able to use, that's not applicable. But what Rear Admiral Lawrence is trying to do now in the Naval Academy and what Stockdale is trying to do in the Naval War College is to create motivation among the midshipmen and officers, to develop an appreciation of what the navy is, what it stands for, what the country stands for, what the navy must do for the country to continue to exist, all these things. So that a man comes into the navy and expects to spend a lifetime, not just to get an education and get out at the end of four or five years, but he expects to stay in for at least a short time - like 30 years.

Q: That's his life work?

Adm. B.: That's his life work, and to do a life's work instead of a twenty-year hitch. I just talked to a navy wife yesterday. She's a very good friend of mine and you know her. She has a daughter who's married to an army officer, a colonel, and she said:

"My son-in-law has had eighteen years in the army - he's in Iran - he's very discouraged with his career, so he's going to get out at twenty. He's got a technical education so he'll have no trouble getting a job, will he?" I said:

"Yes, I think he does have a good chance. But two years from now there might be a hiatus and the army will need good experienced officers. Why in the world is he getting out, he's a career army officer, he ought to stay in. It's not right for him to get out at twenty."

She said, "It's legal, it's quite all right." I said, "Of course, it's legal and it is ethical, but something is wrong with the service when people want to get out at twenty. I can see why they might want to require a few people to retire at twenty, and they should have retired pay after that length of time, but it shouldn't be something that an officer may choose."

Q: It has bearing on that question I raised to you before about pay, however, doesn't it?

Adm. B.: Yes, it does.

This thing of motivation is something that hit me during the war, fortunately very pleasantly. In destroyers particularly, I had this large group of reserve people and very few regular,s and those reserve people were technically deficient lots of times. They didn't know what they should have known. They didn't know what a regular would have known. But every one of those people who stayed in a combat zone was highly motivated. It's true it was for a short time, for a war only, but those people were dedicated. They would do anything they could and they would try. This hit me not as a great surprise but as a warm, wonderful thing to have.

I recognized then what a terrific value, what a terrific asset, motivation is, more so than knowledge, more so than anything else, is motivation.

When a midshipman starts griping and he gets serious about it, I mean if he gets bitter about it - of course, all sailors have got to gripe about something or other, that's all right, it's good, but there's a tone to it when it's good, but when the tone changes and it gets bitter it's anti your service. What most good griping is about is this old scoundrel up here is doing things that are not good for the service, not good enough. Why do they let a man like that continue? That sort of griping. Or why do they put this order out which is no damned good? That griping is perfectly all right, but when they get bitter about the service and the function of the service and similar matters, it's the worst thing in the world. Those people should be kicked out, quick, before they harm the rest of the service.

This is what I'm talking about here on this NAFAC. I'm going down to see Rocco and I hope he has a conference. He says he has a conference with some of the major sponsors, a couple of them. I want to discuss with him the attitude of his lecturers. I listened to one lecture that was a horrible thing to sit through. No old military man could have been effective in refuting the lecturer's statements. It's not the proper place to contradict the lecturer, but he should never have been invited. They knew what kind of a lecturer he was going to be. Most all the people that I heard lecture at that conference, and I didn't hear them all, so I don't know that this is true of all of them, but nearly every man that I heard was lecturing against the interests of the United States, and those young people in the audience absorbed it.

Of course, the audience was primarily university students from outside the Naval Academy, but this has a tremendous effect on the midshipmen who are there, and I think it's an unwarranted and dangerous practice. I think it's very bad. Of course, the answer that I will get from Rocco and from others is that they should listen to both sides. I'm not so sure it benefits the midshipmen to hear the United States attacked and communism defended, for example. But in any case, if that is so - then they certainly should hear the other side too.

Q: Right then and there.

Adm. B.: Right then and there, it should be refuted. When a lie is spoken, it should be refuted, and it should be refuted by a good lecturer. A man like myself, for example, should not attempt to counter the statements of an experienced man who is doing this for a living, who is doing it every day, who's been briefed and has a tremendous background of years of giving that sort of a lecture, so that he knows all the answers, he's experienced in handling opposition. An amateur can't counter that very effectively. You have to get another man who is equally good and who has some positive views.

I'm sure Rocco is not going to like this, but I won't support that program any more unless I can be fairly sure that there's going to be a sufficient number of lecturers to inspire people to do their best for the United States, to stand by this country, and support it. We have to first look after the interests of the United States and not after the interests of Black Africa or the Asiatics or anybody when doing so is wrong for the United States as well as morally. Our action should be for the long-range interest of our country. That should be our paramount thing, our paramount objective.

Q: Rocco himself is the one who selects these speakers, isn't he, with the approval of the superintendent?

Adm. B.: I don't really know.

Q: I think he does, with the approval of the superintendent.

Adm. B.: I don't know, but if he does -

Q: What about the problem of motivation?

Adm. B.: That's the most important problem in the service. Without motivation, you don't have anything. You can't hire a combat soldier, except for specific killing jobs like is done with mercenaries. You can't hire them to do the dull hard work that's necessary to have a good service. Going back to our own revolution, that's what happened to the British when they sent the Hessians over. They were good fighters, they were experts, but there came a time when they didn't want to fight any more and they were all through - they were not motivated.

By the end of 1947, I had been given the job of honchoing a paper. Admiral Towers and Admiral McMorris had accepted the general idea that we could do a paper on national security in the next ten years outlining factors involved, with the understanding that I would guide it. It was my project but they would help, and they did. They did a marvelous job. Everybody helped.

Q: Was your motivation high? Did you enter this project with enthusiasm?

Adm. B.: Oh, yes. I wouldn't have done all this paper work if it hadn't been. It takes a lot of enthusiasm for me to do any paper work, and there was a lot of paper work. I think I probably wrote an average of twenty pages a day for several months, a terrific outpouring of paper.

Here's a paper of 225 pages I wrote, an outline for working papers.

Q: This was the skeleton framework for the thing?

Adm. B.: Yes, a large part of it. Not all of it, but a large part of it. This went into everybody's subject but it gave them a general idea of what could be expected. Sometimes there are misstatements in here, but it was up to them to find and correct those misstatements and make it as good as possible, which they did. This paper was built one subject at a time before then.

Q: Before the June date?

Adm. B.: Yes.

One of the working papers was a study on the Middle East, which was apparently a pretty good paper.

Q: I think you could change the date and a few extraneous things and you'd have something that pertained to the present day. That was my impression, as I read it.

Adm. B.: Did you read the Middle East paper?

Q: Yes.

Adm. B.: Yes, I think it does. I have a chart of the Middle East in there some place, several charts, but I remember one chart on the Middle East and I've seen that in the last three or four years, because the remarkable thing about it is that we've forgotten now what the country boundaries were. There was no Israel then. There was the Arab League and that was a loosely formed league. There's always been an Arab League. There was instability, but the chart is completely different. That's going back to the fundamentals. The geography was the same.

Q: The weather was the same.

Adm. B.: The weather was the same.

Q: People were the same.

Adm. B.: People were the same and the minerals were the same.

They'd had trouble there for the last thousand years and it looked like they were going to have trouble in the future, and they have. But that paper was probably the best paper in the group that I wrote. It was a working paper, and I sent that to Buchanan, who at that time was aide to Mr. Forrestal, who I think at that time was secretary of defense, but I'm not sure. He wrote a memorandum to Mr. Forrestal in which he suggested that this be studied by the other services, he'd try to get the other services to make similar studies, and give it to the president and see if the president couldn't do something.

Well, we couldn't institute studies like this because the basic part of all these papers was that this was only a general idea of what could be done. The overall papers had to be looked at by a small group, but a small group couldn't originate all these papers. They had to be originated, many of them, by people who were expert in the subjects, but this small group had to develop a policy for the country, to develop a course of action for the country, which needed something general like this.

Forrestal was impressed. I'm going to give you his memorandum. You may want to put that in there.

Q: All right, fine.

Adm. B.: He took it to the president, Truman, and from this, I have been told but I don't find it in any correspondence, from the Middle East paper and this paper here, "National

Security and Naval Contributions for the Next Ten Years," was the reason why they instigated in the National Security Council studies on critical materials, the correlation of intelligence communications, and a lot of other groups that we now have. I think this gave them the idea to have such an organization, and somebody to develop possible desirable courses of action.

If that was such a good idea, why hasn't it had a good effect? That's what I've been thinking about since I read this paper in the last week. This is not a bad paper, this great big book.

Q: No.

Adm. B.: Not taking into account that it was done in three or four months by half a dozen people. It's not a bad paper and people accepted it, accepted the idea, not all the details in the paper but they accepted the concept, and they established several agencies because of it. Well, why the devil didn't it work? Why don't we have a policy now? We've got the organizations to develop it.

Nobody had made studies like this, ever, that I know of but it had quite a bit of influence. So various groups decided that what they needed were studies, and they would make studies.

Q: Tell me this. Was it a forerunner of McNamara?

Adm. B.: Exactly. Not McNamara, but the development of

great studies. I'd never heard of an outside concern making a study of military matters before this time. I don't know that they ever did. I don't remember reading about it in history. Maybe they did.

Q: You mean an outfit like Boos-Allen wasn't in existence?

Adm. B.: They were consultants on management. Management, yes, and material problems, yes, research or weapon systems, but not on governmental policy, not on the overall strategy, or the inter-reaction of the various parts of policy and strategy.

When I was CNO, I realized that we needed convincing studies, and although navy people have a talent for finding conclusions from the facts and making sound decisions, but they did not have a talent for convincing people that what they were trying to do was correct. That's where we were weak. We were weak on public relations and on the ability to write smoothly enough, to write well enough, so that we could convince people. In other words, there was too little logical, legal-type thinking in the navy, to make a presentation properly. So we got some studies made by civilian concerns while I was CNO. That was a mistake. I didn't think so at the time. I thought it was a good thing. The studies themselves were perfectly all right, but the sad part was that the outside group picked the brains of naval officers, got all their facts from the naval officers, and then wrote it in a convincing way. They assembled it correctly. They made a public relations paper out of it, and it was good. It was perfectly factual. No facts were changed in their papers. There weren't any lies in it or anything like that. It was just very well presented, so they were successful, those particular papers. Then what happened?

This went on in many areas, so they got tons and tons of paper and none of it coordinated. I believe there are literally hundreds of papers that have been presented within a year to just the Defense Department that are just put to one side. A lot of money has been spent on them perhaps, yet they aren't used. This goes back again to their asking for advice but they don't want to use it. Maybe the advice is wrong, but the papers aren't even looked at, I'm sure. They can't be.

Well, it's overdoing things, making too much of it. This could have been a good idea if they'd had a small group of, say, eight or ten people who didn't want to make a career of it - I mean that their career was to be of service to their country - but who didn't want to make a great big bureaucracy of it. Now they've got bureaucracy in this little project. Large numbers of people's jobs depend upon doing studies that pertain to problems but not to getting the answers to the problems.

Q: Not getting any action on them.

Adm. B.: Not getting any action, not getting anything that an individual like the president can assimilate. That's what went wrong. It grew too big - too cumbersome.

Q: But this particular paper on the Middle East should have assisted greatly because it came at such a timely period, when the state of Israel was being established.

Adm. B.: It did. It helped. It did a fairly good job.

In going over this summary report on petroleum - I'm still, of course, very much interested in this petroleum business - in this study we knew that neither the United States nor any other nation was completely independent for raw materials from some other nation, in peace or war. A nation had to get some essential material from outside the nation or a substitute developed or found for that material. The United States was deficient in many of these materials, but oil was not critical at that time.

Q: Production here was not that great, certainly not as great as it is now, by half.

Adm. B.: You are right, it wasn't all that great. In the last couple of weeks I became interested in that same aspect of the petroleum problem. I tried to compare the situation as it was in 1947 and 1948 with the present one. In those days we were sitting on the top of the world. We were producing more oil than we consumed and exported quite a bit. But it was evident then that there was a limit on the amount of oil we had in the United States. Nobody knew exactly how much reserves we had in the ground and we didn't know how much of that we could recover. We knew that we could get a greater proportion out of the ground in the future than we could then but what that greater proportion was could be only a wild guess. Since then the oil companies have developed secondary and tertiary recovery methods but still we can't get half of the oil out of the ground that we know is there and we still can not make even a guess as to what the undiscovered reserves might be. But there is a limit and we knew then that the world was run on energy, progress was made due to energy, and we had to discover other forms of energy and conserve oil in the United States to make it last as long as possible. We are a profligate nation and we don't like to face problems until we have to, so we didn't do much to develop our vast coal and shale reserves and we burned oil like there was to be no tomorrow. But even though we were concerned about energy in the future and we knew our use of energy would expand rapidly, we had no idea of the tremendous expansion that actually did take place. We greatly underestimated the severity of the problem and over-estimated our willingness to make provision for the future.

In 1947, the world production of oil was 8,688,000 barrels per day, eight million. It's over 51 million barrels per day now. In 1947 the United States produced about six million barrels, and all the rest of the world about two and a half million barrels. Then we exported oil for we used only about 5 million barrels a day. The rest of the world produced less than three million barrels per day. At that time only about one million barrels per day came from the Middle East. It was just starting production.

Q: That's because Saudi Arabia didn't realize what they had.

Adm. B.: No, oil had just been discovered there. The United States produced over 60 per cent of the world oil, and we consumed it at a lavish rate, and it has now about reached its maximum production in this country. We knew it was going to reach a limit some day and some day we would run out of oil in the United States. We couldn't produce at a greater rate. We would reach the limit of production, and that time was reached in 1970, when we produced 11.3 million barrels per day, which is once and a third times the total world production in 1947 - twenty years. Now in the United States we produce about nine million barrels per day and it is estimated that it will go down about half a million barrels per year. The production gets less. But we consume twenty million barrels per day now, versus about five 20 years ago.

Q: That's the figure that was cited by the attorney for the Oil Association this morning, wasn't it?

Adm. B.: Yes. I think it's over twenty million now.

Q: Twenty-two, I think he said.

Adm. B.: In '47 we were not exporters although we imported about 100,000 barrels per day of high-sulphur oil, not very much of it. Now we import 11 million barrels a day, half of our consumption we have to import, and we're producing nine million barrels, so we're using 20 million barrels per day.

At that time we recommended in this study that the United States buy as much oil overseas as it could at that time, in order to conserve our oil in the United States, so that when we needed it we could have it within our own borders. Also, that we should be energy-conscious and get substitutes for oil because eventually we would have to have a substitute for it. We cited the coalfields and oil shale in Colorado and Wyoming. Well, this is thirty years ago.

Q: This was the voice crying in the wilderness!

Adm. B.: Some of this was in the oil magazines in those days, Exxon, for example, Standard Oil in those days. We imported oil, but we didn't buy it to conserve ours, didn't conserve our own oil. We produced our own oil just as fast as we could. We bought foreign oil because it was cheap and, instead of realizing that sooner or later we would run out of it, that candy mountain was not going to stay there, we didn't do anything about it. All this was explained thirty or thirty-five years ago in detail and we didn't do a thing about it. Not only in our country, but in all other nations too.

Now, we're in a sad situation where we can't produce half as much as we use. There is no way that we can import oil in time of war to meet our requirements. There's no way we can do it - I mean from overseas, except from Mexico and Canada and, maybe, Venezuela. There is no real effort being made to convert our coal and shale to oil in an economical manner in quantity, because there are so many restrictions on it. Actually, the government seems to be taking steps to discourage this. And we are going to try to cure an energy problem? We aren't going to do it unless we take some pretty positive action soon. This is why I think the country's in a pretty desperate state, and this is what I was afraid of thirty-five or forty years ago, what is said here at the beginning and why this study was made in the first place. It was a very good effort, I think and completely futile - well - maybe not quite.

Q: I assume that this particular study and that section that had to do with the Middle East did reach the eyes of the president?

Adm. B.: Oh, yes.

Q: What kind of reaction did he have?

Adm. B.: He established a Materials Policy Commission maybe partly because of our study. One of the results that may have stemmed from this study was the Paley Commission on oil in 1952. That was a thorough study on the future of oil, in 1952, and had those recommendations been put into effect we would have been in pretty good shape now.

Q: Was that Paley who was NBC?

Adm. B.: Yes. And there were other commissions that were

formed - I mean that were created, to study the materials problem. The studies were made, but we didn't do anything about them.

Q: There was one on coal, too, wasn't there, an extensive one on coal?

Adm. B.: Yes.

Q: A friend of mine, Eric Hodgins, was the secretary to the thing.

Adm. B.: And we stockpiled for a while after that. We had stockpiles of materials in short supply, nickel, chromium, sulphur, all the things that we would run short of quickly in war we stockpiled. I don't know when we started to sell those stockpiles but we sold a good deal of them in the last five or ten years.

Q: You mean to our own industry?

Adm. B.: To our own industry, and why did we do that? We knew that we were running short of chromium. We don't have much of it in this country, but we sold a lot of chromium. Well, first, we were convinced there was going to be no more war but if there was we could always ship chromium in, which is a fallacy. But the big reason why we sold it was that we had bought that at a very cheap price and it was all paid for, so if we could sell it to industry there was income coming in to the government that would help pay the excess costs of government, and it was a considerable amount. One of the same reasons we sell gold now. We don't have many critical materials left any more. Of course, it costs some money to keep them, too.

Q: To keep them in proper storage, yes, of course it does.

Adm. B.: Yes, but certain amounts of that material in storage we should have. I can see the temptation if you could raise a lot of money, you sell it to raise the money now at a big advantage now and let somebody else in the future worry about the future when the future comes. We're not very provident.

This is what this study was all about in the beginning, to be prudent and to be prepared for possible contingencies that might not occur, probably would not occur, and certainly would have less chance of occurring if we were prepared for them.

This foreword here, this forwarding letter, from the General Board to the Secretary of the Navy is a general explanation of why the study - stating that it isn't a very good study, but that it's a sound concept and why it was made. It goes back to this one statement that's made here, to the conclusion, that a coordinated, overall plan of action for national security should be prepared at the level of the National Security Council, kept up to date, and made available to all working planners of all departments of the government. It was never done.

It's a terrific job to have done that, but looking at it now - I'd forgotten a great deal about this until I went back - and reading it now, most of it is somewhat applicable now. We'd arrived at some very good conclusions. They were pretty good. The last twenty or thirty years have proved that of the things that we were afraid would happen, many of them have happened. The outlook that we presented was pretty sound, and it's pitiful that not a damned thing was done about it, or so little was done about it. It was a futile effort. A good effort that was completely futile. Not completely, but largely.

Q: Let me ask this. Would it have been less likely to be ineffective if it had been sponsored by something other than an advisory board like the General Board? I mean if it had been sponsored and implemented by an operational division of politico-military affairs or something of that sort?

Adm. B.: Well, your key word there was "implement." That's your key word, that's what they now call the operative word. Had it been implemented by anybody in any position it would have perhaps done some good because they could have directed action - but what this thing really is, why this thing didn't go into effect, was because it required some sacrifice at the moment to ensure the future. It required payment now for future security, time, labor, supplies, stockpiles, and so forth, and this is not the attitude of people in general hold.

Q: That is a voluntary kind of cooperation in a society where people have a voice in what is adopted as a policy.

Adm. B.: Yes, but up until sometime before World War II we did have that attitude held by people, as a whole. Individuals had savings accounts. I don't borrow money to this day. Why? Because my father thought that debt was the worst evil that there could be, that no self-respecting man would go into debt, he was ashamed to go in debt. You either paid for it or you didn't have it. There are times, of course, when you've got to go into debt, as he knew. He went into debt to buy land. But debt was a condition to get out of as fast as you could. It was wrong. He felt that absolutely and he instilled that in me.

I know darned well that there are times to go into debt and you can make a lot of money by doing it and by leveraging, but that attitude in general was pretty widely held then, that you paid your way, as you went, you paid not only your own way but you had an obligation to your family, to your community. The country roads that went by your property, there was not county fund to take care of those roads. The county bought the land and that was the end of it. The land owners took care of the road in front of their land, and if you lived in a city you took care of the street, of the trees, and you made sure that the grass was watered. In the early days you each had your own trash people you paid.

Q: It was a matter of conscience and social pressure, I suppose, that kept you to it.

Adm. B.: Yes. It was part of the way of living, part of the way of life, that you did a little more than your part to make sure that your neighborhood, your school, your organization did a little more than it should do. Not how much it could get. That's part of it. Of course, it's not all of it. The big thing is that security ten years from now depends upon what we do now, but what we do now will be done by people who won't be in office ten years from now, and what they do now for something that's going to happen ten years from now will detract from what they can do now that will have an effect the day after tomorrow.

Q: That will bring them votes the day after tomorrow!

Adm. B.: Bring them votes the day after tomorrow, bring them credit or bring them power.

Q: Yes.

Adm. B.: And this is why this study's such a sad thing to look at! But it was a good idea.

Q: And that was probably your final effort on the General Board, wasn't it?

Adm. B.: Yes, and as soon as it was written up I got detached, and before they made a presentation. They made a presentation to the secretary in the middle of July and I think I was detached on the 1st of July. I guess I told you about how I was detached?

Q: No.

Adm. B.: I was detached on the 1st of July and I had written up to the Naval Combat Information Center Team Training Center in Boston, the CIC school, and asked them if I could spend three or four days up there to learn what the score was all about because I was going to command a ship. They said yes, so I went up to Boston, took Bob up there, and enrolled in this school. I'd been there about two days when I got a telephone call from Smedberg, who was down in Washington in the secretary's office. Smeddy said, "Where are you?" I told him, and he said:

"Well, I just overheard something and I'm probably sticking my neck way out in telling you this, but I want to give you a little advice. You'd better be out of the country by tomorrow morning."

Q: Be out of the country?

Adm. B.: Yes, and I said, "Thank you, Smeddy."

Q: Persona non grata! He wouldn't tell you why?

Adm. B.: I didn't ask him. I knew better than that. I thought I knew. He was in the secretary's office and he had overheard the secretary say something that was going to affect me and I'd better get the hell out of the country.

Q: The nearest country was Canada?

Adm. B.: No. I was ordered to command a ship, the Huntington. At that time I was in the naval combat information center team training center, that's where I was. So I went to the skipper that afternoon. I called up Bob and said, "Start packing again." We were living in a boardinghouse or a hotel or some place. I went over to the center and said, "I think I've learned everything I can learn here. I think I've got it." Well, I'd been working in CICs during the war so my lack of knowledge was from '45, what they'd found out between '45 and '48, which was not bad. He thought I knew a lot more than I did because a lot of new things had come in in those three years. Still, I thought Smeddy's advice was pretty good. He said, sure, he'd detach me right away. He detached me.

I had my orders in my hands, anyway, after finishing this school to proceed to the port that the Huntington was then in. She was in the Med. I didn't know whereabouts in the Med, but she was in the Med some place and I was to join her as skipper.

Q: She was a light cruiser?

Adm. B.: A light cruiser.

So he detached me and I went over to Westover Field in Massachusetts. Do you know where that is?

Q: Yes.

Adm. B.: I went over there with Bob in an old car, an old Dodge car, I guess, and a great dane dog. By the time we got there it was just getting dark, and we hadn't had time for anything to eat. I figured Smeddy wouldn't take that chance and call me up unless it was pretty damned important. So I went over there and, of course, the place was mostly closed down. I went into the passenger terminal and said I would like to get transportation to some place in the Mediterranean, London, Lyautey, any place, to get to wherever the Huntington is. They asked me where she was and I said I didn't know, but if they could get me to London or some place in Europe or North Africa, it would be fine.

They said they didn't have anything that night. I'd have to ask again early in the morning. There was just one man there maybe at the desk and he said:

"Why don't you go over to BOQ, check in there, and come over here about nine o'clock in the morning, and I'll see what we can do then, but I don't think I can get you out tomorrow either, but in two or three days we can. In the meantime, you can find out where your ship is."

I said, "No, I don't want to do that. I want to get there just as fast as I can."

He said, "Sorry, but you can't go, Captain. We just don't have anything."

So I said, "Have you got any planes going?"

"I'm just the passenger man here," he said, "I don't know what the schedules are. Try the freight terminal."

So I went over to the freight terminal and there was a man there in charge of the freight terminal. He asked me what I wanted and I said I wanted - well, before that, the passenger man said:

"Look, three days from now there's a flight to Frankfurt. It's a nice flight, passenger seats, a regular passenger plane. That's a comfortable way you can get there at ease, it's got a galley aboard. Why don't you just take that?"

I said, "No, I don't want to wait for three days."

"Well," he said, "I've got one for London in two days," a long time in the future, and I said, "No, I don't want that either. It's not such a good flight."

"It's the only thing I've got scheduled. There are always flights going over somehow, but I don't know what."

So I went over to the freight terminal and asked, "Could I get a plane?" and he said, "We don't have any planes going to Europe."

I figured he didn't know much about it because he was not in the passenger business, either. Here was a navy captain and an air corps man.

Q: He was not going to put himself out!

Adm. B.: He wasn't going to help out much. So I said:

"Do you mind if I go through the terminal here and take a look?"

He said, "No, no, go ahead."

There were piles of stuff, marked to go on planes about to be loaded, within a week or depending upon how much space there was and a lot of other factors. They piled the stuff up in great big piles and labeled it for plane number so and so, flight so and so, put the dope on it, so that people could easily check the cargo in and out. I started looking down the line. "Port Lyautey," I saw, flight No. so and so, next morning, six o'clock or something like that. I looked at the data sheet, checked it. I think it was the 6th of July or maybe the 7th of July.

So I went back and asked about getting on that plane. "I don't know anything about that," he said. I said: "Well, come and take a look." He looked at it and said, "I guess you're right. I don't have that on my schedule, but I guess you're right." I said, "Can I get on that?" and he said, "I don't know. I don't know whether they take any passengers or not. You can come over and ask the pilot."

So I said, "What time will he be here?"

"I don't know. All I know is what that sign says. But I tell you what I'll do. Why don't you go over to BOQ, stay at BOQ, and I'll call you at four o'clock. That will be plenty of time."

I said, "No. Do you care if I stay right here?" and he said, "No, stay here if you want to."

Q: He must have thought you were a funny guy!

Adm. B.: So I went out to see Bob. She was waiting in the car for me the hour or so that I was in there, and I said, "I think I've got a way. I'll get my baggage and you shove off for Washington." She started back for Washington that night. I didn't see her for six months, but she gets her dog and goes off. So I went in and bedded down on the deck next to this sign. I probably had a string on the sign so that nobody could get anything off of that pile without my knowing it!

Anyway, sure enough, the next morning the pilot was in there plenty early, about four o'clock. It didn't take him long to load the baggage and he said, "Sure, but this is a hell of a flight. We've got no passenger seats, but we'll arrange something. It doesn't look like this is a full plane, anyway. We'll see how it goes." In about an hour or so it was loaded and they put in some of these little side seats, a little section, and he said:

"Have you got anything to eat?"

"No."

"We'd better get some sandwiches. We've got to take our own food."

So we went over and got sandwiches and I went to Port Lyautey. I got out of the country by eight or nine o'clock. I never got a telephone call. I was out of the country and nobody called me up.

I got to Port Lyautey.

Q: That's a long flight.

Adm. B.: It's a long flight. They stopped en route.

Q: In the Azores?

Adm. B.: I think so. No, I think they went north to Argentia, then down to the Azores, and then to Lyautey. I think that was the route. The flight was boring as hell. I'd got some magazines and things, but it's hard to read in a cargo plane.

I got to Lyautey and I said to the skipper, Captain Jack Connihan. "Here are my orders to join the <u>Huntington</u>. Have you got any transportation to the fleet?" He said, "No, but let me send a dispatch to Admiral Sherman," who had the Sixth Fleet then. "Some planes come through here. We're servicing the fleet all the time. The planes come through from London or from some place else, or maybe they'll send a plane for you. We can get you there all right."

I said, "Well, I'm in a hurry to get there as soon as I can." And he said:

"I don't know where the hell the ship is. It's some place off Malta. It's at sea now."

So I said, "Well, if you could send a dispatch," so he started to write out a dispatch that I had arrived and was waiting for transportation. I've forgotten who he was now but anyway he was very kind to me. He said, "We've got a plane that's going to Algiers, no, to Tunisia, to Tunis. That's not too far from the Sixth Fleet. Maybe they could send over and get you there?"

I said, "When does the plane leave?"

"That's the trouble," he said, "it leaves early in the morning" this was probably the next day, "because we want it a daylight flight. But we'll probably get an answer back."

I said, "Well, how about just putting me in that plane and telling Admiral Sherman that I am in the plane and will be in Tunis?" He said, "How the hell are you going to get from Tunis?" "Let them worry about that." He said, "You're liable to stay there a long time."

Finally, he devised a dispatch to Admiral Sherman that said that I was going to be in that plane and he would like authority to divert the plane to some other airport to let me off, and would they send a plane to pick me up at such and such a time and take me to Malta. And in flight we got an approval that we could go directly to Malta after putting down in Tunis. So this is the way I got there.

Well, what caused all this hullabaloo?

Later, when I got back from the fleet, six or eight months later, I talked to Smeddy and I said - of course, he never wrote and told me anything, "What was the crisis?"

He said, "Admiral, I overheard Mr. Forrestal asking where you were. He called the General Board to see whether you had been detached and you had been, and he was saying 'Where in the hell is he?' Then I overheard, I guess Charlie Buchanan, say that he'd found out where you were, and he was told to get you down as soon as possible and you'd be put to work. I don't know what the job was at that time, but now I know. The job you got out of was doing the research on his biography for the Forrestal papers."

That was the luckiest thing. I couldn't have refused

the job and if he d put me on that it would have been a year or two years doing research on his papers instead of going to sea, and that would have been disastrous.

Burke #8 - 95

Interview #8 with Admiral Arleigh Burke, U.S. Navy (Retired)
Place: His residence in Bethesda, Maryland
Date: Thursday morning, 21 June 1979
By: John T. Mason, Jr.

Q: Right, Sir. Today, we begin another and an intensely interesting chapter, when you came back from Korea, where you were with the commission working out an armistice with the North Koreans.

You came back to Washington to become head of Op-30, which was the Strategic Plans Division. Later the designation was changed to Op-60. You came back and took over this job in December of 1951. Will you pick up the story at this point?

Adm. B.: You're right, I was on the delegation in Korea, the armistice delegation. I went to this delegation around the 1st of July 1951 and at that time we thought it would be a very short time before we arrived at an armistice.

Q: My, how wrong you could be!

Adm. B.: Yes, like ten days we thought. In the middle of the summer, I received a letter from Admiral Ingersoll,

Slim Ingersoll, and he told me that sometime, when I was relieved from the military armistice delegation, I would be ordered to Op-30, to relieve a classmate of mine, Mickey O'Reagan, and he asked me if that would be all right. He wanted to tell me about it ahead of time.

Well, at that time, my mailing address was General Headquarters, United Nations Command Delegation, Advanced, Munsan-Ni, Korea, and I thought when I received this letter that it wouldn't be too long before the armistice delegation's work would be completed and we'd go back to our regular duties. So I wrote to Slim and told him that I would be very happy about coming back. Well, things dragged on and in October I wrote a letter to Don Griffin, who was on the staff of CinCPac at that time, and I said in this letter that there were no indications at all as to when I might leave the armistice job. The communists were whipped, they should collapse most any time, _if_ we kept the pressure up; they should sign a military armistice within a month, _if_ we did keep the military pressure on them, because our proposals were purposely made very modest, they weren't unreasonable at all and we had not been insisting on any concession at all that we couldn't enforce. So it was a very down-to-earth armistice that we were trying to arrive at. I thought they, the communists, would see this soon.

But I did mention that that might turn out to be wrong

because we weren't making up the armistice conditions ourselves, these were made in Washington and we were only doing the negotiating. We could recommend, but that was all.

The important point there is that I made the statement to Don that the only thing that the communists pay any attention to is power - the use of power, not just potential power. We'd seen that demonstrated so many times in these negotiations. We, as Americans, didn't know very much about the use of power and didn't realize the importance of it, and all Americans have a great deal to learn about the communists' idea of power. The United States at that time had the power, military power, economic power, political power, but we weren't using it. We must learn how to use power and how to capitalize on our use of power. I cited also some of the past conferences that we had had with the communists and, in all of them, although we had a good negotiating position when we went in - we could have come out with an agreement more favorable to us if we had used our power properly. We didn't use it and we didn't get as good terms as we could have gotten, even without forcing it too much but just standing fast. The United States has been talked out of advantages that we could have had if we had just had a little more patience and been a little more realistic.

I also thought that the world would remain in turmoil,

no matter what we did, until the power of communism was destroyed. I was concerned that communism would expand as long as they could create turmoil and then capitalize on it, throughout the world. In order for their control over other nations not to expand, we had to make it difficult for them every time they created turmoil, they had to be hurt for creating it, if we could possibly do it. But we had to use power, not just get angry at the communists, but deliberately set out to hurt them when they started to take control over another group of people, another nation. But we shouldn't do anything unless we <u>could</u> hurt them. In other words, when they were in a position where we couldn't do anything about it, don't cry about it, just keep quiet. In other words, actually use our power wisely.

I think that must have been the time when the Op-30 people were commencing to be concerned about when I'd show up, because I wrote a letter to Micky O'Reagan.

Q: What position did he have?

Adm. B.: Micky Reagan had the job in Op-30 then.

Q: I see.

Adm. B.: He was a classmate of mine and he was a very

brilliant submarine officer and was all American heavy weight boxer when he was a midshipman - a good qualification for Op-30.

Q: And he was about to leave the job?

Adm. B.: Yes, I was going to relieve him, and, of course, he was eager to go.

I told him that I'd heard indirectly, unofficially, that I had been selected to relieve him as a director of the Strategic Plans Division and that the Korean conflict was dragging on and on and I didn't know when it would be over. It could be over in just a few weeks but it was more likely to drag on for some more months, although I didn't say years, as it turned out to be. I did tell Micky that General Craigie, the Air Force representative on the delegation, was being relieved about the 1st of November by General Turner of the Air Force. Bill Craigie and I had gone onto this armistice delegation at the same time when it was formed.

I got a letter from Micky and he said it was all right, I should just come when I could, and he would stay until I did, thinking it would be a couple of months.

About that same time I got a letter from Admiral Harry Hill, who was head of the Naval Academy then, and also perhaps of the Naval Institute. I guess he was president of the institute.

Q: Vice president.

Adm. B.: Yes - vice president, but he may have been at the National War College then, I'm not sure.

Q: He set that up, of course.

Adm. B.: Yes, and he was in one of those jobs. Anyway, he wrote and asked me if I would write an article for the Naval Institute on developments in Korea. I wrote and said I'd be glad to, so I started to write a rough draft of the article and, by the grace of God, I notified the CinCUNC staff, or maybe I talked about it to Admiral Joy or somebody else, anyway, CinCUNC staff found out about it, about the article, and informed me that I should get that article cleared with CinCUNC before I sent it back to the Naval Institute. When you start clearing articles, then you quite frequently lose your article, in the long run. So it didn't sound very attractive to me but I said all right, I'd send them a copy of it, not promising to clear it, but did promise to keep them informed.

Then I got sort of busy because at that time General Hodes - Hank Hodes - of the Army, and I were doing all the negotiating. They had divided the military armistice team, on which there were five people - Admiral Joy, General Craigie, Hank Hodes, General Paik, Sun Yup, who came into town the other day, by the way, and came out to see us, but that was another experience. Anyway, they had divided the subjects up and General Hodes and I got among other things, determination of the present battle line.

One of the most important points of this whole military armistice committee was where is the line that separates our two forces. Where is it, and what should it be at the end of the armistice. By that time, we'd had quite a bit of experience in negotiating with the communists, and Hank and I had a very good system. One of us did the talking and the other one wrote notes, and we had little signals. When the notewriter felt that he had something to contribute, he'd give a little signal and the man who was then negotiating would say that he'd like to ask his partner about this. So we could toss this discussion back and forth, like a basketball game, we could dribble and get the ball into proper hands.

Q: That sounds like the British negotiating tactic.

Adm. B.: That is right, although we didn't know anything about negotiating when we started on this conference. We had no data, no books, in the Far East to start with, but that's another story.

The first thing to do was to determine where the present battle line was, then, from that, we could determine where the final line of demarcation was to be at the signing of the armistice. The communists insisted that the present battle line would have to be the final line of demarcation, and we said no, that cannot be. If we had agreed to that, then all the military pressure would have to be the final line of demarcation, and we said no, that cannot be. If we had agreed to that, then all the military pressure would have come off the communists because it wouldn't make any sense to take areas, to take land, and force them back if, at the signing of the armistice, they would go back to where we are now. We had found that the only way we could get an armistice was to fight for it, not in the tents, not in -

Q: Not in the negotiations?

Adm. B.: Not in the negotiations in Kaesong or, at this time, in Panmunjom. Well, I'll give you an example of how we learned that.

When we started the negotiations on the present battle line, which had to be developed first, before we could do anything more than talk about the final line of demarcation - we agreed to start from the east coast, and we would find out where they were and where we were, our front lines, not outposts, but where the main battle lines were. Then we would determine some place in between there, a point, and then we'd connect these points as we went west and thereby determine the present battle line. Hodes and I had flown all this line. We had walked a good deal of it - 144 miles, if I remember rightly - we didn't walk all of that but a good deal of it we did. We knew that line pretty well, particularly we knew the east coast. The first point was Hill 822, which was its height in meters - I'm not so sure that was the number, but it was right close to the east coast, and we said, "Well, now, we hold Hill 822, you are north of that, and we estimate that you are here." And they said:

"Oh, no, that's not true. We hold Hill 822." We said:

"No, you don't," and they said, "Yes, we do." And then it got acrimonious, and they finally said:

"Either you are lying or your corps commander is lying or your army commander is lying, you do not have the correct data. You do not know what you're talking about. We hold Hill 822."

Well, we had called up the corps commander the night before and we knew our people were on Hill 822. But, we didn't get anywhere in negotiations that day.

We went back to Munsan-Ni and as soon as we got back we called up the corps commander and he said:

We did hold Hill 822 until about eight o'clock this morning, but around eight o'clock they launched a vicious attack, heavy artillery, and drove us back. We're trying to take it now, but we haven't been able to take it yet."

So we said: "Well, bring up your heavy artillery, all your corps artillery, and everything else, and take that damned hill, because it's important in our negotiations."

Well, we went up to Panmunjom in helicopters --

Q: The next morning?

Adm. B.: The next morning, but because we had to know exactly what the battle line was doing we had strung telephone wire from Munsan-Ni, our headquarters, up to the negotiating tent in Panmunjom that night - so that we could have direct communications with all the corps commanders. Before that we could not telephone any place but our camp in Munsan-Ni from the negotiating tent. So we strung wire so we could talk directly to the principal army commands. The next morning we had that telephone up there ready to use. The next morning, very early, we called the corps commander from Munsan-Ni before taking off for Panmunjom and he said:

"We haven't been able to take it." So the communist armies now held Hill 822, "We are at the base of that hill." They held it.

It was clear what the communists were up to. Every time we were going to talk about a point they were going to try to drive us back and make us eat crow. Not a bad trick. We thought we might as well play that game too, so we called Commander Army Eight, General Van Fleet, explained the situation to him and he agreed we would have a battle for every point whether we started it or not and we could drive them back instead of them driving us back. We had the power to do it. He notified the Corps Commanders and asked them to advise us what they could and could not do.

Then we called General Ned Almond of the Tenth corps and he gave us several alternative plans we could choose from and he would be prepared for each of them. The plan to be used would depend on the point the communists and we agreed would be the next point to determine.

Naturally, the communists might have other tricks up their sleeve and some day launch an attack some place else to give us unexpected trouble. So all corps commanders had to know what was going on, both at the battle front and in the negotiating tent. That telephone line was kept pretty busy thereafter.

Well, we had to go to the conference tent and say:

"We were right. We held Hill 822 yesterday, but you hold it today."

They said, "Of course, that's wrong, but if you want

to pretend that, if that eases your position a little bit, we don't mind your deceit. But you do agree that we hold Hill 822."

We said, yes, and they rubbed our nose in it, and they said:

"Well, now, if you agree to that, do you agree to this position of your forces?" And they had it right, so we said yes. We agreed to that maybe in an hour or so's conversation.

Then we started to discuss the next hill west, which was Hill 718, say, and one assumes we will discuss this hill, this point. They said yes.

So I picked up the telephone, got the Tenth Corps, which had the east coast, and said:

"We're just starting to talk about Hill 718, there's going to be an attack on it within fifteen to twenty minutes. Hold it. No matter what, hold it."

They did. We learned there was an attack -

Q: There was an attack?

Adm. B.: There was an attack. Of course, that was battle tactics. Thereafter, there were lots of incidents like that - but we had learned to negotiate by using a military force. We soon took another step. We told the communists:

"Now, we will settle for today, at this point, (pointing

to a map) we'll settle this point for our present battle line, but if you don't accept that today, tomorrow we're going to be two miles north."

At first, they didn't believe it, but we took the next two miles north, because we'd throw an attack in there and take it. Then they'd say, well, we'll take the position you mentioned before, and we said, "Oh, no. We distinctly said that that held only for yesterday. Today, the position is here. Do you accept that now or do you want to wait, because if you don't we're going to take some more today."

And they would accept it. We were doing pretty well in negotiating that present battle line, but we had learned that with military power you had to make them hurt to make them accept what was true, and they were trying to do the same thing to us, only they couldn't do it. We had the power. We were going pretty well. We always tried to understate the amount of advance we would make and actually take more ground than we told them we would do.

By that time, in October, they were coming into the tent dragging.

Q: Not so cocky?

Adm. B.: They were not so cocky. They weren't cocky at all, they were coming in there dragging, and we were fair. We never lied about a position. They did. We never did.

We knew our position and theirs and they knew we knew it. We made it obvious that we were checking right at every point. So we never lied, and they were commencing to comprehend that. I mean they could depend on our word. But they would come in, sheepish, and argue and they'd very reluctantly finally accept our position. We couldn't make fast progress in the negotiations but eventually they would accept it by the end of the day.

We were doing well, but, one day, Hodes and I went up there and they were cocky as the devil. We discussed the point of that day for fifteen or twenty minutes, then Hodes, who was senior to me, said:

"Could we have a recess of about five minutes because I've got to go to the head?"

They translated that, for nobody left the table, whether you wanted to go to the head or not, if the meeting was not formally recessed.

They finally agreed that that would be all right, we'd recess. Hodes and I went out to the head and he said, "These bastards have got something. They've got something - they know something we don't know. This is the first time that they've been cocky in a long time. Today, we dribble, don't try to drive anything today because they're going to be hard to argue with. We'll dribble back and forth, but we don't give anything, either. Let's find out what's happening here. Something is happening, that's quite obvious."

So that's what we did.

That night, when we got back to Munsan-Ni, we had a dispatch from the Joint Chiefs - all of our negotiating positions came through the Joint Chiefs. They originated in the State Department, but went to the Joint Chiefs for transmission to us. That dispatch was our orders to accept the present battle line as the final line of demarcation.

We couldn't believe it, because every day we'd sent a report back on what had happened during the day. We sent back comments and suggestions, so they knew back in Washington what we thought as well as the situation. So we called up General Ridgway in Tokyo - Admiral Joy did - and said what about this, did he know what might have caused those orders. Well, he didn't, it had surprised him just as much. So we said, "You'd better get over here, General, tomorrow."

In the meantime, we wrote a dispatch protesting our instructions, saying that we couldn't accept them, because our whole negotiating position would fail. We had promised the communists we would never lie to them and we hadn't. We had told them we would never accept the present battle line as the final line of demarcation, and now we had orders to do just that. We couldn't do it. We'd lose our whole position - well, we wrote a long dispatch and sent it, but we didn't get an answer back right away of course.

The dispatch probably didn't go out until seven or eight o'clock at night, Tokyo time, and we didn't get an answer back by the time we had to go up to Panmunjom the next morning.

We we went up again and negotiated. They were again cocky, and we had a useless day. We got back late that night. General Ridgway was there and we had a reply back from the Joint Chiefs saying that the United States' position was to be - the United Nations' position was to be, to accept this present battle line was the final line of demarcation.

Well, we said, we just can't do that. We just can't do it. General Ridgway agreed, and we wrote what we thought was a very strong dispatch, but General Ridgway thought it wasn't strong enough, and along about ten o'clock that night he had finished his dispatch, he had changed it, and it was a very strong dispatch. He sent that back, from Ridgway, but stating that everybody connected with the negotiations in the Far East agreed with this dispatch.

That dispatch, I'm sure, is not classified any more. It was then but that's a beautiful dispatch that Ridgway wrote. I don't have it in my files, at least I didn't see it.

The next day we got orders, again with the comment that we hadn't presented anything new in our dispatch. They said they understood our position but for us to accept the present battle line as the final line of demarcation.

Well, General Hodes and I dug into concrete. We said we weren't going to do it, we just weren't going to do it, and if they wanted someone to do that, they'd have to –

Q: Get a new set of people?

Adm. B.: Yes. Admiral Joy said he wasn't going to accept it either, so Ridgway talked to all of the negotiating team and said:

"You are military people. I dislike these orders just as much as you do, but we are military people. We have stated as clearly as we know how our position. We have now been instructed to do something we believe to be wrong but you are military people and you will carry out your orders."

Well, he was right. So we said:

"All right, General, we'll do that, but that makes us liars and so we will not stay on this delegation. We cannot, for the good of the United States, for our own good, for many other reasons. We cannot stay on this delegation any more because we've lied."

Q: You'd been discredited in thier –

Adm. B.: We'd been discredited - "so you'll have to get somebody to relieve us. Well carry out these orders but that's the last thing we do."

He said all right, he'd do that. So Hodes and I went up the next day and accepted the communist position.

Well, of course, Hodes and I and everybody else talked about this thing. We got very little sleep because of what had happened. Obviously the communists knew our orders before we did. They knew what we were going to be ordered to do. They came in to the tent cocky. Well, we carried out our orders.

Libby, who was out there as the cruiser division commander -

Q: That's Ruthven?

Adm. B.: Yes - he was ordered to replace me and he came over to Munan-Ni. Of course, I had to turn over my job and that took a couple of days, for Libby to pick it up. He arrived there about 30 November, I think, and by that time it was getting pretty cold around there. Libby didn't want this job at all and I didn't blame him for that, but I gave him my tent and showed him around the camp - he didn't know anything about living army style.

One of the things that had happened was that I was put in command of the camp a long time before and I ordered that we be fully ready to defend the camp by our own forces there. This is another story, but I'm not going into that, why we did it, but as a part of that deal, we had foxholes built right alongside of our tents so that if we got a sudden attack at night - we were right close to the battle line - if we got a sudden attack at night and our front lines were overrun we would have our weapons and equipment and we could fight a last-ditch fight from foxholes that were right there, very close by. But it was cold, so I sent over to Tokyo and got an electric blanket. We had electric power plant run by diesels - diesel engines on trucks, and when most of the lights were out the diesel could carry this extra power for the electric blanket. I also had a grating in my foxhole, over the fire step. I had a ship's grating that I had had made and I had it on pilings so that if it rained or snowed there were about two feet underneath where water would collect and I could be on a fairly dry grating. I finally got an extra tent fly and put it out so that when I moved into the foxhole this tent fly would come out, I could roll over with my blanket, into the foxhole, and my electric blanket wouldn't disconnect, if it was rigged up right. This was probably the first time I originated something, having an electric blanket in a foxhole.

Q: Plush quarters, I'd say!

Adm. B.: Plush quarters.

Well, I'd just gotten this electric blanket when Libby came and he wanted to buy it. I said, "Sure. It's a brand-new blanket. I've never really used it in the foxhole. It cost me $28.75 and if you want to pay me $28.75, that's fine." He did and you will probably have noticed a lot of letters from Libby about my integrity and cheating, including the charge that the communists had proved I lied, because afterwards, after I had left, he found the price tag on that blanket was $28.25 and I had gypped him out of fifty cents. Libby has been trying to get that fifty cents back ever since, and that's very interesting correspondence.

I came back to Washington, came back angry.

Q: Not the right mood to start a new job.

Adm. B.: No, not the right mood to start a new job.

As soon as I got back I found a letter waiting for me from Admiral Nomura, who had heard that I was being detached. I left Tokyo about midnight and, in those days, transportation in Japan was by streetcar or bus. There were very few private cars and most of those private cars were run on wood gas. Admiral Nomura was the only man who came down to see me off at midnight. It must have taken him two or three hours to get down to the airport to see me off. There wasn't a single U.S. person who gave a damn whether I left Japan or not, but Admiral Nomura came down there to see me off with great difficulty. That's one of the thoughtful things - it's more than thoughtful - it's one of the things that the Japanese are particularly good at, their indication of respect and admiration and affection, all the things that we talk about but they do. That's why I have respect and admiration for them too.

Well, when I got back I had a letter from Admiral Nomura, who commented that he was sorry to see me leave, but he asked me about the U.S. treaty with Japan. I didn't know very much about it because I'd been away from Japan for about six months.

I don't know exactly when I got back but it must have been the first week in December, I think, and I had six or seven days' leave, they said, which meant that I didn't have a job, but, of course, as soon as I came back I reported in to Admiral Fechteler, who was then chief of naval operations. He asked me some questions but he wasn't particularly concerned about my concern that the communists knew our orders before we did. There were several things that I was angry about, really angry. One of them was the communists knowing about our orders and another one was why we would accept their position when it was so obviously not in our country's interest and another thing, who the hell was running the show in Washington?

Who was doing all this? Who, in our government, was responsible for this sort of terrible action? Admiral Fechteler wasn't concerned very much about it and tried to cool me off, but I was still angry and I asked him if I could tell the chiefs what I knew. By that time I had some notes which I wish I'd kept. He arranged for me to meet them but when I went down there to tell my story to the chiefs they weren't particularly interested either.

Q: Was Radford there then?

Adm. B.: Oh, no. Bradley was chairman, Fechteler was CNO, Collins was the army chief, Vandenburg was air force chief, and Shepherd was the marine chief.

Anyway, I went down there and they were completely uninterested. I felt that they had let me come down there at the request of Admiral Fechteler and as a courtesy to Admiral Fechteler but they weren't interested in what I had to say. Vandenburg darned near went to sleep on me. Of course, he was sick then, too. But they weren't concerned. By that time I was furious. I think I said something about them permitting such disastrous orders to be issued but, no? I don't know exactly what I did.

Anyway, on the 17th of December the president sent for me. Dennison, who was aide to the president –

Q: And much more than aide.

Adm. B.: Yes. Dennison told me that I had about fifteen minutes - the president would like to see me for about fifteen minutes. I think I went in about two o'clock, something like that, and he asked me if I'd like to see the president. I said, "You bet I would," so I went in to talk to the president. He asked me some questions and he listened very attentively, particularly when I said:

"Mr. President, who the hell is - are you giving these orders?"

He said: "No, I accept what the chiefs agree to."

So I said, "Who originates it?" and he said the State Department did. So I asked him who in the State Department.

I was grilling the president and that's not what you're supposed to do, but he said, "I don't know exactly." And I said:

"Mr. President, somebody in this government is leaking information because I know that the communists got our orders before we did. I just know it. I can't prove it, but I know it."

He talked about what I thought about Korea and what I thought we should do, and I stayed two or three hours. He kept me. At the end of fifteen minutes - you're supposed, when you're given an alloted time with the president, at the end of that time, to say, "Mr. President, my time is up," and leave, unless he keeps you. Well, he kept me.

The president liked what I had to say. He agreed with it. This was President Truman. He agreed to everything. I asked him about Ridgway. I said:

"Mr. President, General Ridgway is a wonderful man and he submits recommendations he feels are for the best interests of our country, but nobody pays any attention to those recommendations."

He said: "Well, I see him and I agree with him, but we've got to do the things that are best for the government as a whole and he doesn't know all of it."

I said: "That's right, Sir." And he said:

"Well, I agree with Ridgway's stand." The President also said that he was all for more firmness on our part, less giving away, and I felt very happy about it.

The point of this incident is that the president was the only man who would pay any damned attention to what I had to say at all. He not only paid attention to it, he started checking. Well, you know, years later I found out what had happened.

There was a Britisher here - I've forgotten his name, I couldn't find it in the files, and I didn't have time to look it up, but he was on the British Mission. The British got our proposed orders at the same time or before our own chiefs got them. We were working very closely with the British, which was all right, but this fellow was in the British delegation and he sent those dispatches back to Britain and they sent them - not the British government but one of his cohorts in the British Foreign Office - sent those to the communists and their communications were faster than ours. The communists got them before we did.

This came out ten years later. He was a homo, he was finally kicked out of Britain, and he defected to the Soviet Union.

Q: Burgess?

Adm. B.: Burgess, I think it was, either Burgess or Burgess's pal, but I think it was Burgess.

By that time, I'd made quite a fuss. I mean I'd made a lot of noise around here. So, among other things, before I reported in for duty, I was asked if I would please come in and see the public information officer - that they had a program for me.

Q: A speaking program, you mean?

Adm. B.: Yes. They had a list of television shows, speeches, press conferences, and everything, a whole list of things that would have kept me on the circuit for a long time. I said:

"If this is what Admiral Fechteler wants me to do, this is what I will do."

They said they would have some people help me to write speeches and coach me on television programs, because I'd never been on a television program. I'd been on, but never as a speaker, so I was going to be trained on that.

Well, the night of the 17th I got called in - the evening of the 17th - after I'd seen the president. Apparently the president had called Admiral Fechteler or somebody, probably from State. Anyway, I got called in and the PIO said:

"It's all off. You're not making any speeches."

So I said: "What do you want me to do?" and he said:

"We'll give you written orders," and they're in there. I didn't find those orders in my files either, but I found letters. I was to make no speeches for any public audience on Korea because my views on Korea weren't acceptable. They didn't say that, but that was the real reason. They said because the Korean matter was in a state of flux or words to that effect. Nor could I make any speeches on the position of the United States on anything because I was in the Strategic Plans Division and I knew too much classified data about strategic plans. That was sound. That was good enough, and it was probably just as good about Korea, too.

But, thinking it over, I think as soon as I left his office the president started to call to find out what was the matter, and I think the State Department probably called the Navy Department and said, "Quiet Burke now. Don't let him make any speeches. Don't let him out." Anyway, I couldn't, and the only exception to that was that I could make speeches to war colleges, to service groups, but not any place where there were - where I could be quoted, which suited me all right. That was a good decision - for the wrong reason - but a good decision nevertheless.

Q: How do you explain the lack of interest in the Joint Chiefs, though, on this issue?

Adm. B.: They had been batting their heads on that same problem, probably, for a long time. They had used all the arguments that I used with them, probably. They had been over that ground so long in their conferences that they felt it was useless for me to stir it up again. Not that they didn't agree, but, as a young squirt coming back, I didn't know what they had tried to do in conferences with state. They would think that I was young, didn't have much knowledge, didn't know the way things were done, and I obviously showed that I didn't like what I was finding out. They probably resented that and I don't blame them a damned bit. They'd just fought that fight themselves.

Q: How do you account for the attitude of our State Department?

Adm. B.: How do you account for it now?

Q: Was there some possible liaison between the State Department and the British Foreign Office in this?

Adm. B.: Oh, yes, that was an agreed procedure because of the United Nations tie up. The liaison there was perfectly all right. What was wrong was, first, this damned communist in this British delegation, British mission to the United States, and, second, some of the people in the State Department then and perhaps now were convinced that the United States should not use force, not use power. For the last thirty years this has been going on. The State Department is, largely, of the opinion that the United States should not use pressure - not use power but felt that we should use only what they call diplomatic methods with no force behind it, either economic or military. I don't know how to account for it. It's horrible to think that there might be communist cells in there. I don't think there are, but there are certainly communist sympathizers and I don't know who they are, but they are doing things that support the communist cause, whether they are sympathizers or not. They don't agree with the use of power, a just use of power, for negotiation. They just want to talk.

I don't mean by any stretch of the imagination that I have doubts about all the people in State. Many of the very best people I know are, or have been, in State. Many of my friends in State are just as concerned about the stands that State takes sometimes as I am. I have great admiration and respect for the integrity and loyalty and all the other virtues that a representative of the United States should have, of people in the State Department as I do of any other department, but for some reason or other, many of the final decisions on actions the United States takes are not as sound and realistic as they could be. Some of those actions, like this one of accepting the communist position, are contrary to the best interests of the United States and do great harm. Somebody in a position of influence is responsible for our country doing things that increase the status and power of the communists and downgrades our country.

I know some of this is due to the conviction that if we give in to the communists they will be more amenable to our position the next time. I believe this to be wrong for the communists have demonstrated many times they don't operate that way. Still I can understand that a few of our people may still not be convinced of this and sincerely believe that negotiation is the only way to assure success in international relations. They are not disloyal, just mislead. But there may be somebody who is working for the communist cause and not for the cause of the United States for some of these disastrous decisions to be made. The possibility is frightening.

Take the discussion of the Salt Treaty, right now. It's the same problem. Why did we agree to some of those provisions? I don't know about Warneke. He's got a bad history. Why was he assigned to that important job?

Q: All of which was known when he was confirmed.

Adm. B.: All of which was known.

I've got to go down and make a speech a long time from now, in November, on Veterans Day, to a group in Alabama, and the one thing they're going to ask me – unless it's been settled before –

Q: It won't be, probably.

Adm. B.: No. Probably not. But it's the same question that you asked me, why did the Joint Chiefs say publicly that they would support SALT II? This is what was reported in yesterday's paper. I'm going to be asked about that and they're going to expect that I will say the Joint Chiefs are dead wrong. But that's not what I can say, because they aren't wrong. The Joint Chiefs are confronted with a fait accompli and what they have to look at, the one thing that they have to keep in front of them all the time, the one factor, is what is to the best interest of the United States ten, twenty, years from now. They must ask themselves "What can I do that's in the best interest of the United States."

That sounds easy, but it isn't, because you must start from where you are when action is required, whether it's mechanical work, negotiations, or anything else, and the same thing is true of a decision. You start from where the country is, not where you wish it were, and the country had negotiated a treaty. The treaty is not a good treaty, it is not the treaty that we should have gotten, that we could have gotten, perhaps, but it has been negotiated. For seven years they've been negotiating. The president has signed the treaty. He has put the United States' signature on that treaty. He has committed the United States, both in the treaty, and more vehemently by his statements.

Now, supposing a chief disagrees and thinks that's a bad treaty. All of them, I'm sure, as individuals think it's a bad treaty. But they are not just individuals —

they are important officials with heavy definite responsibilities for the security of our country. But what can they do about that? They can't say:

"Mr. President, I'm going to oppose this treaty when I testify before the Senate," because that would be worse for the United States at this stage than accepting it reluctantly and then build up our military power. The important point now for the Joint Chiefs is to consider what can be done within that treaty, within the limits of that treaty, to protect the interests of the United States, and that is, we've got to build up our military capability somehow. I mean we've got to get stronger, relatively, than the communists, which can be done within the treaty. But if the chiefs oppose the treaty, what will the United States administration probably do? They sure as hell won't increase the military capability of the United States. They will decrease it. So if you're a Chief sitting there in this position, you've got to think if I oppose this bad treaty will it do harm or good for the United States, and you've got to come to the conclusion that it will do harm, from the position that the United States is now in, because if the net result, if he opposes it or a group of them oppose it, will be that the relative military power of the United States will be decreased and not increased. Now, they have, by insisting upon getting more military strength, the president has agreed to go to the MX. Maybe that was the reason, and he can do something else.

Q: He hasn't agreed to the manufacture of these things?

Adm. B.: No, he hasn't, but he's implied he will. He's committed to the first step and that's about all that you can ask at the moment.

If the Chiefs opposed this, there would be great dissension. We would end up with the administration trying to reduce the military power or, at least, not increase it. There would probably be a more serious crisis than there is now - and that's bad enough.

Q: And when you say that the president, by signing this treaty, had committed the United States, it's only a partial commitment because under the Constitution it has to be verified by the Senate. So it's only one step in a two-step affair.

Adm. B.: As far as we are concerned that's true.

Q: Well, the rest of the world knows this.

Adm. B.: No, I'm not so sure they really understand it. They may very well believe that when the President of the United States signs a treaty, fanfare or no fanfare and there was much contrived fanfare this time, that our country has made a commitment that at least binds the administration if not the country.

Commitments are very serious matters. When we gradually increased our participation in the Vietnam war for the survival of South Vietnam, there was no treaty or other declaration that I know of, that we would help maintain the independence of South Vietnam. When our troops went into battle alongside the Vietnamese, the Vietnamese accepted that action that we were making a commitment to insure the existence of their nation. We demanded many concessions from their government on the conduct of their government. It was a moral commitment to the Vietnamese. But we did not really fight that war to win. We did not do the necessary things to win. We fought a defensive war and that type of a war is never successful. There were many pleas from our commanders in the field to take action that would result in winning the war. They were not accepted. At the same time we encouraged the Vietnamese to believe that we would truly support them. Eventually we lost that war and pulled out, leaving the Vietnamese to fend for themselves. The Vietnamese people believed in us and we failed them. God knows how many millions of people have died because they believed in us. True, they did not have to believe in us but they did. That was a commitment on the part of the United States whether we meant it to be or not. That is one of the reasons - our failure to win a war we could have won - that has reduced the credibility of the United States.

Another example of a commitment that the United States has abrogated is the treaty with the Republic of China. At least we did this one openly even though we did not inform out friends in the Republic of China we were going to cancel the treaty. This did not add to the credibility of the United States either. Nor did it add to our reputation for integrity.

No matter what we believe about what we should have done in Iran, the rest of the world has many people who do not trust the United States as much as it did before that event. Nations seem to have less confidence in becoming allied with us than they did before. That's not good.

The Soviets know full well that that treaty is not effective until it is ratified by the Senate. But that won't deter them one little bit from accusing the United States of renigging on a treaty the President has signed. They will use all their tremendous propaganda talent to further discredit the United States and try to gain converts from presently uncommitted nations to support them. Unfortunately the President has added to their probable propaganda by some ill-advised statements which will add credence to the Soviet accusations. They will also threaten us with an arms race, a race I think they will continue regardless of what we do, based on their actions in the last decade.

I don't really know whether it would be to the best advantage of the United States to reject this bad treaty or not. I personally oppose the treaty as a citizen of the United States. I am sure the Senate is correct in holding hearings to bring out all the dangerous features of the treaty. I think the retired military people who are testifying against the treaty are correct and are to be commended. So I know you wonder why it is that I can say that I do oppose the treaty and yet think the chiefs did the right thing in accepting the treaty. It is because of the responsibilities of the chiefs to do everything they can to insure the United States can defend its interests. The treaty is not really as important as the actions the Soviets and the United States take in regard to their military strength. The treaty does permit the Soviets to have more advantages over the United States than before but - and it's a big but - neither side now is giving up any significant present capability. Within the treaty the Soviets can build a nuclear capability greater than that the United States can build within the treaty. The real danger is that the Soviets will build up and the United States will not. Without the treaty, the Soviets will surely do as much as they can, both with their nuclear capability and with their conventional arms. So if I were a chief with the heavy responsibility to have adequate military strength to prevent the Soviets from being successful if they decide on an adventure of any kind, I would accept the treaty, not because it is a satisfactory treaty, but because if I rejected it and opposed it, our government would be likely to penalize the military - and the United States - by not supporting enough military buildup to prevent a future disaster.

Q: Well, we're back in Washington. In December of 1951, you're about to take over your new job as head of the Strategic Plans Division of the navy. Maybe it would be well to start out and give me the mission of this office. What was its purpose?

Adm. B.: I just happen to have that here some place, if I can find it.

The mission of the Strategic Plans Division was to prepare preliminary positions for the navy on all matters that pertain to the future security of the United States in which naval forces might become involved. That is a very broad charter.

Q: Encompassing the whole world?

Adm. B.: It encompassed the whole world. There were tremendous numbers of problems - I've got a list of some of the problems which it might be good to read off here. I don't have a list of these problems in my own files, so I went back and asked for the official files of Op-30, and they are tremendous and are divided into various categories. Actual Joint Chief of Staff papers that we worked on, or the papers for the Joint Chiefs of Staff, are in one segment, so I went to what they call the spindles in Op-30, which is only copies of letters that we originated, which Op-30 originated, and I got these topics from those spindles. These are the problems that we had for the first two or three months that I was in office in Op-30, and they're in the order in which they occurred rather than in any priority.

There was an intelligence study on the air situation in Korea; it was evident that the Chicoms and the North Koreans had not committed all of their air, in the Korean War, and what were they liable to do with that air? That was one. The next one was a strategic air offensive in a world war, procedures for determining what the targets should be, the allocation of weapons to various targets, the missions of the various services to avoid duplication of effort in hitting those targets, and the scope of a joint strategic war plan.

The next one was the deployment of elements of the

Fleet Marine Force in the Mediterranean. Should we or should we not deploy a battalion of marines to the Med. You must remember that this was before they had such a command as CinCSouth - there was no U.S. commander in the Med and not very many plans for that areas, we were just developing plans. The bilateral military plans with all nations and which nations we should try to get bilateral plans with first -

Q: Our potential allies?

Adm. B.: Our potential allies, or sometimes, just agreements without alliances, but an agreement that such and such things would be done in the event of a war. The command arrangements in Greece and Turkey - Greece and Turkey were just about to come into NATO - the development of U.S. positions on that, and how much General Eisenhower, who was SacEur then, Supreme Allied Commander, Europe, how much could he negotiate as a NATO commander on the command setup in Greece and Turkey, what should the U.S. position be and what should the NATO position be. In other words, what were the relationships between Greece and Turkey and NATO and the United States, what should they be.

Then another one was the responsibilities of the JCS with regard to covert operations and guerrilla warfare. Guerrilla warfare and covert operations were just commencing to be noticed again by the military services, not so much because the United States originated any covert actions, but they were being used against us, against the United States and other nations by the Soviets. What should we do? What should the responsibilities of the military services be? Should we have anything to do with it at all or nothing to do with it and, if we had anything to do with it, what, and how do you define it. Just what is a covert operation is one of the first things that had to be determined.

The next subject was the control of shipping. This is always a problem. When trouble breaks out in the world, shipping has to be controlled, somehow. The Korean War was in existence and there was danger of war in other parts of the world, particularly was this danger apparent in Southeast Asia. There's all kinds of shipping in Southeast Asia, and how do you control it, who controls it. They had some detailed plans, which I thought were wrong because they were too detailed and we should allow more leeway to local commanders.

Then the emergency plans, the defense plans of SacEur himself. He had just developed those and they had to be gone over although they were written on the spot and they knew what they wanted to do, but they had to be gone over very carefully to see whether they could be supported logistically from the United States, whether we had the shipping to do the things that we wanted to do, whether or not the air transport that he expected to have to support those plans could actually be furnished - all of those things.

The Dominican Republic was another problem, a mutual defense treaty with the Dominican Republic. The next one was reconnaissance of uninhabited regions of maritime areas.

Q: The islands of the sea?

Adm. B.: The islands of the sea and also Antarctica and Arctic areas. Should we have reconnaissance and, if so, what were we looking for, or should we look for anything. But we ought to know what is there and what's not there. How much effort do you put in such reconnaissance, and what value might it be.

Then, of course, we always had to go over budget estimates. Although we didn't have anything directly to do with budget estimates, budget estimates were very important to determine what forces we might have in the future to be able to do anything at all.

Q: Yes.

Adm. B.: Then, another little study, the use of atomic weapons. How should we use them? Not just in a general nuclear war, but could they be used in a local war of some kind, should they be used against cities, should they be used only against military targets, should they be used first, before the enemy used them, or should we wait. What should the United States do? What are the problems involved with the use of atomic weapons? At that stage, that's what that paper was all about.

Now, here's a little bit of a one. It sounds little. The mobilization mission for Massawa in Eritrea. Now, why in the world is the United States concerned about a mobilization mission in that faraway place.

Q: Well, we've heard a lot about the Horn of Africa.

Adm. B.: Yes, recently the Horn of Africa has become a big strategic issue - but twenty-five years ago we had a communications station there, which was a radio-listening station and a relay station, and the mountains of Eritrea are the best spot probably in the world for communications. For some reason, the atmospherics are just right. The station was high and all of our ships could reach the station. It was good for our communications but also it could listen to Soviet communications. It could hear not only our own signals, but hear Russia's signals, too, so it was a good intercept station.

Q: It's sad that now they control that.

Adm. B.: They control that, with our equipment maybe. I imagine the equipment is still there.

The next one was what should the duties be of the U.S. representative on the standing group of NATO. NATO had just recently been formed —

Q: You mean the military commission there?

Adm. B.: No, this was a civilian commission that advised NATO, a standing group, and really the representative of the political entities of the nations that compose NATO. They were political representatives, but you can't have eleven people hold a meeting on daily problems, so although each country has a representative to the standing group, they elected three or four people to a small committee that really runs the day-to-day affairs, running agendas and things.

This is a peculiar one — aerial mining plans in various parts of the world. We should have a mining plan for every area that we might want to mine, so we should know a little bit about it — what the depth of the water is, etc. Well, these mining plans that had been submitted, worked up, were much too detailed. They restricted the local commander too much. They told the local commander exactly what to do.

Those mining plans should have been, and were later, suggestions as to the number of mines that it would take to mine the harbor effectively, the type of mines that were available or could be made available, the length of time that those mines would be effective, all those things, so that the local commander could make the decision at the time as to what he really should do because he would have to use the forces that he had available -- not the forces that we might think would be available and then, four or five years later, find that he doesn't have those forces, or the mines have changed, or something like that. Those things have to be kept up to date, but they should not be too detailed, but they should be complete insofar as availability of material is concerned at any specific time, the types of mines and their various effectiveness and the limitations on mines.

A big problem that we had at that time was the U.S. command arrangements in southern Europe. At that time, NATO had just been formed and they had sent Admiral Carney, who was Commander, U.S. Naval Forces, Europe, with headquarters in London, to take the additional job of CinCSouth -- I don't think it was called CinCSouth originally but it eventually turned into CinCSouth. He moved his headquarters from London to Naples. When he did that, he was unable to carry out the job that he had done before in London. He lost a lot of liaison. So we made this study as to what was the best arrangement the United States could make. Should we separate CinCSouth from what had been Admiral Carney's job before, what U.S. forces should be put under CinCSouth, naval forces, at least, should there be any restrictions. In other words, what should the situation be.

Well, eventually that turned out to be to divide what Admiral Carney had into two parts, one being the NATO part, and leave that separate from the U.S. part. The U.S. part would be moved under another command back to London. Well, of course, Admiral Carney didn't like that very much at first, but it was done. Then, in the next few months, I guess, they formed CinCNelm, which Jerry Wright took over, and moved part of the staff back to London. He had command of U.S. Naval Forces in Europe and the Eastern Atlantic, and CinCSouth would be given that command when the U.S. government turned the U.S. forces over to NATO, because we did not want U.S. naval forces to be specifically detailed to NATO in peacetime because when a ship needs overhaul there's a lot of communication that's necessary just to shift from one ship to another. No two ships are exactly identical. No two ships are in the same degree of training. The army has a very bad habit of wanting something permanently assigned to their command and then they forget about it. They don't keep it up, they don't keep it trained. Well, they don't really know, to do that with Naval Forces, and we wanted to keep our forces ready for combat and, to do that, they had to be under the command of U.S. officers all the way back to the Joint Chiefs. But when a war comes along, they would be turned over to the proper NATO - or alliance - command.

Well, that's what that paper was about.

Then, each commander in chief -

Q: Is this another problem?

Adm. B.: Another problem. Each commander in chief submits war plans for his area of responsibility. Those plans have to be gone over in detail to see whether or not they are feasible, to see if we can find any holes in them, because all the suggestions that come in, some of them good, some of them not so good, but it gets a lot of people's ideas into these war plans so that you don't overlook something obvious like the television show we just looked at where that was not done.

Then the next problem was an interesting one, too, in the present-day situation. The feasibility of holding Bahrein, Qatar, Saudi Arabia, the Trucial states, what was the feasibility of U.S. forces holding them. Op-30 made a study on that and came to the conclusion that we couldn't put enough forces into the Mideast to guarantee the flow of oil. There are too many ways to stop the flow of oil that military forces couldn't prevent. People could destroy the oil wells, among other things. Besides that, the British had the responsibility for the Middle East in those days and if we started to help, pretty soon we would be getting the whole job and the British would be pulling out. They had the responsibility and they should keep that responsibility. If the United States did decide that it wanted to try to protect any part of the Middle East, it would necessitate an augmentation of forces. But that was a study of a long time ago on how we might keep our oil flowing from the Middle East.

The next problem was the defense of Formosa. Should we try to defend it - how can Formosa be defended, in the first place - should the United States have any forces, should it be prepared to support Formosa, what should we do about the problem of the defense of Formosa. Would a show a force in the South China Sea do, should we do any of that, and, if we did, should we be prepared to fight or should we pull out after we'd shown force. If somebody called our bluff, would we retreat or would we be prepared to fight. We ought to know that ahead of time.

The next one was the Cyprus problem. There was trouble even then in Cyprus - I should say "even". I should have said there was still trouble in Cyprus.

There was another paper on the same old problem of U.S. proposals for a NATO naval command organization in the

Med area. That was a British paper that we were to comment on.

Another problem was the negotiations concerning Italian naval forces requirements. Italy didn't have any money and didn't have much of a navy. They were in the Med, they have some wonderful bases. If they had naval forces, they could do more with those naval forces than we could do as foreigners coming in there, but if they were to get any naval forces they had to have help. What help could we, the United States, give them and how much could they use effectively.

Then came another problem, which was an analysis of a previous evaluation, which means another paper, of the offensive and defensive capability of the fast carrier task forces in 1951, which was right then. This was after World War II and we were still having difficulty persuading the other services that carrier task forces were very useful in war, in spite of what they had shown both in the Korean War and in World War II.

The next problem was atomic support operations. If a local war broke out some place, say in the Middle East or Southeast Asia or some place else, should we be prepared for use of atomic weapons under some circumstances and, if so, what circumstances. Or should we decide ahead of time that we would never use atomic weapons under any circumstances in a local situation.

Here's a little bit of a one that seems far-fetched now. Joint military operations programs with Ceylon. Ceylon had just gained its independence and you wonder why in the world should the United States be negotiating there for. Well, Ceylon has a great big fueling base.

Q: Trincomalee!

Adm. B.: Trincomalee, so the rights for air transit, what to do with Trincomalee and Colombo. Would they sell us oil, would they permit us to use their harbor in time of war and so forth. At that time we got a good solution to those problems. They did agree and we helped them in some ways, too. That happy situation no longer exists.

When we first formed NATO —

Q: Is this another problem?

Adm. B.: Another problem, yes.

When we first formed NATO we got all mixed up in the use of U.S. forces and NATO forces, and we found out very early in the game that that caused a great deal of confusion and you had to have one commander responsible for the training, development, logistic support, and everything of his command. NATO didn't have the money, the facilities, or anything to support forces. When you get down to the nitty gritty of military problems they always end up under a national banner, because a nation is the highest organization in the world that can exercise sovereignty. In other words, it can raise and support armies, it can tax, it can order things done. An international body cannot do that. They can request a nation to provide certain forces, and nations can agree to provide certain forces, but if a nation doesn't do it or can't do it, there's nothing that NATO or any other international body can do about it. This is what's happening in the U.N.

So we had to devise some sort of a scheme, some sort of a system, not a scheme, so that a nation had to be responsible for its forces, the support of its forces, and establish some sort of a command to do it. In other words, orders couldn't come from a NATO command to do that supporting job. General Eisenhower was both National and NATO commander at that time, and his staff was getting all confused and there were some mix-ups. So they decided to establish a U.S. CinCEur and that was the very reason that we had divided CinCSouth and CinCNelm.

This is another new problem. Not only do you have dealings - I mean you have to make arrangements for dealings between U.S. commands, U.S. forces, U.S. people and NATO, but you also have to have coordination among the nations, and the most important nation at that time to the United States in NATO was Britain. The British chiefs of staff and the U.S.-JCS operate differently and they have different national backgrounds so they have different concepts. British power was decreasing because of their economic inability to support forces, but still they hated like the devil to give up control.

Q: Their sensibilities were increasing!

Adm. B.: Their sensibilities were increasing, they were sensitive to that, so it was very difficult.

The big trouble that we had on this particular paper was should the French be brought in or not. If you have arrangements with the British, they're bound to be generally known if not in detail. The French are sensitive, too, so should you have similar arrangements with France, and Italy, and all the way down the line. We had had a lot of difficulty with France already. We liked to bring the French in, but the British weren't so sure of that. That was another difficulty.

Another paper was on unconventional warfare, which was not covert operations, didn't pertain to covert operations –

Q: Guerrilla?

Adm. B.: Well, guerrilla operations and also propaganda. There was a study done about that time by some army officer,

I think, but it may have been an air force officer, on the possibility of Soviet psychological plans, programs, in the United States to cause the U.S. people to do the things that would be advantageous to the Soviet Union and the ways of doing this, influencing the education of people, planting sleepers, getting people to do things that the Soviet Union wanted done without their even knowing that the Soviet Union was running the show. That's mostly what the unconventional warfare was all about. Perhaps the Soviets have been quite successful on that thing. I don't know.

Here's a paper that, I guess, was never finished. It is a new subject. U.S. objectives and policy with regard to the Arab states and Israel. Israel was just being formed then, just had been formed.

Q: In '48.

Adm. B.: '48, it just had been formed and there was trouble. The British were having trouble with the Suez Canal. There was an Anglo-Egyptian dispute over the Suez Canal. It hadn't gotten serious at that time, but it was serious enough for us to consider - we've got forces in the Mediterranean, the British have forces, so does Egypt - what are we going to do if Britain and Egypt start fighting. What's Britain liable to do, what do we do with our forces, so that we'd have a general idea of what we could do, one way or the other, both sides. I mean what should we do if we support them, what should we do it we don't support them. That sort of a paper.

Connected with this was the defense of the Middle East. The defense of the Middle East was a British responsibility. We still did not have the forces to commit, enough forces, to commit to the Middle East to help defend the Middle East unless we mobilized, unless we went to general war, then we could provide the forces. So how do the British accept that responsibility, fulfill their responsibility. We wanted to maintain flexibility and be able to commit U.S. forces for local defense some time in the future without being required to commit them, which is a very difficult thing to do. The reason we didn't want to be required was because we didn't know whether we'd have them or not. But we didn't want to be precluded from operating. We wanted to be able to deny the area to the enemy, if we had to.

Another problem was the coordination of Latin-American problems, whether we should do this by bilateral agreements, knowing of the big difficulties among the Latin-American countries themselves. Would it be better to have bilateral agreements or would it be better to try to have a Latin-American group like NATO. This sort of problem was continuously examined.

Another problem was evacuation plans of U.S. people in

various parts of the world. Like you've got to have a plan in Nicaragua right now, so that you can get people out of there in a hurry, even though you don't expect to have to do it, you have to have a plan to be able to do it, so that if something does come up, you're ready to take action. Usually, I think, they do have such plans, but that's when these things were started, after the war.

The next problem was the support that we could give to the Royal Hellenic Navy, the Greeks. They didn't have any money, either, yet geographically they are in a very crucial spot, so there should be some forces there, particularly minelayers, scouts, intelligence vessels, and some defensive forces. That meant that we had to help support them.

Another paper that we had was a determination of what military bases we'd like to have and what we could possibly have in Spain. What would Spain require. That was the preliminary paper for the Air Force getting a lot of bases in Spain later. We later developed Rota, a submarine base. These were the papers that initiated that. We did not initiate all of these papers, by any means. Some of them we were commenting on other people's suggestions but these were the problems that we discussed, had to discuss.

Another problem, a very difficult one at that time, was Indonesia. There were a tremendous number of Chinese in Indonesia. Indonesia is an area of vast resources, very important ones. Red China had then recently made efforts to expand their influence in Indonesia in competition with both ourselves and Russia. We weren't really competing in those days, but the Chinese were making some progress because they had so many people there. We made a study on that.

This study slopped over because Indonesia became so interesting that we did a similar study on Indochina. Of course, the French were in Indochina and it looked like they were going to stay there for quite a while. At that time, General de Lattre was in command in Indochina and he came over here and briefed, first, CinCPac and I think he briefed the Joint Chiefs. Anyway, we got a lot of his papers, a lot of his suggestions, and one of the things that worried us was what should we do, what courses of action should we develop, in case the French withdrew from Indochina. They denied they ever had any plans for withdrawing, but they were catching hell and, so, maybe they would.

Another paper was the evacuation of Hong Kong, the forces available. This became an important paper because, to evacuate Hong Kong, we had a lot of naval forces out in the Far East. Those forces were under the command of CinCUNC, but CinCUNC said, "You can't use my forces for the evacuation of Hong Kong."

We said, "Well, the only forces that are available are

the forces that are already out there. If Hong Kong has to be evacuated, it has to be evacuated quickly. We don't expect that it will have to be evacuated, but it may be attacked, and, in case it is, we want plans so that we're all ready to do it."

"You can't use my forces."

Well, there was that little problem that had one chance in a thousand of ever developing, but you have to plan for it. If you think of it, it can be done, and you've got to have a plan to do it.

This brought up the bigger problem of how much control should a unified commander have - when you assign forces to a joint commander, does that mean that those forces are gone irrevocably, does it mean that they can't be used for anything else. This goes back to a fundamental problem between the army and the navy that has been present ever since there have been armies and navies. The navy is a mobile service. No navy, no nation ever has had a useful navy that hasn't been able to have multiple-purpose forces, and use them for one thing one day and another thing some other day. You've got one ship and it can do a lot of things. An artilleryman is an artilleryman and he can't become an infantryman overnight. This was that kind of a problem.

Then we had the continental air defense system that was just being developed, and another problem was what should we do about the Black Sea.

The Black Sea up until that time had been a sort of Soviet lake. We didn't have any forces there. Should we or should we not, what could be gained by doing anything.

Q: We had international rights, but they were latent?

Adm. B.: Yes, that's right. In international law, you have no rights you can't enforce. Was it worthwhile to send in ships to the Black Sea in accordance with the Montreaux Convention and make the Soviets unhappy -- or not? The oilfields of Baku are on the shores of the Black Sea. Baku could be an important point in time of war with the Soviet Union. We could destroy Baku or capture it to prevent the Soviets from using it. What should naval forces do in the Black Sea. Also, what intelligence, what information, could we gain in the Black Sea that would be useful, about what the Russians were doing.

Well, those were the general types of problems.

Q: Certainly, you had enough to sink your teeth in, and it must have been quite a challenge to you.

Adm. B.: Well, not so much. In that outfit, they were all bright people. Many of them had not had much experience in planning before, but all the people in that Op section had either had some sort of a command or an important staff position and they were realistic people who recognzied the importance of their job. And they worked together very well - and above all - they were all hard workers interested in their jobs.

Q: How big a staff was this?

Adm. B.: Fifty or sixty, I guess, commanders mostly, commanders and captains. For example, in my own class there - I relieved Micky O'Reagan. I didn't relieve him in December, when I arrived there. I had to have some time to break in and I relieved him I think about the 1st of February, some time in early February. Don Felt was there, a classmate of mine named Carl Hensel, who's a brilliant submariner, was an administrative lad and most of the papers, I notice, he signed. Ken Ringle was liaison officer between us and SACLant.

Q: Such a disparate number of subjects and the scope of them is so tremendous, it certainly called for some kind of organization and concentrations; I see that one of the first things you did was to issue a white paper, so to speak, on how you planned to deal with these subjects.

Adm. B.: I did. First, as I said, we had a very good staff. It was well organized. The only thing was I didn't know enough about my job, I didn't know how to get a handle on my job. I had to be informed and I had to learn how. So for about a month, I worked on what I didn't know and how to correct the wrong things I thought I knew, so I came up with a paper of about five pages, I guess, about such little things as - well, they had no general meetings because nobody had time for a meeting. So we'd have a meeting early every Monday morning, and the reason for Monday was that that was before the papers started flowing and we could discuss improving our own performance and exchange information on our problems, because all the problems were interrelated, and the action officers themselves had to know about the interchange, what similar problems were in the hands of other people.

Op-30 was divided into sections like 301, 302, and so forth -

Q: At that point, it was called Op-30?

Adm. B.: Yes, it didn't change while I was there. It was never Op-60, until after I had left. I don't know when it was changed. Obviously it had changed to Op-60 before my files were sent to the archives for they are all marked from Op-60.

Each one of these sections had to bring up its most important problems at each meeting, and if they didn't have any problems, then they could tell a story or something like that. They were not compelled to attend. If they had something to do that they felt was more important, they didn't have to come to that meeting. The reason for that was that just as soon as it is made mandatory it becomes a great bore. Everybody did come.

Q: Naturally.

Adm. B.: This was the guts of the thing. I said that the responsibility of this division is tremendous, for it is our responsibility to determine how the navy will fight its next war. It is our responsibility and ours alone to ensure that U.S. Navy plans are sound. There is nobody else in the navy who has this responsibility, including our seniors. Therefore, it is essential that we do some sound thinking and that we do our best to make certain that the papers that are accepted are correct. That means that it is not enough just for us to have good ideas. We must fit our bosses with the data in such a manner that they can sell those ideas, after they're convinced.

Q: Your bosses being the Joint Chiefs?

Adm. B.: No, the chief of naval operations and the senior Navy people. I was a very junior rear admiral then.

I said this brings up a corollary. The ideas of our seniors or the words of our seniors are not sacrosanct. What we want is the very best possible solution, and sometimes the words given to us by our seniors are not that best solution, because they have not been well considered. Those seniors realize this. Sometimes their words are based on vast experience and are absolutely correct, but do not make that assumption. If this be true in any individual case, and we modify their words, we will be told about it. But it is our duty to present the very best paper with the very best ideas that we can. It is our further duty to make certain that our seniors understand what we are trying to do and why we think it is sound. In short, there is no room for a yes man in any outfit like this.

This is very important because a lot of people have an uneasy feeling that a proposition or a paper is not quite right, but they don't feel they have enough data to go in opposition to somebody, either senior or junior to them. They can't prove their case, but they should still bring up their doubts. This is what makes an organization work, because one man has a glimmering of an idea he's not sure about and it may be that somebody else can pick it up and eventually a good solid idea is developed. Something else may come out of it and that is also good.

I also mentioned in that order that we were in a

series of perpetual crises. We worked our heads off solving day-to-day problems and we have neglected our long-range problems. We don't tackle the major problems soon enough, and the bigger the problem, the less time we spent on it. Because we work so hard on short-range problems, we don't work on the big problems because those are not immediately urgent, and we've got to correlate the whole series of little problems in the major categories, some of which probably have similar characteristics. We can't solve our problems piecemeal, we've got to develop some general policies, see if we can get some general policies accepted so big decisions can be made and thereby everybody can have a general idea of when the Navy wants to go and how to get there.

One of the things that I had was the command difficulties that we might be faced with in the future, the relationships of national commands and international commands. We discussed already the command situation in Southeast Asia, for example. I said that problem was going to kick us in the teeth and soon, what about a standing group in Southeast Asia. There are some advantages to this and also some grave disadvantages. Would it be possible to develop a system that could incorporate many of the advantages without the disadvantages. Our major problems should be studied in advance of the time that they become critical, and the most major one is what can we do in Southeast Asia. At that time, nobody was concerned about Southeast Asia, except France. But just as soon as we failed to use our power in Korea, it became evident to the communists and evident to us that it had become evident to the communists that we would probably not use our power in Southeast Asia, and so they could take control of Southeast Asia. And that's when they moved in, a long, long time before the French were defeated. They decided that the French would not be able to get support from the United States and therefore they could throw the French out of Southeast Asia, which they did. That's when Southeast Asia became important to them. This was evident in '51.

Q: How widespread was the evidence in high commands?

Adm. B.: The evidence was there.

Q: But the understanding of it was not?

Adm. B.: The significance of it was not. The possibility that this would happen in three, four, or five years - this putting off consideration of a problem until it becomes acute is an American trait. It isn't restricted to the military solely, it's an American trait. We haven't done anything about our energy problem although we knew what was going to happen if we had stopped and and thought about it cold-bloodedly. Everybody has known about energy problems for seven or eight years but we didn't want to take action because we didn't have to do anything about it right then. We know right now what problems we're going to have with the Soviets. It's inevitable that either we're going to fight the Soviets some day in our defense or the Soviets are going to crack. We know exactly that they're not going to crack as long as they're successful, as long as they can get control of a nation every year or so, they aren't going to fold. We know that. Everybody knows it. They know it, they know we know it. But the effort to stop the Soviets from getting a nation is tremendous and it doesn't pay off right away, and it doesn't solve anything because there's another problem right after that we're going to have to face, too. We aren't willing to face those things, we aren't willing to do that.

We hope that maybe, if we're good enough and can rationalize what we do, the problem will never occur, but the evidence is all there that it will occur, except we can't prove the future, so we don't do anything about it. It's very plain that, barring an internal catastrophe in the Soviet Union, they are some day going to feel themselves strong enough so that they can tell the United States just don't bother us any more, you stay out, let us run the world, you just stay over there in your own little corner, and if you don't you'll get hurt. They'll tell us that some day, and maybe we can't do anything about it by that time. Maybe we will have weakened ourselves so much that the only thing we can do is say, "What do you want us to do, Mister?" and do it.

Q: Understanding that, as you faced the problems in the Strategic Plans Division and others in there must have understood it also that this is a national characteristic, that we do not face up to our problems until they're forced down our throats, it must have been rather discouraging to go ahead with these plans of every description, knowing that they called for the exercise of power and energy and knowing full well that in most cases it wouldn't be applied.

Adm. B.: Well, they might be applied. Whether your bosses use what you provide for them or not is not something you can control. You can't make them do it, just like you can't make the government of the United States, as a government, do anything, anything at all. You can't make them do it, you can only persuade them. If you don't persuade them, you've failed, but if you don't try to persuade them, you've failed miserably. You've got to do the best you can do and that's all you can do.

Q: In this division, as you reflect on it, did the personnel generally share your point of view on the exercise of power?

Adm. B.: Oh, yes. Those people in the division had studied their problems long enough to know that and, in discussing their own problems, whatever they were, they would soon come to the conclusion by being asked questions about what are you going to do if this happens, "We assume that's not going to happen."

"You can't assume that, son, that that's not going to happen. It can happen, can't it?"

"Yes, but we don't think it will." So I said:

"What you're doing is discarding all the things that make it tough, and the enemy's not going to do that. They're going to make it tough for you."

Then they all came round pretty fast, but most of them agreed with it a long time before I got there. It's something that I think most military men agree with.

We are a democratic nation and we're brought up very carefully to make sure that the military does not get itself into a position of making national decisions, and that's sound. But the other side of that is that the political people, who do have the responsibility for making national decisions, have the knowledge and integrity to do it. Our democratic system won't work if people are not conscientious, I mean the majority of people. If most of our people don't live by the rules that they themselves provide, our people cannot be depended upon in general. In other words, what's usually called law and order. Most people do know the laws, and they try to obey them. They make the laws and they try to obey the laws that they have made, either directly or indirectly.

If a country develops where self-discipline, a feeling of responsibility among citizens become so weakened that most of the people don't agree to that, it falls apart, and that's when dictators take over. That's always the basic reason why dictators take over, and once they have, once a nation divides itself up into a group of divisive parts, small parts, antagonistic towards each other, protagonists for their own little thoughts, they no longer can seem to get together. Just like Italy now doesn't seem to be able to get a concerted view.

Q: That's the argument that's leveled against our Congress, too.

Adm. B.: It is, exactly, like the trucking controversy now. The independent truckers are raising hell, they're killing people. Why? Because they demand that, no matter what happens to the rest of the economy or to anybody else, they get cheap fuel for their trucks when they want it and they're going to raise enough hell so that the government had got to do this, or the consequences will be so great and they will destroy so much that we'll pay more heavily than if the government gives into them. Well, that can't be done, because another group is going to do the same thing if it is a successful tactic. Whether the truckers are right or wrong on their need for more fuel doesn't have much of a bearing on the problem. It's a question of can a group defy, the whole government and to provide for its own interest against the interest of the society as a whole. If it can defy it, then you lose the society as a whole. That's what has happened years ago in Italy, it's happened in France. That's why France has only been successful when a man like de Gaulle comes in and lays down the law although they are doing better now. This is a democratic government fails, and it only fails when a people fail. When the people fail and lose their self discipline in a democratic government, you don't have a government any more, and it seems to be beginning here now. You're right, not so much as in Britain, but maybe Britain can snap out of it. We hope so. Maybe Mrs. Thatcher will be able to do that. But we in the United States should learn from the experience of other nations.

But this is a thing that all those people in Op-30 understood. They worked their heads off.

Q: They were divided, they took different subjects. They didn't all work in the same area?

Adm. B.: Oh, no, there were probably three or four people working on one subject only. They all had different subjects. They were all interrelated. Some were closer together than others. And this brought up the question of relationships with other divisions, too. This division couldn't be run in isolation.

Q: No, indeed it couldn't.

Adm. B.: So one of the things that we had to do fast – although we had pretty good cooperation with the other divisions like operating divisions, like Op-05, Aviation Deputy, research and development, to know what equipment is being worked on. We wanted to get them into the problems sooner and we were able to. They helped very much, particularly those under the Op-03 umbrella, 31, 35, all those sections worked very closely with us. They helped us and we helped them, and gradually we got a few better ideas. The same thing worked with commands outside of Washington. We also tried to have unofficial contact with the senior naval commands, the other service commands, NATO commands too – although not so much NATO for we didn't get any inkling of a NATO paper sometimes until we received the completed paper. NATO commands were all new and the new staffs sometimes originated papers that had serious defects in them that the NATO staffs did not recognize because they did not have enough knowledge of opinions or conditions in the individual nations. These could have been corrected with fast unofficial liaison with planners in the separate nations and thereby would have eliminated much unnecessary controversy and much paper work later on.

Well, how do you cure that? Our group coldn't start a paper and say, look, this is what we're going to study, like I did with a General Board paper, for example - "This is what we're going to study, please submit your ideas on it." We would have to write an outline or something like that and then submit that for comments. Some comments would get them in on time for us to use them, a lot of them wouldn't. Such a system is a lot of extra work for the commands and they would feel we were asking them to do our work. They had enough to do already. Yet a problem is more easily and quickly solved if all hands concerned with it know the general thinking of all others concerned early on - as the British say. So how do you solve that problem?

Well, we solved it on a personal basis, usually. All of us had friends in all the staffs. First we'd write to the top commander and say "who do I write to on your staff," on little problems, "I don't want to take it up with you. You shouldn't use your time handling these problems, but who do I write to on your staff, tell him about these problems, he can get your ideas, he will tell you about this if he thinks it's important. He'll know and he can give you all the dope, and he can get dope for us so that your input could get in in time to be most helpful.

This is what I wrote to Don Griffin and other people. I'd send a rough draft paper to them and say:

"This is a rough draft. It has no official standing at all, yet. It hasn't been signed. It's just thoughts, but it's generally what's going to come out with some modifications. Have you got any ideas on it?"

You can get back some pretty good ideas that will help him and help the whole paper. This is a burden because it means that we would have to have voluminous correspondence. We would have to generate possible solutions fast and submit them to many people before they had been fully considered — and sometimes before we knew all the ramifications. The final paper had to be our responsibility and we could not ask them to be responsible for our interpretation of their comment.

Q: It's outside of their bailiwick.

Adm. B.: It's outside of their bailiwick and we could not wait sometimes for their answer. But such preliminary work does improve the paper, not every one but most of them.

Q: Did you have a project system manager?

Adm. B.: No, that doesn't work all the time with plans. It only works in specific cases. If you're thinking of a project like Polaris -

Q: Well, I'm thinking of it as it worked out in BuOrd or some place like that.

Adm. B.: Individuals handled specific types of problems. One individual or maybe three or four people, for example, would have to do with, say, atomic warfare. Maybe there would be a little section on atomic warfare, nuclear weapons, anything to do with nuclear weapons.

Q: There are a couple of topics there in that list.

Adm. B.: Yes. Another one might be command relationships. Now nuclear weapons and command relationships intertwine frequently, so they must get together often. People became experts in certain fields and those fields were defined - and often modified.

Q: Your specific role was to ride herd over the whole thing, and to be knowledgeable in each area?

Adm. B.: No, one man can't be that good, but to be sufficiently knowledgeable to be able to explain what was happening and to be able to help the people who worked on each project. Sort of a house mother. Not to ride herd but to know who had the most knowledge on a subject and help him do his best work. How can you help your outfit, how can you help the individuals in that outfit. This is the same basic idea as a commander's job. The commander's major job, is how to help his people, his command, do the best job they can do. That's about all he can do. If he can direct in such a manner that he can help them improve, if he can improve their performance, then he's a good commander, if he can get a little more out of them than they think they have, not by his great intelligence, but by his ability to draw out their intelligence so that they can produce more, his command is usually successful.

I don't think that I have had very many original ideas, but I do think I have been able to encourage other people with original ideas to get those ideas moving and help them get their ideas accepted. As an example, we had to brief both the chief of naval operations and the deputy chief - Op-03 - all the time on each of these papers. He would take them down to the Joint Chiefs for their action. The Joint Strategic Plans deputy, was the CNO's standby who handled the minor problems that the Chief didn't want to handle, or all the problems when the Chief wasn't there. We had to brief them on all these papers. We got nearly all the Joint Chiefs of Staff papers for review, comments and to recommend action the Navy should take and we'd have to brief our seniors so they would know all the reasoning behind our recommendations. Well, one man can't do that very well. So we had the action officer do the briefing, usually a commander or a captain. I sat in on all of these briefings. If I had something to add, I would add it, or if our questioners disagreed with our solution which was not at all unusual, I would take over if the briefer started to get into deep water. Naturally, and correctly, the chief asked demanding questions and took nothing for granted. He had to be sure he had a firm foundation for his subsequent discussions. He had to know the subject throughly.

The lad who wrote the paper can deliver it better than anybody else can deliver it. He knows more about it than anybody else, so he ought to be there to brief it. This also gives him a sense of responsibility, because if he comes up and briefs me every day on something and then I go and brief somebody else, it's bound to get somewhat changed. He knows that, everybody knows that. If he goes up there, he knows exactly what happened at the briefing. This procedure cannot be carried to extremes because an action officer cannot go to see the president, for example, the Joint Chiefs have got to do that, but it's important just the same when it can be done.

This is what made Roosevelt such a good administrator. When I was a lieutenant in the Bureau of Ordnance, the <u>Mississippi</u> had an accident, a gun blew up. I'm a lieutenant, it's evening and I happen to be in the office. He sent for somebody who knew something about this explosion. I didn't know much about it but I was the only one there. I was on the ammunition desk and knew something about what might have happened. I tried by telephone to get some senior people in BuOrd to go but they could not get there in time and the President wanted somebody to brief him - right now. So as a lieutenant I went to the White House - scared to death. That gave me a terrific feeling of responsibility, and my bosses at that time supported me completely. It's perfectly all right they said, you go over, you know what you're talking about, so go over and tell him.

This maybe has changed a little bit now, and the reason why it's changed is because the bosses themselves can not take action any more. The problems must go clear up the line of authority before there is a man who has authority to act. He can't know all about all subjects so nothing is solved there. Then the problem goes down to a staff, and so it goes from one junior part to another junior part with the name of the top man of each part apparently being responsible, and none of them knows very much about it.

Q: As you reflect on this list of problems that you outlined to me, can you say offhand which one was most successful in development?

Adm. B.: Oh, no.

Q: What were some of the highlights, as you look at the list?

Adm. B.: I didn't run into any highlights in the files that I examined. There was nothing there that highlights a particular broad problem. Take the problem of the Middle East, that problem is still with us. Also the problem of geography.

One of the studies I don't think I mentioned was a study of Russia, her geography, her resources. Just now I read in U.S. News and World Report that in the last few years the Soviet Union has realized that Siberia is their support base, and this study that we made years ago indicated that some day that would happen.

Going back to old Admiral Nomura again, we undertook a study of the rivers, the climate, the geography, the resources, that is there. These factors stay pretty constant. What are they going to do about it? What can we do about it?

Southeast Asia was one of the important highlights. It was obvious that we didn't win in Korea because we were unwilling to use power. It was obvious that the communists were bound to try that again in a very vulnerable area, and the most vulnerable area in the world at that time was Southeast Asia because France was having great difficulty. The communists were bound to do something there. They did. We had pretty good ideas as to what we could have done to control the situation there and not let the communists have it. Now they've nearly got it. But the worst thing of that distressing situation is looking at the reports of these boatloads of refugees with all these people, all of these millions of people looking to the United States as their savior because they thought we were going to save them, now they're dying, and maybe there's nothing much the United States can do now to help those people who thought that maybe somehow the United States would help them. They go to sea in little boats and keep being shoved off and drowned or starved.

Q: One gets the feeling almost that some of them at least are being forcibly evacuated.

Adm. B.: I think they are.

Q: I was struck with one itme in one of your files, a letter that you wrote about this time, 1952, in which you said you were becoming more and more concerned about Afghanistan and Iran and perhaps this was the next area that would be a hot spot.

Adm. B.: There again, that wasn't because a lot of people were concerned about that area then but geography indicated it would become a problem area, but it wasn't immediate.

Q: The proximity, too, to the Russians.

Adm. B.: Yes, trouble was bound to happen. They were vulnerable areas - and it was then evident. Just like it is evident that the Soviet Union and Communist China may come together and maybe within three or four years. They can very well come to some sort of understanding that they can act in concert or in agreement with one another, and they will do it when they think it to be to their advantage. It's not sure and it's a long way away and we aren't doing much about it, because it isn't a current situation. I would dread to think of what would happen if someday Mr. Brezhnev, or probably after he's dead, his successor said, "Mr. Hua and I have decided that we're going to do this," and we suddenly find ourselves lined up on one side and all the rest of the world, at least Russia and China, on the other, and most of the world sympathetic towards them, not because they believe in the form of government that they have, but because they may be strong enough to enforce their will by then and people want to be on the side of the winner. It wouldn't be at all surprising to see that happen, and yet we aren't doing anything about it yet and I don't think there are very many people who recognize the possibility that Red China and the Soviet Union might come together, or if they do recognize the possibility, who will think about what we might do if it happens. We hope they won't and believe there's no need to borrow trouble, so we just don't do anything about taking steps in case they do.

This is not unique to the Americans, but the Soviets are a ruthless planning group. They think of things like that.

Q: I wonder if you could summarize the paper you wrote for the CNO, Admiral Fechteler, in May of 1952, which is a crystallization, I would think, of your point of view on the Korean conflict and our involvement therein? This was after you had been back in Washington and in your job in Strategic Plans Division for some months and had a chance to reflect on what you had learned out in the Far East.

Adm. B.: Yes. This paper was written in desperation, just to express views that I held very strongly and I wasn't able to get anything done about them. We weren't doing anything about it, but I felt very strongly.

Q: Earlier on, in relating your experiences when you came back and talking before the Joint Chiefs and so forth, you didn't meet any great encouragement. The only one, you said, you said, who did listen intently was President Truman.

Adm. B.: Yes, so as a result of my frustration, which, I guess is what it really was, I wrote a paper for Admiral Fechteler and gave copies of it to a lot of other people, including General Shepherd, who was commandant of the Marine Corps. The paper was on Korea, on possible U.S. courses of action in Korea. It was based upon regardless of what we wanted to be, our wishful thinking, and in spite of rationalizations such as calling it a police action, we were at war. The United States was at war. The United States had committed large portions of its armed forces to action there. The United States was largely instrumental, solely instrumental, I think, in causing the United Nations to take a strong stand in Korea in June 1950, to oppose the communists. We committed ourselves to the principle that our resources, our military strength, along with our political assistance and financial contributions would be devoted to the security of South Korea and the security of free nations, at least those free nations who would fight to maintain their own freedom. We made a lot of statements about that and many small nations believed them. We had taken action in support of those beliefs and they trusted us. Our enemy was a cold, ruthless, very clever nation, which had no justice, no scruples, and had avowed plans to dominate the world. They had said so over and over and they were telling the truth.

Q: The enemy being Russia? The Soviets?

Adm. B.: Russia, yes, the communists. The communists at that time because the Soviet Union and China were very close together then, but primarily Russia. Their policies were clear and unequivocal. The only question was how they were going to try to do it.

The negotiations in Korea proved that the communists would agree to an armistice or to accept any of our ideas only, first, if they were forced to do so by military pressure, or, second, that they gained an advantage by doing so. There should be no longer any question that the communists do expect to gain their ends either at the conference table or on the battlefield and, unless they are prevented from doing that by military action, they expect to win one way or the other.

So I outlined some possible courses of action. We want to win this war in Korea as cheaply as possible. We want to win in Korea with the least jeopardy to our security in other parts of the world. No man can predict what forces will be required to win, but it must be evident from our past experience and throughout all history that either we have not committed sufficient forces to Korea to win or we have not utilized those forces to the full extent of their aggressive capabilities. It is also evident that we must win in Korea and that we must do it by fighting, and we must commit additional forces, if necessary, in order to win. Since that is so, we must increase the intensity of our military actions by all the armed forces and we must reinforce those armed forces as rapidly as possible in order to win as soon as possible.

The commanders on the spot should be given the authority and the means to carry out aggressive campaigns in the manner that they desire and that they find necessary within broad limits set by the government.

Q: And was this to continue, in your own estimation, under the banner of the United Nations?

Adm. B.: It didn't matter whose banner it was under. We had to win it. No other nation could win it. We had to win it. As a matter of fact, although this was under the banner of the U.N., it got that way quite by accident and by a very clever move on President Truman's part. By taking quick action, he got the U.N. to act in a hurry and the Soviets in an aberration walked out of the meeting, abstained, and that made it a U.N. action. But actually the forces that were provided were all either supplied by the United States or they were supported by the United States. Other forces that came in were actually U.S.-supported for the most part. We had to win that war or we were going to fight another one. Well, we did fight another one, and the next one was in Vietnam. We lost that one even more than we lost - we really lost that one, we had something of a stalemate in Korea. We did not win in Korea. But in Vietnam we sadly lost.

One of the things that was interesting in those Op-30 days of twenty-five years ago, and this paper brings it to mind. In the Mediterranean, for example, all the littoral of the Mediterranean were friends of ours, all the nations were friendly to us. At least all the littoral states of the Mediterranean except maybe Egypt —

Q: Who?

Adm. B.: Egypt, maybe friend, maybe not, but she was not unfriendly at that time. Algeria, Tunisia, Yugoslavia, Italy, France, they offered bases any place we wanted them. When the fleet went over there, it could go into any port it wanted to. It was routine. I mean you didn't think anything about it. The Middle East, Iran, Iraq, generally friendly towards us, Iran particularly. Afghanistan, India, Southeast Asia, all friendly. Now many of those nations are under absolute communist control. Cuba was a friend of ours at that time. Now it's a communist satellite. Nicaragua. The power, the influence, of the United States on the world is much less now than it was in 1951, 1952, and we thought we were having trouble then. The central power of the Soviet Union was great then, relatively, but they did not have much influence internationally. We were afraid they would have and they have done what they said they would do, as you said, to gain control of the world. They felt that they had to destroy other governments and take those governments over and build, build their own governments under their own rules, under their own domination. They would accept nothing less. This is what they're doing. Now they're having some trouble. They're having trouble in Afghanistan, they'll have trouble in taking over Iran, but eventually, unless something happens that I don't anticipate, they will be able to take over Iran, after they get rid of Khomeni and some of the other people.

This is in regard to that article that Admiral Hill asked me to write for the Naval Institute.

When I came back I talked to Roy Horn - he was very enthusiastic about an article on Korea. He was editor of the Proceedings. I submitted a rough draft of part, maybe nine-tenths, of the article to him, but I had not put a finish on it because the armistice wasn't completed by that time. But the Institute people were all in favor of it. I worked on it and tried to improve it a little bit. The Naval Institute didn't want to publish it unless they could get general approval. Well, that's correct. So they tried to get approval from CinCUNC, but he didn't want to approve it and nobody back in the State Department wanted to approve it. Nobody said they disapproved it, but it just died. I said I didn't care whether I finished the article or not:

"If you want that article, you get it cleared and you get it approved. I'm not going to fight for it. I don't care whether it's published or not, but if you think it's a good idea, you go ahead."

They couldn't get to first base on it.

Q: What was the real deterrent to approval?

Adm. B.: I think it was the same thing I've been talking about here. I was preaching the wrong philosophy. I felt that we couldn't solve this question of Korea unless we whipped the enemy. You had to oppose the force of communism with force, not only military, not necessarily military, economic would do just as well, or political, but we couldn't do it just by giving in to them.

I think that was the general underlying reason for opposition to it. I don't know why, though, I'm just guessing. I just dropped it. I had quite a few meetings with Roy Horn. As a matter of fact, I can't find the article now. I don't know where it is. Maybe they've got it at the Naval Institute.

Q: Maybe they do.

Adm. B.: I don't know that I ever kept a copy of it.

We, Bobbie and I, did have some pleasant things happen to us.

During the Easter vacation in 1952 we had visitors at home at 4529 Hawthorne Street in Washington. Miyoko and Tadashi Nomura came to stay with us for their vacation from Northwestern University. It came about this way.

I mentioned that when I left the Military Armistice Delegation in December 1951 I went from Munsan-ni to Tokyo where most of my gera, which wasn't much, had been delivered. I collected my gear, made calls on ComNavFe, CinCUnc and as many others as I could see in the one day I had there and went down to the airport to catch a military plane that was to leave about midnight. While I was waiting for the plane Admiral Nomura came down to see me off.

But Admiral Nomura had not told me that he had sent his son, Tadashi, to take graduate work in Northwestern University. Tadashi had been a lieutenant in the Imperial Japanese Navy, in the Supply Corps. Admiral Nomura knew that the future of Japan depended on close cooperation with the United States and wanted his son, only son, to speak English fluently and to be familiar with American ways. Early in 1952 I received a letter from Admiral Nomura telling me about Tad being in Northwestern University in this country and added that he was not doing well, was not able to adjust to our ways, and he thought something was wrong someplace. He asked me if I could quietly find out what the score was and advise him on what to do.

Well, I was right busy and did not have time to go

to Chicago to take a look for myself, so I called the Commander of the NROTC in Northwestern University and asked him to quietly investigate without letting Tadashi know about it and let me know the answers. It didn't take him long. I had not met Tadashi in Japan so I was surprised when he told me that Tadashi was very shy, lived with an American family but was most reluctant to participate in their activities, spoke English poorly, had made no close American friends, did not participate in student activities unless required and similar remarks. He ended up by saying that the young man was so timorous he was reluctant to take part in events, was fearful of using his poor English, the war was not long over and some of his American classmates did not have a good opinion of Japanese, there were no other Japanese there to associate with him, but mostly the young fellow was just mighty lonesome and suggested that his wife be sent over to go to school too. I don't think I knew he had a wife but I wrote to Admiral Nomura and suggested that his wife be sent over just as soon as possible. I knew this might not be easy for him financially but I knew he would do it if possible. He did — and in a couple of weeks he reported that Miyoko was on her way. I had asked the Captain in the NROTC to look out for them in a quiet way without them being aware of it, and if any money problems became apparent to let me know. There weren't any.

Of course we then wrote to the young Nomuras and asked

them to come down to see us during their Easter vacation. We arranged tickets, I think. The Captain had told me before they arrived at our home that Tadashi was doing much better by then and was pulling up his grades and apparently enjoying things. Miyoko had learned English in Japan and spoke very well. They were to stay with us only a week so we decided to Americanize them as much as we could and laid out a schedule of housework, sightseeing and blocks of little activities. We met them and I saw that Tadashi was uneasy, very restrained and seemed to have no sense of humor. He was polite but wary. Miyoko was more outgoing and entered into everything with fun. Although I don't like houseowrk any more than any Japanese man, I did help with the meals while they were there and insisted on Tadashi helping too. (A deceitful act on my part). I don't think Japanese men usually do that, housework, I mean. He tried though. I made jokes and the three of us then usually explained them to Tadashi. I played a few practical jokes too against my good wife's advice for she thinks they are the lowest possible form of humor and bad taste.

In a couple of days he started to loosen up, though, and about the fourth day at breakfast, as soon as we sat down, he announced, "Now I tell a joke." I remembered that joke for years but I have forgotten it now. He had arrived.

I have been told that the young people's marriage

was arranged in the old Japanese manner. I don't know if that's true but if it is, Admiral Nomura certainly picked a good wife for his son. I got up early and one morning while I was coming down the stairs very quietly I saw Miyoko fingering the keys of our old piano. Not touching them enough to make a sound but playing just the same. I watched her for a few moments and then went back up and came down noisily. I asked her if she played and she admitted she used to but had not been near a piano since the war. After some urging she played and quite well, too. I'll never forget the longing look in that girl's face when I first saw her sitting on the piano bench. After they got home in Japan in the summer we sent her that old broken down piano, with the great help of Lieutenant H. L. Prestview, who was going to Japan to become the aide of Admiral Shein.

When they were leaving and we were taking them down our front walk to their car, Mikoyo-san stopped and turned to me and remarked "I have learned many American customs too" and put her arms around me and kissed me. She had indeed.

I doubt if they know yet that Admiral Nomura had checked on his son and sent Miyoko over when she was needed.

Tadashi-san later went into a Japanese bank, is now retired. Of course, we see them every time we go to Japan.

I note in my files several letters from Randy Lewisohn. They reminded me of a question I am sometimes asked by some of the young officers i.e. did I ever think about getting out of the Navy during my career. Well, I did, and Randy nearly persuaded me once that the opportunities outside the Navy were more rosy than inside.

Randy was a member of the Lewisohn family who built the Lewisohn stadium and other important edifices around New York. I was in the inspection division of the Naval Gun Factory just before the war and during the early days of the war. Young Lewisohn, in his thirties I would guess, reported to my antiaircraft gun mount section as an assistant, either just before the war or shortly after it started. We were looking frantically for manufacturing facilities which could possibly make gun mounts. After several months training Randy made a pretty good inspector. We had found that manufacturers of printing presses were accustomed to fine workmanship and were used to holding to the very small tolerances required in the manufacture of accurate gun mounts. So we got all the printing press plants under contract as soon as we could. There were quite a few. Of course we made contracts with other plants too and we had maybe twenty plants manufacturing antiaircraft gun mounts and parts within a few months after the war started.

One big trouble with those plants was that they had been manufacturing one type of apparatus for so long that their plants had grown like Topsy, without recent overall planned layouts, and they were not used to flow sheets, fast work, large outputs, etc. The workmen were all very experienced in machining on the work they were used to but were not very susceptible to the needs of getting accurate mounts out in a hurry. They were willing enough but it was just like teaching old dogs new tricks. Many of the plants were family owned too and the leading men and supervisors had built up little systems they thought were pretty good but we knew wouldn't get the job done either soon enough or good enough. Family owned businesses meant that there was more than a little nepotism around too.

We had to have new machines put in, arrange flow of material, make machinery layouts, adapt their old machines, arrange for work loads, possible bottle necks, and all the other things necessary to start up a plant and get it operating at full speed in a hurry. The technical and mechanical things were bad enough but the worst difficulty was in getting new systems introduced and having supervisors who could get the people to continuously turn out good work and not resent the supervisor and go balky when he rejected a piece of work. We worked out, because we had to, a good system of supervision and inspection and ways of handling these good men who were 'sot' in their ways. Although I spent most of my time in the Gun Factory I was usually at a new plant when they first started to roll mounts or when something happened and the local inspector sent for me. For some reason or other I took Randy along on many of these trouble shooting trips and since he learned fast and was good, eventually, I sent him out by himself. He became very good and could usually get a plant rolling without help from me.

Well, after the war Randy recognized that there were hundreds of plants that had to convert from manufacture of war material to peacetime things, and they would have as much trouble doing that as they did to convert to wartime manufacturing. He got an idea that we could form a partnership to manage plants which might have trouble, insure we would make them profitable or no fee, buy a share of the plant, and in addition have the fee based on the degree of profitability. Good idea, especially when he would put up most of the money. I had no money but he said I could arrange to borrow it. He was certain we would be millionaires within three or four years. I was pretty sure it would work too and I was tempted to get out of the Navy and give it a whirl. But I still thought Navy life was better.

Randy urged me quite a bit but I finally convinced him that was not for me. He went into that business by himself and sure enough, within three years he had made his million and it came in faster thereafter. Only he died from overwork and a heart attack within 10 years.

Although the story of Chief Yeoman George Guzowski has not a thing to do with Op 30 I'd better talk about him a bit because all the correspondence with him was during my tour in Op-30 and if I don't tell it now I won't be reminded of it any other time.

Guzowski was the Chief Yeoman on the Staff of ComCruDiv 5 when I took command of that division. When I received orders to the Military Armistice Delegation I was informed we would have to form a supporting staff and it would be much easier if we each could bring several officers, yeomen and radiomen from our present jobs. That made sense for we would be working with people whom we knew and who knew the routines of our own services. So before I left Los Angeles I called in Guzowski and asked him who the best yoeman was in the ship. He proudly stated he guessed he was. Then I told him to get ready to go with me to Munsan-ni when I was ordered to go and that I hoped he would improve in taking dictation for there was going to be a lot of that in that new job. Then he tried to get out of it by saying I should know better than to believe him when he was boasting, there was a better yeoman who was a first class and he could take dictation real good. No soap. He added that he got land sick, he didn't like the army, he was needed in his present job and other similar very good reasons. It didn't work.

After we had our camp shaken down and got a little bit squared away, Guzowski found himself as the chief yeoman for the negotiating team but he griped all the time about living in a tent, the lack of heads and too many latrines, nobody in the other services worked hard enough or knew what to do. I always agreed with him and gave him dictation until he was mighty good. Among his other duties he always brought my own mail to my tent after I had returned from Kaesong. I soon found out why. Bobbie didn't know anything about the army either and thought I might starve out there so she had formed the nice habit of sending me a box of candy or cookies about every three or four days. If Guzowski handed me a package I always opened it and gave him part of whatever it was. He liked cookies even better than I do - broken cookies included, and probably ended up with his half all right.

One of the oversights of the army in establishing the camp at Munsan-ni was no barber. Excusable for they didn't think the negotiations would last long enough to require a barber there. As you must know the army is a stickler for detail and when they establish anything they have a T, O and E, which means a table of organization and equipment. If if isn't on the list you don't get it, and there was no barber on the list and the army officers in the camp needed haircuts just as much as we did after a couple of weeks. But Army Eight wouldn't relent for them either. So I called up the Navy headquarters in Tokyo and asked them to buy me a complete set of barber tools and send them over to the camp. They did, and of course

Ski brought the package around with his tongue hanging out for cookies as usual. He hadn't looked to see where the package came from. I opened it. He asked what in the devil all of that gear was. I told him. He asked me who was going to use them and when I told him I was, he got the idea right quick and said, "Admiral you wouldn't do that to me would you?" He needn't have asked that question for he needed a haircut even more than I did. I told him I had to practice on somebody and it might as well be him. As a matter of fact after several false starts I soon got the hang of it and Ski ended up with a pretty good haircut - a little short maybe. But good enough so that my next customer was General Hodes who got a better one. By the time I was through everybody who had to face the communists at Kaesong had presentable haircuts but Burke. Hank Hodes was the only man who would attempt to cut my hair. It wasn't bad either. Very shortly after that there was a barber assigned to Musan-ni.

When I was detached in December from the delegation Ski was left behind and that he did not like at all. He just wasn't cut out for army type duty and before I left he pointed out all the sacrifices he had made on that duty, like the haircut, having to practice every third day with his carbine, the cold weather in a tent, and all the other strange things that a sailor should not be subjected to and asked if I would help him get recruiting duty in the Los Angeles. I said I would and that was what all the correspondence was about in my Op-30 files.

I know you were a good friend of Herb Riley. I have found many letters to Herb in this set of files. You know Bobbie and Herb were distant relatives. They both descended from Ann Lovelace Gorsuch. She was a sister of Richard Lovelace and left England in the 1650's with some of her children after her husband, who was a Loyalist and supported King Charles, the first, was killed as a result of Oliver Cromwell's purging of all loyalists. They didn't know they were relatives for years after they had known one another but finally it came out. Bobbie gave Herb's daughter one of the Gorsuch family rings. Bobbie was a Gorsuch.

Interview #9 with Admiral Arleigh Burke, U. S. Navy (Retired)

Place: His home in Bethesda, Maryland

Date: Thursday morning, 16 August 1979

By: John T. Mason, Jr.

Q: Today, as a continuation of the discussion of your tour of duty in Op-30, I think the subject you want to lead off with is the thinking process that goes into navy planning.

Adm. B: Yes, I would, but I'd like to make a comment on the last interview because that was probably the worst one I've ever done. In going over the transcript, I realized I had covered too many subjects to discuss any one of them completely. Many important points were not covered, and those I did mention were mostly the less important personal ones.

Q: Yes, and it was not your intention from the start to concentrate on any particular one.

Adm. B.: No, so what I wanted to say before I started this interview is that there were a lot of very important subjects that I haven't had time to investigate, like the establishment of SacEur and consequently I did not discuss them at all. My big fault though, was not covering the most important aspects of the incidents I did mention. There is much more to them than the remarks I mentioned in the interview and I hope people interested in those subjects go back to the basic files, too.

Well, to get into this thinking process in Navy planning in Op-30.

That organization, as I said last time, when I joined it it was composed of very fine men, really brilliant men, hard-working and with all the qualifications you could possibly expect. But the problem was that they were handling so many problems on an urgent basis that they couldn't coordinate very well. They needed policy, they needed direction, and there wasn't time to give direction on individual matters.

Q: That was back of your Monday morning sessions, was it not?

Adm. B.: Right. There's always a tendency in any

organization to follow the directions that come down from on high, from a senior, and doing so without really questioning them or examining the direction very closely. In effect, that attitude can be fatal in an organization like a planning section. If this attitude becomes habitual in any planning organization, it becomes deep-seated, and the directions that are issued by the top had not only better be right but the originator should also have thought out all the possible contingencies and side issues that might arise from those orders, because those orders, if they're in detail, are very apt to be carried out blindly and without much intentional deviation from them.

Q: That is a danger in a military organization, isn't it, I mean to follow?

Adm. B.: In any organization, not necessarily military. Surprisingly enough, I think the military are more aware of that pitfall and try to avoid it, but it is a danger of course. But I found this is equally true in civilian organizations. It is probably the major cause of Chrysler's trouble right now - that's what's happened to Chrysler. They did not examine the assumptions adequately - the assumptions on which their directives were based.

An organization that doesn't examine its directives from the top will eventually turn out to be a yes-man organization. They will do what they're told, they will do it very well, but they don't go beyond that. Dictators run into that trouble very soon because they got their office by being forceful and by giving detailed directions, and they suffer from the same faults as anybody else because no one man and no one group can know all the ramifications of any complex problem, any major problem.

Quite frequently the senior commanders themselves do not intend to have their detailed orders carried out absolutely. Yet the assumptions of the commander and his staff when they drew up those orders turn out to be erroneous assumptions. What commanders frequently do not understand is that their juniors just as frequently don't know what those assumptions were. They don't have the background that the commander and the staff have. But if an organization is usually issued detailed instructions, then that organization commences to have the opinion that such details would not be included in those orders unless the boss meant exactly what he said, he intends to have those details carried out, and they follow his directions exactly.

Q: Now you're going to give me your role in this process as head of Op-30?

Adm. B.: Yes. This is an abstract of a memo that I wrote then. Even when a junior may think that those orders are not as good as they could be, in a case where he's used to getting detailed orders, he's apt to carry them out as written and also without commenting on them, without anybody being informed that he really doesn't think they're very good.

The more detailed the instructions the more blind submissivesness permeates the thinking of the recipients of those instructions. Just blind obedience.

The other side of that coin is that all units in an organization must operate in support of the common plan and toward a common goal. If that doesn't happen, then there will be absolute chaos. This is particularly important, of course, in the military. It's absolutely essential in a military organization.

Q: And a diplomatic one, too. We see the incident today.

Adm. B.: Yes, exactly. However, it a military organization coordination of plans and operation is essential or some units are likely to be destroyed and the whole operation fail with disastrous results to the nation. In a diplomatic organization you'd fire the man and usually the operation can be recovered. In a military organization sometimes you can't recover if you don't have common plans.

So the local commanders and even great commands like SacEur, SacLant, and CinCNelm cannot operate completely successfully without direction and support from their own seniors, and the bigger the command the more important that is. There must be cooperation and very loose cooperation between nations. between commands and between the services, as well as between the lesser commands. This has been the problem of alliances throughout all history. This is the reason why military men in all nations, because they do study history, feel that they must know the policy, the goals, the aspirations, and the intentions of their government. They want to know the parameters in which they can function, in which they might be required to function, and they want not only the parameters of such general things, or such attitudes really, as general intentions and other perhaps rather abstract matters, but they want to know what they've got and what the government expects to make available to them.

This is what's causing the trouble in the navy now, to a large extent. This is well-known, of course, it's known to all governments and that was one of the reasons why the NSC, the National Security Council, was formed in the U.S. government. After the war, it was formed under the guidance of the president to develop the policies, the goals, and the intentions of the United States. Now, there are many conflicts that are apparent when these are written out. Those conflicts must be reconciled in the development of a national policy and there must be input into that national policy and the development of that policy by those very subordinate organizations whose future directions and orders as well as their future capability to carry out those orders will be determined by the national policy.

Q: And you imply that the national policy has to be — there has to be continuity in it, it can't be like shifting sands?

Adm. B.: That's right, and this is why it's important when one administration relieves another that the national policy stay essentially the same. This is what we used to have. We have less of it now, but still government leaders do try to do that. This is the big advantage of the British government in having a shadow government. International relations remain about the same, although it's not true with Britain right at the moment.

This is why those NSC papers were reviewed with great care by all of the departments when I was in Op-30, and especially the military departments. It was also the reason why long arguments occurred in the wording of a single phrase sometimes, the exact wording, because the interpretation of a paper must be clear, and, above all, the interpretation must be the same for all the people using it. Government papers, policy papers particularly, are sometimes waffled to get an expression that will cover several divergent meanings, and the proponent of each one of those meanings thinks the paper is satisfactory to him because it covers his point. He can interpret it the way he wants it to mean. But different interpretations of that paper can be very bad, so it must be clear.

Q: I suppose this is back of the president's effort in this administration to deal with jargon, lots and lots of words!

Adm. B.: Yes, jargon can be interpreted to cover both sides - or all sides. A politician, of course, is adept at finding words and expressions that will mean different things to different people, but it's dangerous in a government policy paper. That policy doesn't have to be widespread. I mean it doesn't have to be known generally, but it has to be written so clearly that the people who have to carry out the policy do know what it means - exactly - it isn't, but it should be.

Of course, a big trouble in a policy paper is that if one group has a different interpretation from another group then that trouble is bound to occur in the future at a critical time, when the policy is being applied.

Now, it's most important to have the inputs from the concerned organizations before a policy paper reaches its final form. This is frequently not done. If not, there will be dissension in the future, or more importantly, when the time comes to carry out the policy it may not be possible to carry it out because some critical factor has not been considered that should have been considered or, worse, it may be carried out and the results may be completely different from what was expected because the possible effects of that policy were not considered enough in the formulation of the paper, which is why subordinate organizations should have an input in that policy before it is finalized.

Q: I suppose that's back of the effort to get some very bright people involved in the whole thing?

Adm. B.: Exactly, but what I'm trying to emphasize here is that directions and instructions issued by higher authority, such as a government or a military command, must be complete enough so that the recipient knows what the policy is, what the intentions are, and what forces and equipment will be made available to him to carry out that policy, but they should not be so detailed as to unnecessarily restrict the action commander in how to carry them out. For example, you can't have the president deciding the bomb-loadings in Washington for striking targets in Vietnam. He doesn't know what the situation is. This is the evil of centralization of detail in high places.

Q: And the ease of communication!

Adm. B.: The ease of communication.

All hands realize that there must be, should be, a mutual and even cordial understanding between the boss and his subordinates, not antagonistic. This is a very important factor and was very important in Op-30. The junior commander is subordinate, but he understands what his boss is trying to get done and he knows that his own initiative and innovation are depended on by the boss to carry out the Boss's intention in the most effective manner he can. That's the ideal. That's what everybody always tries to do - I hope I said "should" back there, instead of "must." I say "must" but it's very seldom achieved exactly.

Q: Because it involves a lot of personalities!

Adm. B.: Right. I guess what I'm really trying to say is what everybody has said before, that all hands in an organization should have the feeling that they are all part of the same team, that they're all working toward the same end, and that the subordinate realizes that he will have to use his own brains to be sure that the most effective action is taken and that the boss knows that he, himself, can't do it all. He can't give detailed directions and he knows that no other man, none of his subordinates, will do the job exactly the way the boss would do it. It's going to be done a little bit different, sometimes quite a bit different, but in a good oranization he's got to feel that a subordinate is doing what he can do with what he has available and he's trying to help the boss out all he can.

That's an exasperating problem in all organizations, civilian and military, how to get the solid support and understanding and willing cooperation from the subordinates and, above all, in the application, to get the subordinates to apply themselves with their own initiative, their own innovation, to further the achievement of the common goal.

Q: I can see where in the navy you do have an advantage in that the concept of teamwork is paramount on board ship. It's a team and so the men have this experience in their background.

Adm. B.: That's exactly right, and it's not unique in the navy but we do have it more than the other services. The Navy does try hard to get this cooperative attitude, all trying to work toward a common end, doing your best for your boss, but at the same time without that slavish acceptance of directions without question.

However, this matter of how best to direct subordinate organizations to carry out the policies of the higher commands in coordination with other commands and organizations has always been controversial. There are strong differences of opinions between armies and navies, and not just the U.S. Armed Forces either, but all armies and all navies throughout the centuries. It's always been that way. Armies are usually prone to develop more centralized control systems, central general staff systems, to direct the detailed operations of their subordinates much more than naval officers are. The army doesn't have to give those subordinates as much leeway on how to do the job as navies must do because of the medium in which they operate. .

Q: The distances that are involved?

Adm. B.: And the mobility particularly. Navies nearly always rely on more general directives, which outline the purposes and the goals and supply the intelligence, all the data that are available for subordinates to accomplish the operation in the manner they determine to be best, based on the conditions and the circumstances in which the commander finds himself and all he can determine at the scene of action.

This is the guts of Jasper Holmes' book. Jasper Holmes said a dozen times in that book, Double-Edged Secrets, which is a very good book, that it is the function of the intelligence officer to give to commands the data, but it is not their function to tell the commander what to do. This slops over —

Q: Yes, he underscores that point.

Adm. B.: Yes, because he found it out from bitter experience and he did a great job in doing just that. That's one of the reasons why CinCPac was so successful.

It's natural that there should be these differences of opinion between armies and navies because armies are not so dependent, not nearly so dependent, on mobility and rapidly changing circumstances that might occur as are navies. It's feasible, for example, to draw meaningful, specific lines to separate corps boundaries of operational areas for land warfare, but you cannot do that at sea at all. That's why armies can never understand how we operate our logistic forces because in the same areas they intermingle and yet with different commands. So it's a natural source of contention.

There are many other differences, too, that are germane to the differences in philosophy of warfare on land and warfare at sea. But the point of all of this is to bring out that armies seem to naturally assume that a centralized command system is proper. It works well for them and so they think it should work well for navies, while navies just as naturally abhor over-centralized control. Navies usually develop decentralized systems that permit proper advantage to be taken of local circumstances by the local commanders in time of action or stress. Let subordinate commands make the decision on how to do the job whenever possible.

That's a long and probably unnecessary explanation, but I want to bring out that this one problem was constantly reappearing, over and over and over again, in Op-30, all the time, and it's still a big difference among the services today. The Navy had strongly opposed unification of the services in the manner proposed by the Army in 1949 for the very reason that it was fearful that the establishment of a general staff system, with all the power and direction being concentrated in a general staff, a general staff that would be dominated by people who were convinced that detailed centralized control of all armed forces was necessary, that is the army would operate under a philosophy of a command that would destroy the navy's ability to take the action it was necessary be taken. It would throttle successful naval action, because naval actions require rapid adaptation to local conditions, to enemy changes, because the enemies' navies can change just as fast, as they always have.

The Department of Defense had just been established at that time and when it was established, because the navy had brought out all of these dangers, it was established with a lot of safeguards to inhibit the formation of any system leading to the formation of a general staff. It was the law. There were many proposals for change in the law after the DOD was established for increasing the power and control of the Department of Defense and reducing the ability of the services, all the services, to make decisions on matters unique to those services or of particular interest to those services. They wanted to make everything alike, the DOD did. At this time, there was concern that these proposals would push more and more decisions up to a higher level with consequent long delays in making those decisions because they had to go through so many hands. There would be a substantial increase in costs. There would be a lot of extraneous inputs, some of them political, which would increase the costs without increasing the effectiveness. But, most importantly, eventually the responsibility for making those decisions, because one man could not handle it, the secretary of defense himself could not handle it, would be passed down to his staff, and his staff would be composed of inexperienced members who were brilliant young men but not cognizant of service needs, not having practical experience in the services, and who would eventually form a self-perpetuating bureaucracy after they had been there a long time with all the evils that come with such a bureaucracy.

Q: And you certainly saw a major step in that direction with the amendments to the National Defense Act in 1958, didn't you?

Adm. B.: That's right, and this is why it takes ten years to build a ship now instead of three, this is why a Polaris project could not be instituted now. It's impossible because the bureaucracy would kill it. All the delay, the increased costs, the ineffectiveness, is not done intentionally. It's just the way such a system works. That handicap was known then and it was something that we were trying to avoid or at least to reduce as much as possible.

The navy was especially concerned with that, but there were also members of the other services too who pointed out the gross mistakes that had been made in World War II by the Germans and the Japanese by requiring that all decisions be made by centralized authority. I have just read Ruge's book on Rommel and he describes the actions of the OKW, the Obercommando der Wermacht. The OKW, for example, required that Rommel not have direct command of German army forces in France - they tied Rommel's hands before the Normandy landings in the early days. They wouldn't let him move his forces the way he wanted to move them, particularly his Panzer divisions. They ran the show from Berlin and Rommel was always given authority and control of forces too late. The Germans failed in the Battle of Normandy. Maybe they would have failed anyway, but they ensured that they would fail by maintaining detailed direction of combat forces in the OKW. They did the same thing on the eastern front. They did this because they were highly successful at first because there wasn't very much opposition in the early parts of the war and the opposition did not make any surprise moves. The German Army didn't have to innovate, they could bull their way through.

The Japanese did exactly the same thing. They directed the details of war operations from Tokyo when they should have realized that it would have very unfortunate results. They tried to decentralize control in the middle of the war but they never could succeed.

Those past examples were brushed off by the proponents of centralized control who wanted more power in the DOD. The examples were not applicable, they said, those things are going to be different. Events don't have to happen that way. This time there will be bright people in the central organization who know of these dangers and they wouldn't become bureaucratic.

Q: That's a bit naive, isn't it?

Adm. B.: It's a bit naive, but that was still their primary premise. They believed conditions are different now, faster communications, faster everything, but they still would rely upon just one man at the top and his staff for all decisions and the decision makers are not held responsible for what happens. They make the decisions but they do not have responsibility for executing the plan so they're not held responsible for it. Of course, this was a long time before McNamara became SecDef, but we were afraid that a man like McNamara would become SecDef –

brilliant, hard-working, self-confident, preemptory, feeling very certain that his opinions were the only correct ones and that if he surrounded himself with brilliant men he could make all the decisions right at the top. We were afraid such a man would not listen to the men who had to do the job. This is the fundamental flaw that we tried to avert in Op-30.

Now, it's twenty years later, after the Vietnam War. The secretary of defense and even the president took action in that war, made decisions, in the greatest detail, which they shouldn't have done. They were wrong decisions. The most unfortunate result in that procedure was not that any one particular decision was wrong but that all the subordinates had to wait for orders from Washington. They waited for details. They could not use their own judgment. This was what we were trying to avoid then in Op-30 because we could see what the results might be. It had happened before in other nations. It had happened in our own nation before. Our great concern then was that naval officers were commencing to lose their initiative, lose their innovative capabilities, and were tending to restrict their thinking to the ideas and the plans and the data to those that were being promulgated by the JCS and the DOD. In other words, they didn't think for themselves because they had to submit all proposed actions to Washington for approval where they were either rejected or delayed or modified.

There were many papers even in those days that attempted to get more centralization, more power in one office or another, always at a higher echelon, and that, I thought, was wrong.

Q: And that you discerned clearly in Op-30?

Adm. B.: Yes, and so did a lot of other people, but we certainly did then.

At that time, one of the most energetic and independent and aggressive lads in the navy was Dan Gallery. You probably saw quite a few letters in the files about Dan in those Op-30 days because we'd been discussing this danger of over-centralization. He was most vehement. He felt very strongly about the danger, the increasing danger, of resigned, passive, compliant, obsequious attitudes among naval officers. There was some evidence of it, not much, but enough to indicate that subordinate commands were not submitting new ideas because they thought they would be squelched or not considered and not worth the trouble. You probably saw one letter particularly of 12 August 1952 where he made an astonishing and perceptive blast at what he thought would happen if this consolidation of all decision making power in DOD went through and it's exactly what I was after.

All of us had noted a tendency within the navy to restrict our thought processes to within the assumptions and the conditions contained in the papers that came down from on high - it's easier to do it that way. If the assumptions were incomplete or in error, the whole conclusion would also be in error, and we thought that some papers had been purposefully based on erroneous assumptions, sometimes hidden assumptions or assumptions that weren't stated. Those papers were sometimes to accomplish some purpose of special benefit to a single group or to a single service, but usually to a group, at the expense of the effectiveness of all the other groups. Navy people weren't very alert to that sort of working business. We weren't alert to examining the basis for the letter, the basis for the assumptions, the assumptions behind the plans in the paper, and we weren't very alert in examining the conclusion that that paper had reached as well as we should have been, we weren't quick enough, or perhaps skeptical enough. We were not used to doing things that way. So we tried to correct that, to be critical. Not antagonistically critical, but as effective as we could be. We tried to examine the reasons for the changes. We wanted to make sure they were right. If we didn't know they were right, we'd ask the organization why. We tried to find out why. Why the devil is this particular statement in there? How do you know this is going to happen? What is the basis for the conclusions? What can be the result if the conclusions are not correct?

At that time, we thought we in the navy were probably getting tired and we were just taking it easy, taking the easy way and the wrong way, and becoming compliant, complacent.

All naval plans were necessarily restricted to conform exactly with the approved plans. That is, our navy plans had to be in accord with —

Q: The master plan?

Adm. B.: The master plan, the JCS plan, and that is good. But, if the master plan is wrong or if it could be changed to improve the ability of the navy to accomplish the objective, then that master plan should be changed. This we had not done much, so we started being critical of master plans.

Q: Yes, but how could you avoid that with the kind of staff you had, who were very bright and innovative? They would see these flaws in the master plan, would they not?

Adm. B.: Yes, sometimes — but not always — and when we did then we'd take exception to them. That caused a lot of purples, a lot of split papers, and we'd get a lot of papers changed, but it was always a fight. It's always difficult, particularly after the plan had been issued.

If we could get the dope on a plan ahead of time, we could avoid much controversy and usually we could get a better plan.

We felt at that time that we'd reached the stage where we were unnecessarily limiting our interpretation of those plans. We weren't examining them carefully enough and we weren't using our own thinking process.

Q: The CNO at that time, was he aware of your dilemma, so to speak?

Adm. B.: Oh, yes, we kept him informed all the time. That's one of the things we did early - to tell people in positions of responsibility in the navy of what we suspected as well as what we were sure of.

Q: Who was CNO?

Adm. B.: This was Admiral Fechteler.

So I put out a memo that we had to retain our ability to think for ourselves, our ability to determine what was best to do with the forces that the navy had available for battle or any other emergency, and in the context of all other U.S. policies and in consonance with the other forces. I know I'm beating this to death but this was the fundamental that Op-30 was working on. We couldn't have a unilateral plan that would conflict with those from the other services, I mean that didn't support the general plan. We had to support the other services. We should, so they had to know about our plans. They had to know about what we were thinking. We had to know about what they were thinking. And this is what we started. This is why that voluminous personal correspondence you found in my files. It all comes back to the basic principle of a good command philosophy in any organization, the necessity to have the basic concepts of naval warfare and the control of naval forces widely promulgated so that everybody knew it, so that all naval commands would understand and be familiar with them and, hopefully, that all the U.S. commands would understand and support them. This is exactly what we had at that time, but that means the concept's got to be right. You can't just get a bright idea and put it out as a plan. It's got to be right and all people must know and be convinced it's right and must be kept current with new developments and new equipment. Particularly at that time, there was a lot of new equipment coming along, and changes in alliances among nations, changes in attitudes among nations, and changes in the amount of support that nations were going to give to the United States. So we had to have a planner's concept.

Op-30 was divided into a great many sections with about three or four officers in each, for specific projects. All of those projects interrelated one with the other, so there had to be a general planners' concept of what the whole outfit was trying to do on naval warfare, and so - one of the first things we did was to put out a planners' concept of the different types of naval warfare, such as ASW, antiair warfare, surface warfare, amphibious, and so forth. We knew those planners' concepts weren't exactly right, but we set them up, gave them wide distribution and asked for comments on them, corrections, suggestions. We got a lot of suggested changes and after a while those concepts were improved. But the big thing was not so much that we knew the general concepts, but that everybody knew them so that they all could work towards a common purpose. This sounds as simple as it is, but Mr. Young got himself in a wringer because he didn't follow a simple concept that the State Department thought he knew. He probably did know it and just violated it because he thought he'd get away with it. It's a good example of what happens when people in an organization work at cross purposes. Mr. Young should have tried to get State to support that concept, if he thought it was correct, but he shouldn't act in opposition to the government's concept.

We hoped that with these concepts we could get more and more navy people to think about what might be required, what more could be done and what forces we should have. What kind of forces we should develop and when might we have those forces available, and what improvements were needed in equipment, particularly in communications because at that time our communications were not good enough. That was a weakness. We thought that if all the commands in the navy did that, we'd be better prepared for war operations, so we asked for comments. We got them, but it required an awful lot of work, a tremendous amount of correspondence, not just from me. I had a horrendous personal correspondence, but all the other people in the section did, too.

Our big difficulty was keeping the papers limited to concepts because we could get into details pretty fast ourselves. The papers had to be concise. We just couldn't write long letters to cover all points, and so when the letters were concise they cover all the possible contingencies. We hoped the letters would be about 95 per cent right. If they were short, they would necessarily not have all the background information, so if somebody questioned it we would have to furnish them with background information, and they ought to question it if they weren't sure of it. But what these many letters did do was generate better ideas and create a common understanding of the various concepts.

Of course, as those comments came in, a lot of them were dissertations like I'm giving now, instead of concepts, but they did some good.

Along about '52, '53, the NATO staffs were expanding. SacEur started with a very small staff. They were expanding into huge organizations and they required many U.S. officers. The SacEur command, except for CinCSouth, which was just being formed, was composed largely of army and air force officers and the reason for that was that basic requirements in Europe were largely ground operations. But those ground operations could not take place unless the navy could do its stuff, unless the navy could get them there, support them, and they had very little idea of what naval operations were all about.

Q: That's somewhat traditional, isn't it?

Adm. B.: It's traditional and so frequently forgotten by the other services, and there were very few naval officers in these staffs. We had to get naval concepts in them to prevent the formation of plans for their operations without consideration of what the navy had to do to make them succeed. The ground staffs were apt to just assume that the logistic support from across the Atlantic was going to be there and our gunfire support would simply be automatic because that's what seemed to happen. So we had to get some excellent and experienced naval officers in those staffs so that faulty ideas and concepts could be corrected right at the beginning and not be incorporated in the plans and then have to go through the difficulty of getting them changed.

At that time, the navy had many fewer officers than the other two services. People have forgotten that. We had maybe two-thirds of the officers in either of the other services. We did not want to increase the size of our officer corps much and this was particularly true in the higher ranks, captains to flag officers, where our percentages were much lower than those of the army and air force.

Q: What was the reasoning back of that? I mean you could see the advantage of increasing them and having more representation on these joint staffs.

Adm. B.: Because if we got too much representation in staff jobs, pretty soon we would have more staff people than operators. Also, officers ought to be overworked a little bit. For strictly naval operations, we didn't need any more than we had but we had to get somebody into the other staffs, the other commands. Those people wouldn't be doing any navy job, they were just introducing navy concepts. Our personnel authorization was based on the navy's requirements to support itself, but it was not built on large staffs which we had never had, and now we had to have large staffs in OpNav and naval commands to answer the questions by the DOD staffs and we had to have people to send to non-navy staffs. There was great reluctance within the navy to lessen our own naval combat effectiveness by detailing experienced senior officers from sea duty because they needed these officers for commands at sea. We'd lessen our own effectiveness in naval operations by assigning a considerable number of these very good officers - they had to be good officers or they wouldn't be any good at all - and particularly experienced senior officers to any staff duty, especially any joint staff duty.

Q: But simultaneously the navy leadership must have seen that they would lose out if they didn't have their representation?

Adm. B.: Yes, but you can't make an officer, you can't make a captain overnight. It takes quite a while to create an experienced captain. It takes most of a lifetime.

So we were short and our senior naval officers did see it. That's why the laws were changed eventually, but even then there was a reluctance to take those good officers out of good navy jobs where they were doing good jobs and send them over to SacEur's staff, for example in the hopes that they would change SacEur's plans.

Q: Just as a footnote, was there also an understanding of the need to have an adequate naval point of view represented in the White House?

Adm. B.: Yes, we had to get good people there too and we did better on that.

Also, all naval officers then felt that the most important duty in the world was duty in a combat unit and in command. That was the goal of every naval officer, every naval line officer, to command of a combat unit. Staff duty was to be avoided if it possibly could be. We'd been brought up that way. My whole life, I balked at every staff job I was ever required to take. I kicked about it, but I got them, anyway, and that was typical.

By assigning those officers to non-navy staffs, the navy operating forces would be greatly handicapped, but if we didn't assign them we would handicap our future by the lack of understanding the other services. So we finally got them. We worked on it. We had to work on people, individuals, not just the top people but everybody to get a change in attitude, so that a young officer who had been brought up to think "I'm about to get my command and now I'm being ordered to a staff" would not think that he'd failed. I did that, you know, when I was detached from the General Board, I was offered the choice of going to the National War College or as the captain of a ship. Of course, I went to sea, as every other naval officer would have done. This change of attitude was where we had to work. That was the hard part. We didn't have much encouragement to start with and we had a lot of downright opposition, mostly from the people directly ordered!

We didn't get much help from the NATO commands,

either. They weren't particularly eager to have naval officers over there. They did have a few but those people always found themselves - were apt to find themselves, not always - not in a position to influence a decision or to help in a problem - even in the very problems that their knowledge and their experience ought to have provided a lot of help. They weren't given jobs where they had much experience on plans. Some of them were insulated from the important staff activities, and all too frequently they were insulated from planning activities especially, even those affecting naval participation. They were shunted to deputy jobs with no authority. They had no access to what was going on in the command. They were not consulted and sometimes they were only tolerated. In other words, they were bypassed or ignored.

There were many plans involving the navy some way or another that were issued without the knowledge of any naval officer, without the participation, at least, in the formulation of those plans. They didn't know about them. Sometimes those naval officers on the staff of a joint command were given copies of plans that had been worked on for a long time but without their help, and then they were asked to comment on complex matters within a week, or a very short time. There are many ways of bypassing people on a staff and the navy was being given a very good course of sprouts in all of them.

Q: I would think there were many examples of people asking to be reassigned?

Adm. B.: There were quite a few. We had to somehow stop the short-circuiting of navy staff members on all of these staffs.

Q: And this was part of Op-30?

Adm. B.: No, it wasn't our job. A planning job can't be done, though, unless that can be done.

Q: Well, you were cognizant of it?

Adm. B.: We were ocgnizant of it.

Q: You were working in other directions to effect it?

Adm. B.: We were the ones who were mostly affected, our product was affected right quick, and so we were concerned about it. But you can't just put out an edict or a letter or a directive or any other order to a commander and say this is what you ought to do. The only way to accomplish that is to prove to those commands that are run by a sister service, the joint commands, that naval people could be a help to them and not a handicap. That's not done by talking about it. It requires examples. Senior army and air force officers had to be shown.

So, first, we ran up against the reluctance to use naval officers properly, and then we ran up against another old custom that's different between the army and the navy. If the navy had a very well-qualified junior officer, we gave him an important job as a junior officer. His rank didn't count so much. He got important staff jobs particularly. But that was not the custom, and isn't now, in the other services. Rank counts in the other services more than it does in the navy, even more than competence sometimes. In the navy we had the quaint custom of thinking that a staff man's idea was what counted, not his rank, but we found that didn't work in joint staffs. The effectiveness of his advice was partially dependent upon the rank of the man who gave it. We found that out, particularly in joint commands.

Gradually, the navy started to assign its best captains, to joint staffs. The navy commands didn't want to assign them and the people didn't want to go, but those captains had to realize that they were in an important job. Their duties were important, they were good, we knew they were good, and that's why they were there, and they were lonesome. That meant they had to be supplied with material. We had to write to them. They had to be kept informed. They had to write to us.

Q: To keep their morale going?

Adm. B.: Keep their morale and keep them updated on the status of plans, data on prospective problems, so that they could prove to their bosses in the other services that they knew what they were talking about, that they knew their job.

The navy had another little custom that we always had followed. If a task looked like it required three or four officers, we assigned two and overworked them.

Q: That was your philosophy, certainly!

Adm. B.: It was mine, yes, but we had to do that because we didn't have the officers.

So we gradually got a few experienced officers but quite a few officers inexperienced on staff duty, but very capable officers to fill the billets that required tremendous knowledge and above all great persuasive ability with persistence to keep in there, plugging, but it also meant that every one of those officers was terrifically overworked, every damned one of them.

You probably noticed in these files Abe Vosseller's correspondence.

Q: Yes.

Adm. B.: He was on the staff of SacEur. He's a wonderful, brilliant man. Never once in all of those letters did he say that he was overworked, but we got the word from other naval officers that Abe was working sixteen hours a day. "He doesn't have enough sleep, he's heavily overloaded," they reported to us. So we'd write to Abe and say, "Do you need some help?" Of course, he did but it took time to get people over there. He finally got help but not enough. He recognized the importance of the job that he was doing and he did a magnificent job. He changed a lot of ideas in Eisenhower's mind, Ridgway - Ridgway already had a pretty good knowledge of naval operations, but his staff sometimes did not. Abe Vosseller was a typical example of - no he wasn't typical, he was better than the typical officer, but he did a magnificent job under great handicaps without much assistance.

This heavy workload of Abe's was self-imposed. This was true with all of them. They went out looking for jobs, looking for work to do. They could have been by-passed and had a very happy time doing nothing. Their commander didn't lay that work out for them, they found it. They were self-driven men. They didn't do just what they had been told to do, they did what their experience and their knowledge told them should be done. They were the only people in a position to do it, so they did it.

I'm emphasizing that, too, because that is a quality that I think our naval people have to a greater extent than any other group of people that I know of around that era.

Q: Going back to the people you had in Op-30, I have a question that I'd like to pose. These men were working in small groups on specific plans for specific areas and very often they must have felt that it was highly improbable that the plans would ever be put into effect, that it would be almost a miracle if they were. What effect did this have upon these men, highly motivated, original thinkers? What effect did it have upon them when they couldn't anticipate the fruition of their work?

Adm. B.: I don't think any. I don't think any effect at all. They knew before they started that their plans, 99 per cent of them or a large percentage of them, would never be used, but one of them will be used, and they know very well too that the plan that is used will have to be modified a great deal. A plan will not be followed exactly when it is executed. Circumstances have changed. All the things can not be foreseen. A plan is only a guide. This is a condition that naval officers, particularly senior officers, must recognize, that a policy or plan can only be a guide. It's not something that will direct everything that should be done. It's a general guide and it must be changed from time to time as circumstances change. The ability to carry out a plan changes fast, too, just like most of your personal plans. You have contingency plans about what you will do when you take a vacation and you don't go on all those vacations, but it doesn't bother you much. The same thing was true of the people in Op-30 and on joint staffs.

Q: I wondered how long a tour of duty a man could take under those circumstances.

Adm. B.: About two years. It takes him six to eight months to get acquainted with the organization and the way it works, so he ought to be able to produce for at least a year —

Q: To be motivated?

Adm. B.: They were all highly motivated in the first place. Dedication like that has no reward. The only reward that such a job has is more work and a sense of achievement, the satisfaction he has that he did a pretty good job. There's no way that you can reward a man for plans because —

Q: Well, that's a pretty intangible reward and it runs counter to human nature, doesn't it, in a sense?

Adm. B.: Yes. Of course, there's a thrill, an excitement, in making plans, even little plans, seeing if you can arrange for the contingencies, seeing if your estimates of the situation turn out to be correct. You practice on plans. There is a great deal of satisfaction out of of being able to foresee the problem and developing plans on what can be done about.

One of our big problems there is the next subject and that's how do you get good officers.

Q: Yes.

Adm. B.: I inherited some wonderful officers but we had to expand somewhat. I had to get more. Above all, we had to get people in the staffs, our own naval staffs, who were very good, in joint staffs, and in NATO staffs, too, and our allies' staffs. We had to get good people to start with and then we had to encourage them to do their very best. We didn't know who had the motivation and skill to become good planners, so the first thing we did was to consult our own people in Op-30 about possible candidates, "We ought to get Joe in here. Joe's pretty good at this stuff, I know him." So we try to get Joe. Well, first it's hard to get specific people. Joe's already got a job and his boss is not about to let him go if he doesn't have to. So you have to get people who are just about ready to change, anyway. We did get a few specific individuals.

One of the first things I did was to write to all the war colleges, not always to the head man but to other people and say, "Can you give me the names of the five men who wrote the best papers in the last term, and put them in order, if you can, who you think is best, not just on that paper, but who'd make a good planner, a good thinker." Frank Virdun, for example was in the Naval War College, he sent a list to me. We had a few people going to the army war college. I had army officers grade our naval officers. "Burns is a very fine bloke, he'd be pretty good." Surprisingly, they helped like the devil - staff colleges, all the war colleges, all the staff colleges. Then, all of our alumni, all the old planners, we'd write to them and say, "Do you know anybody suitable in your area?" We got a few that way. We had people on the lookout for possible planners.

We didn't get enough, so we started asking for student papers at naval war colleges. First we started suggesting to the war colleges a subject that they ought to be writing on, ought to be studying. They took it pretty well and did it. Then we asked for copies of their papers.

Q: So you could make your own evaluation?

Adm. B.: We made some evaluation.

This was not long after the war and so we had a retention problem, too. During the war nobody retired. They brought back a lot of people, and we ended up the war with many more officers than we needed later. We had to bring the navy down to size, and there's always turmoil after a war. People have had enough fighting and some of them want a different field. So we had trouble with retention and a lot of very good people getting out. They want to make money or they want to be home - or something, so we had to work on retention, and this, with my own people, was one of the problems, to encourage them, - to find out what's bugging them, what's eating them. The same things were probably bothering other people, too. So we had to discuss with them the navy, their careers. Not their own individual careers, but what's ahead for their service.

There are three things that are important to an officer. First, that he belongs to an organization that has pride in itself and achieves something. Second, that that organization will develop good people within it. And the third one is that he can be one of those good people if he works hard enough. In other words, he's going some place in an organization that's going someplace. You can overdo that a little bit. We did. People wanted to come to Op-30 and were not quite capable of doing the job. It's hard to tell a good man that he just hasn't had that sort of experience or he doesn't quite have the writing ability or has some other lack. We had requests from very good captains who were about to retire. You probably noticed quite a few letters in there. They had an idea on some papers that they wanted to write, they had about six months or a year left on active duty - they felt that they could contribute more to the navy by coming into our shop and working on those papers, and asked would that be possible. Well, I tried to work it out and I couldn't do it because we were assigned a certain billet structure. We couldn't have more officers than that. It would be very bad ball to have somebody come in for a year to write one specific paper and take up a billet, because normally that would be all he would be good for. He wouldn't be able to help carry the rest of the workload that was already there. It would take six months, about, for him to get into the job well and then he would have to have about two years to produce.

Q: The situation had to be more flexible than it was.

Adm. B.: That's right, and the navy couldn't make it flexible because these people have to be paid, and our needs have to be weighed against everybody else's.

Q: A dollar-a-year plan might have worked!

Adm. B.: Some of them would have done that. They were willing to retire and then work on their projects. There were a few who did, not to work in an office but work on their projects at home. It happens now too — like Dave Rosenberg's problem here on the Bay of Pigs. He doesn't have background enough to write an abstract paper on that event in a short period, so I called up Krisel and said, "Will you write about six pages of summarizing the Bay of Pigs story. He said sure. He said, "When do you want it?" and I said, "Tomorrow." He said, "Get the paper to me and I'll get it back."

There's no reason on God's green earth why he should do that. It's just he does.

Tom Sisson was a lad who wanted to come in. He's a wonderful man but we couldn't take him in to Op-30 for just six months.

Well, we had to have vast correspondence with a lot of people. We had to have direct correspondence with foreign navies, people in foreign navies. We had direct correspondence with SacEur and all the other commands of NATO.

The CNO had to know what we were doing, but we shouldn't send every letter up to him because he can't read that much. He had to trust us, so we had to give him an outline of what we were trying to do, keep him cognizant of what was happening. We were careful to warrant his trust in us. For example, we put a file on his aide's desk and said, "This is a SacEur file, these are the naval officers on SacEur's staff, these are the people we're corresponding with, these are the subjects that we're corresponding on. This is the gist of the important items."

When we received a letter that was or might be of interest to the CNO, he ought to know about it. We would sent it up to him, marked so that he wouldn't have to read the whole thing. After a while, he used us as a conduit. For example, he wouldn't want to write a letter to General Ridgway to obtain information on a simple matter — he did not want to make an official request for information, so he would ask us to obtain that information. We could — and did.

Q: So you become similar, in a sense, to the Central Office that once existed in the navy?

Adm. B.: Somewhat, for the planning process, but the important part there is we had to keep our own bosses informed, and each naval officer out in the field in another staff had to keep his boss informed. This was something that can't be done under the table, I mean this private correspondence. Our job was to get an understanding of naval requirements into the plans while they were in the formative stage and that required much correspondence at lower levels but with the commanders full knowledge and approval. This could not be done all at once. Trust and confidence had to be built up slowly so that the joint or NATO commanders knew they could rely on the judgment of the naval officers on their staffs and in their commands. The commanders had to know our navy people had correct data and knew what to do about it.

Q: This is just a footnote, too, but this kind of development, this kind of system, would not have worked in the marines, for instance?

Adm. B.: Yes, it does. It works fine in the marines. There was one other problem, though. We were dealing with high security matters. War plans have about the greatest security there is and it's very difficult to discuss such matters in personal correspondence. We had to keep the security of classified material, and to do that we had to classify our own personal letters "Confidential," "Secret," or other appropriate classification and to ensure they were sent through proper channels so that we didn't violate our own security rules. This is one of the things that worried me all the time, security. We never did find any breaches of it, though.

This is another good conclusion in Jasper's book, the matter of letting people know what is happening so that the information can be used appropriately. If it's kept too secret, it doesn't do any good.

Q: It doesn't do any good anywhere!

Adm. B.: Right - not any place. If you don't keep it secret enough then it gets known and you mess up your own problem, so this thing of the proper amount of security, the proper amount of secrecy is always difficult to judge.

There were dangers in this personal correspondence, great dangers. All of our people were aware of the dangers and were very careful for they wrote letters just like I did. We had to know to whom we were writing, and to know that he had good judgment.

Q: Almost had to have clearance!

Adm. B.: Yes, and great integrity. We relied on the kind of experience he had, his judgment, whether he was cautious or reckless, whether he had great integrity. We had to know a lot about our correspondents.

Another thing was that these were complicated matters and we couldn't cover all the aspects of the problem. I think I mentioned before that it is very difficult for a very junior officer to write to a senior officer giving his early thoughts on a subject when he was not quite sure he was on the right path. He could not be certain his ideas were sound – and he had not yet examined the whole problem. Yet his early impressions – or off the cuff judgments – could be very useful. And of course sometimes he was bound to be in error.

Q: You inherited this organization, Op-30. Had that kind of system been in existence before?

Adm. B.: No. There was some personal correspondence but

not to that extent. I got this idea from my experience with Admiral Mitscher and in Japan. That's where I really found that it was necessary for people to know what was being considered early and to take earlier steps to deal with the possible contingencies long before the plans were completed.

For example, the mere mailing of a letter - if I mailed a letter to Abe Vosseller, for example, to his post office address, it went into the army's or into SacEur's post office and it was sent, not to him, but was opened and distributed to the staff. It went into the official files. Sometimes it didn't make any difference, sometimes it did. It's not that we wanted to have him - and him only read it, but we wanted to make sure that he read the letter first and became the action officer. Then he would take it up with his bosses or make other suitable disposition of it, of course, it did have to remain secret - but not exclusive.

We had to go to great lengths sometimes. I sent a lot of letters to Abe via Bob Pirie, who was in London, and the next time they flew a plane over to London he'd take the letters to Abe -

Q: He'd deliver it by hand?

Adm. B.:, and we got some back that way, too. Those

personal letters were not to be generally distributed, not so much because we wanted to keep the information restricted - there was some of that but not very much. The big thing was that our correspondents would know how to handle it and how much credence they could put in it. It might be absolutely right, it might be just a possible contingency. If we had written for example, that the navy proposes to do so and so to a personal correspondent, he would know that that's just what it means. The navy may not do it but it was a proposal the navy was considering.

These personal letters were not to be generally distributed. Distribution depended upon the recipient of it. If he thought it should be distributed, okay, if he didn't, okay. They were not official, they were not final, they were all preliminary to get information before things froze. The funny thing of it was, copies of letters were very difficult to get. Everything had to be mimeographed. There was not such thing as Xerox, so that if you wanted a copy of a letter, you had to retype it somehow. That's one thing that has changed greatly in thirty years.

We tried to understate our case. Always understate, never overstate, particularly was this true in our official letters. We always had a better case than the one we presented, so that we could always live up to our promises. We never promised anything that we could not do.

Q: That's a very difficult point to put across to people

generally, isn't it?

Adm. B.: Yes. It's very difficult for Dave. He wants to make his case and he wants to pound it over the head. He doesn't realize that if you understate people get confidence in you, justified confidence.

Q: You certainly have much more latitude under those circumstances?

Adm. B.: Yes. Our big trouble was half-promising. I mean giving an indication so that the navy was actually starting a project when we only were considering it. We had to watch that and never imply a future promise, that if an event occurred we would take a specific action when we were only contemplating taking that action. This is particularly true with foreigners. We never promised anything we could not deliver, and not just that the navy could deliver but that that man could see that it was delivered. If we couldn't do that, we would have to say, "I will try, but it may not happen."

Then, we never overadvertized our new weapon systems or anything that we did because it reduces public confidence. It reduces the confidence of other people in what you do, if you overadvertize or overstate -

Q: It raises their expectations to a high point, too.

Adm. B.: Yes. There was a great tendency then to overstate the danger of war - nuclear war is just about to come, the whole world's about to go up. Those are wolf cries and when such statements are made often, people correctly discount them. Then, when the danger is imminent, there is nothing left to say. You've said it already.

One of the things we had trouble with in our own commands when they were uncertain about an action they were taking, they would sometimes conceal it by an attitude "I know best, I know what I'm doing." This was particularly true when a commander issues an order to a subordinate, and the subordinate questions it. Some commanders may say:

"Look, I know what I'm doing. I gave you that order. Carry it out."

The subordinate does - but may lose some confidence in the jdugment of his senior. The junior has got to be able to, not to protest the order, but to make sure he understands it, and if he thinks it to be in error he should inform his senior with his reasons for doing so. Confidence of juniors in their seniors builds military effectiveness. The commander has got to generate that confidence.

Then, another thing, some people can't write a letter without provocative phrases, so we had to try to keep our letters from being provocative, unintentionally provocative. We also had difficulty in not keeping our letters overly secretive, to hold things too close to our chest, and still not be a blabbermouth, either. To do this, we had to develop some systems. The "eyes only" letter was used to limit distribution to the addressee.

Q: That was carried by hand?

Adm. B.: Yes, carried by hand. Then there was "no foreigners" - this was both official and unofficial - or "blue flags only" to flag officers only, being very careful to restrict this just to flag officers and not to -

Q: We might say that many of those instructions, those markings, show up in your files.

Adm. B.: Yes.

Q: Especially the personal stamp, classification stamp. It shows up quite frequently.

Adm. B.: Yes. Well, this whole business was trying to get data quickly and to obtain other people's ideas. In addition to the letters, we had conferences with our own commands, and foreign representatives. An example of that is when I went eo England for any reason, I always talked with the British planners, too. I got so I knew the British planners, Balfour, and they came to know us (you see a lot of letters in there from Balfour.) He got a lot of dope from us, and a year after we started that cross fertilization scheme we could draw up a British-American plan that had a good chance of being accepted by our British colleagues. The British could also draw up a plan that we wouldn't have any comment on. They had our views before.

Q: Did they operate with some of the same concepts as to how the thing should be done?

Adm. B.: Usually not.

Q: Did they correspond, as you did, with individuals?

Adm. B.: Yes, but not to the extent that we did and not exactly for the same purpose. Our idea was to get ideas from them, and to give them our ideas, and that was not too darned usual.

One of the subjects that I kept harping on, as I usually do, was don't kid yourself, be realistic, be analytical and not wishful-thinking. You've always got nasty realism facing you and you'd better by a damned sight take it into account.

Q: So, no self-delusions!

Adm. B.: No self-delusions.

There was difficulty in getting navy ideas across to the president, both President Eisenhower and President Truman. They weren't exactly navyphiles, so I wrote a little memorandum once that I found in the file to Admiral Dennison because I didn't think that President Truman really understood the navy, why the navy operated the way it did and why it was the way it was.

Q: Did he have any army concept?

Adm. B.: Yes, sort of. This was a memorandum to Dennison, who was aide to Truman, as you know. I told Denny why don't you tell the president that the navy is very much in the same position with regard to public relations as a virtuous woman. Virtue is very seldom spectacular, it has very few cases that cause long editorials, and naval philosophy and maritime strategy are not spectacular either. Naval strategy offers no panacea, no one thing that will cure the ills of the world. Success depends upon long, dull hours of hard work and there's no action that's clearly decisive by itself. Final success is dependent upon a series of previous small actions.

Q: What action was taken on this memo?

Adm. B.: It had effect. Dennison just showed it to the

president and it worked pretty well, it did have some small effect.

Our major duty in Op-30 was, of course, war plans, handling Joint Chiefs of Staff papers. We proposed papers to the Joint Chiefs of Staff and we had to comment on papers that the other services proposed and on what the Joint Chiefs of Staff were doing and make sure that all those papers were distributed in the navy properly. We originated quite a few of those. There was literally hundreds of these papers in a year, so I don't want to go into any individual paper, but the same process that we used for our own command and other commands; that is, exchanging ideas and getting ideas before papers froze, we tried to use with the Joint Chiefs of Staff organization too, and that worked pretty well, except on questions of force levels. It didn't work at all on force levels. We dealt with the actual force levels that we had, plans based upon those actual force levels, we determined what force levels we would require to carry out certain plans. Then we had our druthers, desirable force levels to carry out additional plans. But exchanging ideas in advance there never was very successful because we were in direct competition with the other services.

Q: Yes, I can see that.

Adm. B.: That was one place where this exchange of ideas

did not work.

Q: I take it you worked through the chief of naval operations for the JCS?

Adm. B.: Through the chief of naval operations and through his deputy. The chief of naval operations handled all the important papers and his deputy handled the less important papers. That was Op-03. The JSPC, the Joint Strategic Planners, that was a committee of the deputies - they met on Tuesdays, I think, and Thursdays, the Joint Chiefs themselves met on Wednesdays and Fridays, if I remember rightly, and there were special meetings quite frequently, too, but they divided the workload. Sometimes they both sat in on the same meeting. But we did give them a lot of information. We started the procedure of giving a lot more information than was actually required in order to acquaint the other services, other people, with what we thought about things, and we started to get a lot more information back too.

A big trouble with war plans for the navy, one of the basic troubles, was again a difference of philosophy. All navies wanted to keep war plans pretty flexible so that the commander could have quite a bit of leeway in what he did. There are certain things that cannot be kept flexible like force levels, the forces that he has available, but how to get something done we'd try to leave up to the commander. In nearly all the papers that problem would come up sooner or later. We would try to cut out the details, cut out the specifics that we didn't think had to be in so that the commander would have the authority to make his own decisions on how he would take action. This was true even for the commands of the other services because we thought they should have that authority too. It had a little effect, I guess.

Q: That was entirely acceptable as a philosophy when you were head of Op-30? It came not to be later on, though.

Adm. B.: Well, it's not so much now. There's a tendency now, psssibly because of experiences over the last twenty years, for the navy to accept the desire for centralized control probably because they have to. When I became CNO, I put in a naval electronic command system to protect ourselves, I mean for quick communication and to exchange information within a command or among commands very quickly. But information is so easily obtained now back here in Washington that the people back here think that they can run all details of operation. It is true that the local commander does not know the president's idea or the governments ideas altogether. It is true that the government is responsible for what a local commander does and they don't want to let him use his own discretion on many matters because of the "wild major" complex, but we took the view then, and I think it's correct, that a commander who has any significant authority has also had experience and he is very cognizant of the limitations on his authority and of the tremendous responsibility that he has in committing his forces to a particular course of action. He's going to stay within that responsibility and he's probably going to be a lot more careful and have a lot more knowledge of the local situation than the president.

I'm sure that the biggest mistakes that this country has made in the last two decades, both in international relations and in the use of its military forces, and its economic power, too, has been in the overconcentration of responsibility and decision-making in the hands of the president and the bureaucracy. Among other things, he cannot disavow what he has done. That's one nice thing about Andy Young. The president can fire him but nobody can fire the president if he made those same statements. But, more than that, the people on the spot usually can do a better job.

This brings up one other point, though. One of the big differences of opinion between President Eisenhower and myself - I thought that man was one of the greatest presidents we've ever had and I liked him personally, everything about him, nearly, but this trait I did not like. He kept harping at me all the time and the rest of the chiefs, too, that the chiefs should get together and have a single opinion. They should not present a split paper to him, "You have got to solve your own military problems and solve them down in the Joint Chiefs level. If you come together and have a single opinion, it's a much better solution all around."

My standard reply was that, "It's your job, Mr. President, to make the decision. There are differences of opinion and if we get a solution that we all agree to, it will be a compromise solution and that is never as good - very seldom as good - as a single solution. These are complex problems. There is no simple solution. These fights, these differences of opinion, have good effects, because we have to justify before our peers all the time and to you - when we do not agree with one another. We get good ideas from the other services. Sometimes we take them reluctantly, but it's much better to have three different opinions, or four or five different opinions, than it is to have one. When you get just one opinion from a group of people, then you don't need all those people."

Q: He wouldn't buy that?

Adm. B.: No, he didn't buy that, and he was right sometimes. It is unpleasant to have those continual fights all the time, but it also has some good aspects. If you can coordinate when it comes time to do something, if you have a friendly difference of opinion instead of being antagonistic, you can be a proponent without being antagonistic.

We had pretty good luck with the JCS papers and we had some fairly good war plans.

Q: Might I ask were any of them implemented at any time?

Adm. B.: Yes, not the war plan itself. It's very seldom that a war plan is actually implemented completely. The plan is there so that parts of it or all of it can be implemented. Take Lebanon, for example, we had a lot of contingency plans, and the landing in Lebanon was based on a pretty good, well-approved plan. At that time I, as CNO, had the responsibility for carrying it out. I was in command of the fleets. I was executive agent of the Joint Chiefs of Staff for carrying out that plan. That meant that it only took about ten minutes to get approval to execute a plan. Everybody knew what it was and it worked very fine. I pushed the button and said "Execute," then things started to roll. Replacements, logistics started to flow, the whole thing. It didn't take a whole series of dispatches, all it said was go, and everything started to go. The support of Taiwan - yes, quite a few portions of plans were carried out.

The next subject is SacEur. I've gone over many detailed papers on the early days of SacEur. General Eisenhower was SacEur first but in '52 General Ridgway took over. General Ridgway had come from Japan. His deputy was General Schuyler, and General Handy was U.S. CinCEur. USComCEur was formed - I'd better go back a little bit.

When NATO was first formed, they formed SacEur as a permanent command, the important command, but NATO itself had limited authority. It had no authority to tax, no authority to raise armies, no authority to provide logistic support, no money, it had no people. It was dependent upon the support of the nations involved. The Supreme Allied Commander was an American, General Eisenhower, and he had tremendous authority that the nations gave to him initially to carry out war plans if anything happened. But he didn't have any authority to raise forces or supplies. He had to rely on nations to do that. When the command was first started they didn't have any separate American element of that command and General Eisenhower found himself both as the NATO commander and as the U.S. component commander. He could order things to be done by the U.S. component, which he could do all right with the U.S. but it didn't work with a Frenchman, or other nations. One man was exercising command over both international forces and his own countries forces - and he and his staff sometimes got mixed up on which hat he was wearing.

Q: But it probably worked better with Eisenhower making the request than anybody else?

Adm. B.: Yes, that's right. So they found out that Caeser's responsibilities had to be separated from everybody else's responsibilities - give unto Caesar what is Caesar's, but don't give him anything else. That is, the United States had to retain responsibility for the logistic support of its own forces and it couldn't be well done through an American who was responsible to NATO and not the United States. That responsibility couldn't be delegated to a NATO commander and yet the NATO commander was absolutely dependent upon those forces being supported.

So they established a U.S. CinCEur, United States Forces, Central Europe - Commander in Chief, United States Forces, Central Europe. He was responsible for the lines of supply, everything except the combat operations and the plans for combat operations although, of course, he had to be cognizant of these plans. But there had to be extremely close coordination between SacEur, CinCEur, and the other allied national commanders. The French national commander had to supply French forces and so forth. The NATO command had all nations in the command, the supporting commands were national. This had a particularly bad effect on the navies.

In the Mediterranean we had a few ships now and then but there wasn't any such thing as a Sixth Fleet in the Med. Most of the ships in the Med were British, there was a British naval commander, based on Malta. CinCSouth had responsibility for the land forces of

Greece and Turkey and the protection of the Mediterranean. He had to have naval forces available to carry out that responsibility. Admiral Carney then had command of U.S. forces in the eastern Atlantic and the Mediterranean, U.S. naval forces, based in London, so he then was appointed CinCSouth to be the southern component commander of SacEur. So he moved down to Naples and he took his London staff with him. Well, they found that U.S. forces and NATO responsibilities got mixed up again. In addition to that, he could not carry out some of the national duties that he had been able to carry out when he had his office in London, so they decided to split the NATO command and national command of naval forces. This was a very great and difficult problem to solve, split the command, and CinCSouth was formed, which would be a NATO command, and then a CinCNelm, which would be a U.S. command, to support the NATO command but who would actually command U.S. Naval Forces in Europe.

The British, who had the big naval force then in the Med, did what they wanted to do before _ I mean tried to do what they wanted to do before. They always like to take control and so they were interested in controlling the Med. They had CinCAFMed, CinC British Med is what it really was, but they finally conceded that Admiral Carney would be CinCSouth and that they could have the BritAFMed in the Mediterranean, too, and would coordinate and cooperate with NATO but would be assigned to CinCSouth only under certain conditions. That was all right, but it took a lot of doing to get the responsibilities straightened out.

Admiral Carney didn't much like at the beginning to split his command but he finally did and Jerry Wright took over CinCNelm. Abe Vosseller was the naval representative on SacEur. The U.S. Joint Chiefs of Staff depended a great deal upon the recommendations submitted by NATO commanders on the forces that they would like to have under their command, the forces that they felt were required to meet their responsibilities. Well, SacEur had one captain, very few naval officers on his staff. CinCSouth hadn't been really established yet, and one of the first questions that Abe Vosseller asked was how many carriers should we provide. Well, we answered him that the United States could perhaps provide as many as eight but not constantly. We could supply those if all the war activities were in the Med and there was no war any place else. We couldn't guarantee eight under all circumstances. This is the big trouble always in the provision of naval forces. We cannot guarantee that those forces can go to a specific point, a specific place, for a specific duty in case of war.

Q: That they'll be constant?

Adm. B.: Yes, they can't be. With armies, you've got to do that because it takes a long time to get them in place.

The strength of the navy is its mobility. The reason why navies are cheap is because you can use them in different places at different times, but you can't use them in different places at the same time. No nation can have that much navy. The army, ever since I've known them, have always objected to the fact that the navy cannot make a specific commitment, a total specific commitment. We can guarantee that we can have two carriers in an area but we cannot guarantee what we might be able to provide, such as eight or ten.

Q: That's a simple enough concept to absorb!

Adm. B.: It is, but you can't plan on all the carriers, you see. Take the delivery of atomic weapons. These were the days when carriers could carry atomic weapons, and they would want to assign to the navy certain specific targets. Well, we could guarantee some of them, but we couldn't guarantee all of them. We wanted it understood that sometimes we would have a capability far greater than that and we could take care of extra targets. The hell with that, the army and air force would say, they're not your targets, they're our targets. In other words, the atomic strike plans couldn't be flexible enough to handle an increased strength that might be there but might not be there.

To get back to the force-level business, they wanted

to request twelve CVs. That's good. I mean that's a lot of CVs, and a request from the Supreme Allied Commander Europe is of some importance, not overriding but it's a big factor. They want to know if that was reasonable. Well, we wrote back and much to their consternation, said no, it's not reasonable, we cannot provide twelve. We can provide eight but that's the maximum.

Later on, I had to get a captain relieved because of the philosophy that he had. He had similar problems and he said:

"Why can't we just say that we could do it. Just have papers. We might be able to do it. It's not really a total untruth because we might be able to do that."

He argued about that too long. I said you've got to be able to deliver what you promise. You cannot promise unless the navy has the capability of delivering because, you know, some day that emergency may arise. That's what plans are for - to take care of a possible contingency. If that day should come and people had depended on us and we failed, the United States would be guilty of lying. We must be able to deliver what we promise.

Q: It had to be a bona fide promise?

Adm. B.: Yes. This was one of our troubles, but its also become a great advantage. They commenced to rely on our word. They would trust Vosseller, for he always delivered what he said he could do.

Another thing is that you can't make a plan for an unlimited time. Our carriers get old and they run down, and if you don't get a replacement carrier, you can't continue the old plan. Our force levels were always dependent upon our budget. That was not for just next year. Plans have always got to be four or five years in advance, war plans particularly, or action plans, and sometimes we couldn't guarantee naval forces until we had approval in the budget for the carrier to be built. In those days it didn't take ten years to build a carrier.

There's one letter here, I notice, where Vosseller said he worked too hard and got so little accomplished.

Q: I saw that one, too.

Adm. B.: CinCNelm's initial problem after Jerry Wright took part of the staff back to London was its relationships with SacEur and CinCSouth. He had to have good relationships directly with the Supreme Allied Commander and CinCSouth and also CinCNorth. But he had only one naval force. It took a long time to get that squared away.

Q: And a certain amount of experience, I suppose, unfolding, too?

Adm. B.: A certain amount of experience. One of his

problems there was a peculiar problem. We had a lot of U.S. Minesweepers in Germany, sweeping the Rhine and various places. Those minesweepers belonged to the United States. I don't think we built them, they were manned by Germans and they were under British control because they were in the British zone. We wanted to start a German navy and who the hell owned those minesweepers! We finally got it squared away. We all, the British and ourselves and the Germans came to one conclusion. We gave the minesweepers to Germany and the British gave control to Germany and the Germans said they would take them.

Q: In that connection, there's a story which I have been told which doesn't appear, at least I haven't seen it, in this particular file about giving a destroyer to the Germans in which you had a very important role. Do you recall that story?

Adm. B.: Yes, that was when we gave three ships of DesRon 23 to Germany, and I'll talk about that on the German Navy.

Q: Oh, you will, fine.

Adm. B.: One of the limitations SacEur has, and there's a big debate going on on this right now, is the geographic limits of NATO. NATO has geographical limits and those limits do not include the Middle East, the South Atlantic, or any place other than the North Atlantic, the Med and Europe. So what can NATO have to do with the Middle East? It doesn't have anything to do with the Middle East. A NATO command cannot direct anything for the Middle East.

Q: Except that it reaches as far as Turkey now and Greece.

Adm. B.: Greece and Turkey and the Med but that's it, not any country in the Middle East. So, who in hell looks after the Middle East? Nobody. There wasn't a Joint Chiefs of Staff directive because nobody was interested in the Middle East. CinCNelm had to pick up that responsibility which he could do as a U.S. commander. We had had ships over there before and we had been interested in it when it was solely an American command or British, I mean solely national. The only national command we had that was interested in the Middle East was CinCNelm. Nobody else wanted to take it. Admiral Towner was commander of the Middle East force there. Do you know him?

Q: I don't know him.

Adm. B.: He's a great big tremendous man, a wonderful man. Well, he was Commander, Middle East. We put him under CinCNelm and we had him, I note here, draw up plans for the defense of Bahrein and the Bahrein oil complex.

I don't know whether they're any good now or not. We were fearful of a Tudeh coup in those days in Iran, and just like they are now, like Khomeini is. I think I said this last time, Khomeini is going to have a Tudeh coup or maybe a coup in coordination with the Feydayeen.

Q: Where did the Persian Gulf Command fit into this picture?

Adm. B.: That was ComMidEast, that was Towner's command. He had an old seaplane tender and a destroyer or two sometimes. That was twenty-six years ago and they had the same problems to be planned for as they have now.

When CinCEur was formed, Charlie Wellborn went over there as a rear admiral, to that joint U.S. staff, so we had to cut Charlie Wellborn (and U.S. CinCEur) and Jerry Wright in on the problems of the Middle East, and see if it would be possible to send troops under some circumstances from Europe to the Middle East if we needed them there quickly. That never got solved.

Another problem that CinCNelm had, which did have to do with the Turkish strait, the international law in the Turkish strait.

Q: The Montreux Convention?

Adm. B.: The Montreux Convention. I wanted to send U.S. ships into the Black Sea. We hadn't done it since the war - so did a lot of other people, too. The first thing we had to do was go to the JAG to find out what the restrictions were on U.S. navy ships entering and leaving the Black Sea in peacetime, in time of war, with Turkey as a belligerent or nonbelligerent in war and what the Potsdam Agreement had changed in that agreement.

Q: All the ramifications.

Adm. B.: All the ramifications. Of course, most of State Department people wanted to make it as limited as possible so that we were permitted to do just as little as possible, and we had to go back to the JAG and say:

"Look, the letter you've written you don't really mean, do you? Maybe you want to take it back and rewrite it and tell us the reasons why it can be done instead of the reasons why it can't be done."

That took a lot of doing. We finally got some ships into the Black Sea but not at that time. It took a couple of years to get that straightened out in our own shop.

Q: It really is a privilege that you have to keep on exercising, isn't it, in order to maintain?

Adm. B.: Yes, exactly. A right not exercised is a right soon lost. You have to worry them a little bit. If we went into the Black Sea we didn't have to do anything real, but we wanted to keep the Soviets a little bit on edge as to what we might do, just like they keep us on edge. They're very good at that. They sometimes show themselves, their submarines show themselves, because they're afraid maybe we haven't really detected them and know that they're there. I'm sure they do that and it does cause us worry.

One of the liaison officers we had was George Campbell who was with the RAF Coastal Command in Northwood, a navy captain and a public-relations expert. He had been on Admiral McCormick's staff and he was a very good writer. He could find out from the RAF just in conversations, he'd hear rumors about what was going to happen in our own country and he would inform us of the rumors. Sometimes that was the first time that we had any inkling that the subject was being discussed or being thought about in our own air force. In other words, it was a pretty good working system. Some foreign organizations we learned as awful lot from. Several nations had a good propaganda mill going in those days. They'd start rumors and could get a lot of opposition going. We were so naive we took those rumors as having some basis in fact, and sometimes they didn't, they were just straight fiction, but they had an effect. Psychological warfare is something that I never really knew about until I went on the Korean armistice negotiating committee and on that job I found out that people used psychological methods to influence friendly nations to do the things that they would like to have done, and it could be done indirectly through our own people if they were careful.

Q: What reliance did you in Op-30 put on foreign publications?

Adm. B.: Quite a bit, but we always tried to check them. It's like the publications now about President Carter. A lot of those stories about President Carter have a basis of truth, some of them are completely true, but some of them are conjectures for political purposes, and nobody knows what they are.

There was a whispering campaign there at one time against General Ridgway. General Ridgway is a soldier, an operating soldier. We checked to see if it was just a whispering campaign against him. It was - and we helped stop it by warning our people that this was a possibility and be careful. They became alert to that type of influencing propaganda.

One of the things we got from our people in England was a possibility that the British, because of their lack of money and lack of equipment and forces, were hoping to develop plans so that British forces would be used solely for the defense of England, that they would withdraw gradually back over the years to defend England, and they would want as many U.S. forces, as many foreign forces, too, as possible, to defend England. They would want somehow to ensure that England would be defended first. That's normal. I mean that's not a wrong idea for a Britisher to have!

Q: It's a little England concept in contrast to the empire?

Adm. B.: Yes. We had to watch for signs of future movement of forces. This was before the British had withdrawn from the Mediterranean. This was the first indication of it, about that time, and so we warned our people not to depend on the British where they were in a position to withdraw unilaterally. If any nation once gets back to defending only its own soil, then their allies don't really have much help. But now that's about all they can do and they might not be able to do that.

I've got here a letter from Towner who said that the United States was unpopular with the Arab countries —

Q: So were the British, he says.

Adm. B.: Yes, giving more help to Israel, and that the Arab leaders distrust each other and they're so conniving and bickering that there's no cooperation among the Arab countries, except in opposition to Israel. The one nation that holds all the Arab countries together is Israel.

Q: I noted that, too, because it pertains today.

Adm. B.: It's worse today but that, I think, was the first time I'd ever heard that the single nation that's a unifying force for the Arabs is Israel, and I think it's true. He said then that the Arab countries know and they fear communist control but they aren't going to do anything about it so they put their faith in Allah and remain neutral. I don't think that's true with Iraq and I don't think it will be true with Iran very long. I think I'm going to tell you a story about that.

Q: All right, fine.

Adm. B.: It's about putting your faith in Allah. I had a good friend in the army, Paul Guthrie. He was sent down at the beginning of World War II when Russia got in it, when we got in it, to supply Russia through Persia and he helped build the railroad, truck routes, and so forth. One of the things that he had to do with was training truck drivers - he was in Teheran and he'd trained a lot of truck drivers - have I told you this story?

Q: No.

Adm. B.: He trained a lot of truck drivers and explained to them that in spite of the fact that they were educated Arabs, and therefore not accustomed to manual labor, they had to be able to look under the hood and find out what was wrong with the automobile if it failed, because there couldn't be two classes of people, one that didn't get their hands dirty and one that did - not with trucks. He had taught every day in his driving school and his students were very well indoctrinated. The first class came out of school and so he had a little test. One of the tests was to send a driver in a truck from Teheran down to the oil port, Bandar Shahpur. The truck driver didn't get there. He found out by telephone communication, no truck driver arrived. So he started out finally with his own jeep, Paul did, went down the road and pretty soon he ran into this truck stopped alongside of the road, hood buttoned up. So Guthrie got out of the car and said, "What's the matter?"

"I don't know. The engine stopped."

"What did you do when the engine stopped?"

"I got out of the cab and I faced east and I prayed to Allah to send help."

Paul said, "Didn't you look under the hood?"

"No, I just prayed to Allah."

Paul gave him a long lecture that you've got to look under the hood. It's probably some simple little thing, it didn't do any good to pray to Allah. After he got through the lecture, he raised the hood and looked in, and, of course, it was a little thing, he fixed it and started the engine right off. Then he told the driver:

"Now you see, don't you, that what you did was wrong, and you now know what you should have done?"

"No, Sir, I do not. When the thing happened, I got out of my truck and prayed to Allah to send help, and Allah did."

Q: Can't dispute that! Or, disprove it, at least.

Adm. B.: This was the trouble with the Middle East then and it's the trouble with the Middle East now.

Instead of going through these other commands, perhaps I'd better get to the building up of foreign navies.

I came to the conclusion, as did a lot of other people, and we made a little study on it, that the United States could not possibly do all the necessary things with only its naval forces, in spite of the fact that we were the great naval power that was left. We would not be able ever to have the forces to control the oceans the way they needed to be controlled. We would have to have help from foreign navies. They could do things near their own territories better than we could do them, cheaper than we could do them, and more reliably. We would have a tremendous number of ships in mothballs, they were old ships, they would probably stay in mothballs until they were scrapped. I thought better than putting them in mothballs, why don't we give them to somebody, just give them, don't try to sell them, but put those ships to work as training platforms, if the nations will take them not force them on them. If they want ships, they're there.

Q: And promised to man them?

Adm. B.: If they promised to man them and keep them going. And this was particularly true with antisubmarine warfare and minesweepers, for even if it didn't increase their military capability very much, if they wanted the ships, it would improve relationships among the naval services. If they got some help they would give some help. We thought it would be a big improvement. We also wanted their suggestions, their ideas, their plans and force levels. This was the time that I first met Robbins, chief of the Belgian Navy. I talked to him about relationships with foreign navies and he said:

I want a particular kind of navy. Belgium had no navy before World War II, it was dependent upon foreign nations entirely, and we need a navy. Particularly, we need minesweepers.

Nobody had minesweepers to spare for Belgium. If we just had a few, we could have done a tremendous job and it cost us millions of francs because we couldn't clear our harbors. All we needed was a few ships. I want a minesweeping navy. I want the best minesweeping navy in the world. We'll concentrate on this thing."

Well, I thought he was right. We needed minesweepers, why got give them to him. They used them well and they improved on them.

One thing I could never get through in our own government. I wanted to give these ships to a nation with no strings attached to them. I don't think it pays to loan ships. I had to loan them, that's the law. I don't think it pays to loan ships or to have strings attached. I think one of the saddest things we do is to loan arms, loan arms, or whatever to a foreign country and then tell them how to use them. In the first place, I think that's degrading to a nation, where they have to say, "Sir, may I quell this riot now," or "May I use them against my enemy who's just coming over the gate?" You can't do that. In the second place, they get all mixed up on what is allowed and what is not, and the third thing, spare parts come in - like we gave the Israelis engines for airplanes and they put those engines into an airplane and then they'd fly that airplane on a relief expedition that they did. Was this a misuse of MAAG material or not? I don't think it was. But anyway it caused confusion, so I think that we should either give it to them or let them buy it, but don't keep tugging, don't nag them.

Q: There is a modern version of that, too. They buy things but we still keep restrictions on them?

Adm. B.: Put restrictions on. Now, it is perfectly all right to say, "I will sell you these things, but we expect you not to use them for these specific purposes. If you want to buy them and tell us you're not going to use them for a certain purpose, that's fine." But we shouldn't nag them afterwards.

Q: This is one of the irritants that works in the opposite direction with Israel and our selling of armaments to them?

Adm. B.: Yes, that's exactly right.

The most important foreign navy was the Japanese navy, which I had tried to start a little bit, a little bit of a maritime force, when I was in Japan. It didn't get very far, but a little bit, and this continued. To get the Japanese interested themselves, I suggested to Admiral Nomura and Admiral Hoshina, the two people I knew the best, that they write articles. They said "Who'd all publish them?" and I said, "Write them for the Naval

Institute, if you can't publish them yourselves. Even if they don't get wide distribution, get your articles published a little bit so that your ideas are considered. It's a Japanese idea."

Well, Admiral Nomura did write several articles for the Naval Institute - this was in 1951 and 1952 - on Japan's defenses and the Maritime Safety Agency organization at that time. He also wrote "The United States in a Soviet War and Japan" for a Japanese research institute. These articles had very minor effect, but they did have some effect. They caused a few Japanese to think and a few of our people to think. Admiral Hoshina wrote some, too.

You mentioned ships that we gave to them. Japan had minesweepers, period, and a few patrol craft. They needed something more than that, so we tried to get two types of ships to them, frigates that were coming back from Russia and LSSLs, small landing craft. We finally got them both to them but it took a lot of letters to get little things like LSSLs that we were scrapping, and to get them given to Japan instead of scrapping them, shipping charges to get them over there sometimes.

I notice that I wrote in 1953 to thank Admiral Hoshina for sending over to this country Captain Oy, who was a commander of destroyers and I fought against him once. He's written several books. Makasoni and Mr. Maki came over to this country to study our navy's situation and to see if they could develop some ultimate goals for Japan's naval defense, see what they thought after they'd looked at what our situation was. They made a pretty good study on Japan's imports, their need for a navy, and the ships that they would need. Eventually, in coordination with Admiral Briscoe, who was then ComNavFE, and Rosey Mason, who was also in Japan.

Q: He was doing intelligence work there?

Adm. B.: Yes, he was doing intelligence work.

I wanted to give them some old destroyers. They did take a couple. Then we were putting old carriers out of commission, and I thought that Japan of all the countries in the world is going to need air defense and ASW defense, it's going to need airplanes, it's going to be Japan who will have a need for ASW and they're going to need carriers, so why can't we just give them one of our old carriers and let them get a good platform to train on.

Rosey wrote back and said the Japanese didn't want them. Why? He said, "It's too much, it would take too much of an effort, too many people, too many Japanese to man these ships, too much of a change. It's not a gradual growth, it would be a tremendous big jump, and there would be great resistance among the Japanese civilians who had just been told and believed that they would never be permitted to rearm or to have any war material, and certainly not an aircraft carrier. It's just too visible, too expensive, and they want to build up gradually."

They were absolutely right. That's what they should have done and that's what they did do.

Q: The papers on that subject also bring out the point that the U.S. Air Force people were opposed to turning over a carrier.

Adm. B.: Yes, because what they had hoped to do was to have all aircraft of any kind under the Japanese Air Force. That's one of the things they always tried to get accomplished, patterned after the British, but they didn't want to admit that.

You know the story of the Japanese Navy. I think I've given that before.

Q: Yes.

Adm. B.: The ROK Navy was about the same, continually trying to increase the size and the effectiveness of the Republic of Korea's navy, and to get the people on the spot to think about what they needed and try to do what they could do with what they had, to do a little bit more, particularly to concentrate on those weapon systems with which they would be confronted, like mines and small craft.

We assisted them in starting their naval academy at Pusan. Did I tell you about my experience at Pusan?

Q: I don't think so. In connection with the academy?

Adm. B.: Yes. This was when I was in Japan, too. They had a few naval officers but most of their naval officers had come from the army, with some naval experience. So they started this naval academy in Pusan and they asked me to come over whenever I could. So I went to Pusan one time. It's not really in Pusan, it's in Chinhae, right next to Pusan. I went over there, and it's a beautiful harbor, one of the most magnificent harbors you've ever seen, deep water, just wonderful. I went up on the hill - the airfield is not far away - to inspect it and here were perhaps fifty midshipmen in overcoats - it was in the wintertime, fall, and I was to stay in Chinhae that night. I got there late in the afternoon and there were about fifty midshipman in this great big barracks. They had windows but all the windows had been knocked out and no glass in the windows, no heating, no blackboards, no books, just a few books, a few instructors. These people were sitting there. They had a little box that they had their gear in. They were sitting there in overcoats and gloves and hats and so on, and the professor would write on the homemade blackboard the lesson. They would copy that in notebooks.

Q: With their gloves on!

Adm. B.: With their gloves on or maybe just taking them off. They had no text to study. He was writing the textbook and they would copy it down. They were very interested in what they were doing. I was impressed, I was really impressed, so I immediately wrote back and asked for books. I asked the Naval Academy library and a lot of other people. They sent a lot of books. I started their library out there, that I did.

Q: Did you get glass put in the windows?

Adm. B.: No, I didn't do that, but I asked what time they got up in the morning. Well, they got up at 5:30. What do you do first? They take a little exercise. Would it be all right for me to join them. Oh, sure. "We've got to have you."

Well, at 5:30 in the morning I got up and went to take their run. They damned near killed me. They ran about five miles. I thought maybe they'd go a mile or so, but they ran about five miles. I was in fairly good shape, or thought I was, but nothing like that. Cold? Ooh.

After an experience like that, watching those people trying to learn something about the navy, you want to help.

So I tried to get the ROK navy to get frigates, training, to get some training in the United States. Because of that experience, I wanted to get them back here to go to school, back here so we could give them some books. They got mobile training teams started over there, but it's hard to get - the ROK is a little different from the Japanese. The ROKs want a little bit more than they need and so you give them a little bit less than they need. Germany is the same way.

The EDC, the European Defense Committee, first started to make plans for German armed forces. We were not part of the EDC, the United States was not, so how could we help the Germans. The European Defense Force at that time, with the Germans, was land-minded only. It didn't have any consideration for anything at sea, but they needed a small navy, particularly for the Baltic. I talked to a couple of German officers, including Admiral Ruge, at that time. I think I went over there. And there again they started, just like the Japanese, damned near the same system. Let us start very small and let it grow. We'd like to have naval aid, we would like to build as soon as we can, but let us grow ourselves as fast as we can.

Germany had patrol craft, mine craft, coastal aviation, and they wanted some bigger ships and destroyers. Ruge came over, and I said:

"I'll tell you what I'll do. I'll give you my squadron, my own squadron, DesRon 23, which is about to go out of commission.

They've had a hell of a beating during the war, but if you'll take care of the squadron I'll give it to you."

Well, they didn't want it all. I think they took four ships, and so we gave them those ships.

Q: How did you surmount the legal problems in doing that?

Adm. B.: There weren't very many. The big problem with Germany was submarines, and large ships and that sort of thing, but there were no insurmountable problems on the destroyers. It just took a lot of paper work. You had to get a lot of permissions from people, from the British, the French, that's where the trouble was. The British particularly were - eventually, they did give permission but it took a lot of letters.

I didn't get those destroyers to them until I was CNO. I told Ruge that we would train his crews, if he'd send them over. That does us a lot of good because it gets them U.S.-minded. We were doing most of our training up in Newport then, and Ruge accepted all those things.

Q: What was his official position?

Adm. B.: He was inspector general then. In the German Navy there are two channels that a line officer can go in and he can shift from one to the other. Under the inspector general label, he inspects installations and makes plans and suggests, but he has no command authority. Then the other one is a commander. He has authority to give orders to his people but he accepts and seeks the planning data, information, that he can get from the inspector general. We have our inspector under the command organization. He was inspector general then of the navy because they didn't have a navy so he had nothing to command at the beginning. Later on, he became their chief of staff.

He came over for the commissioning of the Charles Ausbourne. We had a U.S. Navy crew aboard the Ausbourne.

Q: Was that a troop ship?

Adm. B.: No, a destroyer. She was at the dock with, of course, U.S. flags flying, a beautiful ship, and they played the U.S. national anthem, hauled the flag down, our crew marched off. Admiral Ruge and I were on a platform right opposite the ship on the dock. As soon as the last of our men left the ship, the captain stood at the ladder to wait for the German captain. The German captain was in a building perhaps 100 yards from the ladder so that he had a little time to walk. He walked down first, his officers following, and then - I mean his executive officer, and then each division came down, marched down.

I wanted this to be a good German occasion. "Lili Marlene" had been forbidden in Germany, so I asked the bandmaster of our band, "If you can play three or four measures of an innocuous march, just about the time the men start marching - the captain of the ship will have gone maybe twenty or thirty feet. He will probably start off first, but just about that time, can you do that?"

And he said, "Yes, Sir." So I said:

"Then, can you play "Lili Marlene"?

"Yes."

Well, this is what happened and it caught the Germans completely by surprise. I've never seen anything like that because you could see - I was watching the captain and Ruge out there, and when they broke into "Lili Marlene," the skipper of the ship - tears came in his eyes. He had the hell of a time getting aboard his new ship. Ruge did, too. We'd forbidden our own forces to play "Lili Marlene" and the German forces, too, after the war. He never forgot that. I still get letters. Who the devil was the skipper of that - Von somebody or other, he was the son of a German army officer.

That's what Fritz Harlfinger was talking about because he was there. He came over with Ruge.

Q: Yes. Well, he was attached to Conant over there.

Adm. B.: Yes. I think he came over with Ruge, I'm not sure. But, anyway, that was the story of "Lili Marlene," or the German story.

Is this getting too long?

Q: No, no, no.

Adm. B.: I was going to talk about the Brookings Institute. They had a seminar in Dartmouth from 18 to 30 August in 1949.

Q: Yes, and that's a very interesting one.

Adm. B.: A very interesting seminar. I joined the Brookings Institute. Leo Pasvolsky was the head of it then. He was a wonderful man, and he asked me to come up to give a paper on major problems of U.S. foreign policy. I was at Round Table No. 2 in the Baker Library at Dartmouth. The interesting part about that round table was the people who were there. A lot of those people are still active - Walter Ryan, Rostow, Clayton Ford, Liversey, but the most interesting man was a man named Jay Lovestone. He was a Russian.

Q: Lovestone?

Adm. B.: Yes, Lovestone. That's probably not his real

name.

Q: Anglicized.

Adm. B.: Probably. Jay Lovestone was an ardent communist, fell out with Stalin. He was a hatchet man for Stalin, one of them, and he somehow escaped, got over here, very anti-communist, I think. I never have been sure. Anyway, he's very high up in the AF of L-CIO hierarchy, now he is, has been, was then.

Well, Jay Lovestone and I tangled right away because he's very positive, but he knew his stuff. I learned more from him than I did from anybody else up there. I remember we sat up all one night, the whole damned round table, arguing, and we got about two hours' sleep before the next day broke. But mostly it was Lovestone and me. I had a lot of fun.

Q: Was this covering the waterfront or did you have one particular thing?

Adm. B.: I've forgotten, but we must have covered the waterfront. I found some notes there but I can't read them. I remember this was in the Hanover Inn, that's where we stayed. I think that probably he's really anti-communist. I had great doubts at the time whether he was really so anti as he pretended to be. I got a lot of ideas from all these experienced people. I had a whole list of things that I would want to take up with them, what do you think of this -

Q: What was the general theme of the seminar.

Adm. B.: U.S. foreign policy all over. They had various round tables. This lasted for ten days, I guess, 18-30, so it was probably a ten-day conference.

Another separate subject that doesn't have much to do with Op-30 was about a month before the coronation -

Q: Of Queen Elizabeth II?

Adm. B.: Of Queen Elizabeth II, yes - Admiral Fechteler sent for me and said:

"I want you to go with me to the coronation, on my trip to Europe, to the coronation. Unfortunately, it's just you alone."

He wanted me to do the work, of course. That's fair enough. So I said I'd be very happy to go. I don't think it was a month, I think it was only a couple of weeks, but I wrote to Vosseller on the 7th of May and told him I was coming to London, I would like to go to Paris - SacEur, of course, was in Paris then - on the 30th and 31st of May to get all the dope I could down there but I did not want to see General Ridgway until the 10th of

June, when I was coming back to Paris again.

I wrote to Neil Dietrich and asked him to see if he could find me a place to stay, to arrange my flights to Paris and stay in London. He set me up in the Lancaster Court Hotel. He asked me to stay with them and, of course, I said no, I couldn't do that because he was going to be busy as all get out. He gave me the full schedule of all the receptions, and every time that I had left over I had conferences with people like Holland Martin, who was a British planner.

That was all right, but I came home and told Bob I was going to the coronation. She's of British extraction and she said — she came down to the plane. She took it very nicely, but she wished she could go. I'd fought a couple of wars and left her on the dock, and I'd never seen her cry, but when I left on that airplane to go to the coronation great big tears came down. I've never seen her want anything so much as to go to that coronation, and here I was, it didn't make that much difference to me, but that was one thing that she was deprived of.

I got in on all the official affairs but I was a big nuisance because I couldn't go with Admiral Fechteler to the coronation because he had a seat, so they got me in with the CinCNelm crowd up in a corner of Selfridges, looking down the whole street of the parade, not the start of it, but close, and we had the best seats in all London for that.

But that trip was one of the most hectic I've ever had. I didn't have a yeoman, I didn't have anything but what I could carry myself, I had to make all my own arrangements, I was an adjunct every place I went. I did go to Paris first and then back to London, and after London we went to Scandinavia and then down to Paris, Naples, and so forth, and Germany. I remember one of the troubles that I had was when we got in to - where was it, in Germany - Orem put us up.

Q: Howard Orem?

Adm. B.: Howard Orem. He knew I was coming - oh, yes, Jane Fechteler, the Fechtelers' daughter, and I were put on the third floor. There were two rooms on the third floor and one bathroom. I said:

"Damn it, you make the arrangements here so that I don't get embarrassed on this thing."

So Orem had water hours for me and water hours for Jane, but there was always some difficulty like that that I caused, but I had a very interesting time and learned an awful lot, and I did see the coronation.

The next thing here is about an Argentine visitor, but maybe I ought to stop this. This is about Senora Maria Ema Santillan de Aignasse. You asked me before about the large number of letters I got from her. When I was skipper of the Huntington, we put in, among other places, to Buenos Aires, a beautiful harbor and we anchored out in Rio Plata. We were there I think for four or five days. The Argentines were just wonderful to us, but, among other things, we got an invitation - I got an invitation - from Maria Santillan, Senora Maria Ema Santillan, to come to a barbeque with the ship's company, 900 or 1,000 people she was asking. She had everybody, the whole ship, come to a barbeque in a great big public park in Buenos Aires. Naturally, we couldn't have all the ship do that. She had about 500 people and it was a tremendous barbeque. She had beer and bread but, above all, this beautiful, beautiful meat. She was obviously very rich. She was a woman perhaps fifty, forty-five is probably closer, red-haired, German extraction, and I think at that time her husband was alive. I think this was from Santillan but I'm not sure of that. Anyway, we were very grateful. I went, the exec went, the operations officer, the engineer, the people that she mentions in her letter.

Well, I was very grateful for all that she had done for us. She offered us theater tickets and other things, too, her help, and I said:

"If you ever come to the United States, please let us know," and I gave her my calling card, so did the exec, and King, who was the operations officer, and Bachus, the engineer - we all gave her our cards. I wrote her a thank you letter and so did they all and let it drop.

This was years later, on the 17th of December of 1952, I got this letter saying that she was coming to the United States. She would leave the Argentine about the 20th of February 1953 and she wanted to know where to stay, what kind of bags, crocodile bags, which are very expensive, what kind my wife would like, could I make arrangements for her to be met at the station. She was traveling alone - I remember she said she was traveling alone, so I think she was widowed and she would need help. Her letters to King and Bachus and the exec had been returned, and she wanted to know what happened to them, could I make arrangements in New York for a place for her to stay, and so forth, and would I, please, arrange to have a spanish-speaking friend meet her when she got off the ship in New York and take her to her hotel.

I sent a pretty nice letter. I said certainly, we could do that, we'd be very happy to, we were glad she was coming to the United States. I didn't think my wife wanted a crocodile bag, she had lots of bags, appreciated it very much. Bachus and King were at sea, apparently I was the only one in the ship who was in the area. When she came to Washington, of course, she would stay with us. I had called New York and arranged for a Spanish-speaking officer, I didn't know who it would be, but I would find somebody.

So I called New York, Hillenkoetter, and asked him to arrange it. His aide did speak Spanish.

We had several exchanges of letters, telegrams, cables and things saying when she was arriving, and finally I learned that she did not speak any English at all. Her letters were all in Spanish and I had to read them and then have them translated to make sure I got them right, then write her back in Spanish. So I knew by that time that I had to be very careful to double-check everything so as not to get things messed up, which I knew I was going to do anyway, somehow, I was going to get it messed up.

I got the name of the ship she was on, the hotel that she thought she was going to, and then I called the shipping line and the hotel to make sure that I got her room number and everything. I thought I had that pretty well under control. Hillenkoetter's aide said he would take care of her in New York, he would meet her, get her there, make sure she was either with Spanish-speaking friends, or he'd arrange something.

Then I got a letter that should have tipped me off and didn't. She said that she would like to exchange things when she arrived in Washington for dollars. As I knew, the exchange rates were very high and very difficult to get in Argentina and she would not have very many dollars, so she was bringing some material that she would like to exchange for dollars, did I have any suggestions on small U.S. things for her to buy to take back, or to bring up to sell - she didn't say "sell," but for her to bring up. Well, I smelled something, but not enough!

I wrote back to her and said I didn't know anything anybody wanted. I didn't know anything about that, and the best thing to do was to arrange it through the Argentine embassy, but I didn't call the Argentine embassy and she never said anything about the Argentine embassy any more.

She then wrote me a letter saying she was leaving the Argentine on the 14th of February, things had been delayed -- she reminded me of Rosenberg on that - a little bit and she would send a telegram or a cable when she arrived from Trinidad. She had made reservations at the hotel, which I had checked on. She wanted reservations either at the Hudson or the Tudor and I had found out that they had made them in the Hudson, she was squared away. She was going to be in New York for about three days and then she would come to our house for a few days, and she had a very valuable gift for us.

Well, I thought, if she said she was going to stay in New York for three days and she was going to stay at our house for a few days, I said, that's three or four days, I thought. I April she got into New York, they called me that she had arrived and she had been deposited at the Hudson Hotel. She was with Spanish-speaking friends, so she was doing all right, and he would see that she got on a train that would arrive down here at a certain time. Well, she arrived down here. We met her, Bob and I did. We knew by that time, we'd gotten a double-check, that she spoke not a word of English, so we had a lot of our Spanish-speaking friends - I've forgotten who now - with us. We met her at the train. She had everything that she could check on the train, hand luggage that she could check, she had checked and there were tons of it, more than our car could take. We got all of that arranged with lots of bell boys and lots of express wagons that the red caps had to take. Then I got a spare taxi driver to take her stuff, then I found she had a couple of trunks that were checked. Fortunately, they hadn't come in yet, the next morning.

We got her home. We lived on Hawthorn Street then. We had a little house and no help, of course. I knew this woman was rich or she couldn't have given a party for 400 or 500 people. I didn't know how rich. I just assumed she had lots of money, but I didn't know, and I should have known, that she had absolutely no knowledge of people without servants. She had no knowledge of people not waited on, and here we were, the only servant I'd had I'd married and the only cook I had was the same girl. There was a bedroom and no bells to push. She did have her own bath and bed, but it was a small bedroom and it was not posh at all.

I'd bought two dictionaries, one for Bob and one for me, Spanish-American dictionaries. Bob spoke a little Spanish and I did, too, damned little, so we got along fairly well, and we had parties for her, with all of our Spanish-speaking friends that we could gather, anybody we could entice who spoke Spanish, whether we knew them or not we'd ask them in to take care of this girl. Billy Miles was one of the best and Sally Mendenhall, they were the two people we relied on primarily because they were both experts in Spanish and both had good common sense. Billy or Sally was usually there.

Well, we ran out of parties, we ran out of money, conversation was very difficult. She never even learned to say hello. She was polite, courteous, and demanding as hell. I mean she wanted things done exactly right. Bob tried to help her out. Bob was her chauffeur, drove her every place. Bob was learning Spanish pretty fast, but it reached a stage where Bob was just about to be driven up the wall, and after about a week or so Bob asked me: "When is she going to go?"

I said: "I don't know, she was going to stay just a little while."

She said: "One of us has got to go pretty soon," and I said:

"Well, we'll have to get - my Spanish is not good enough, yours is not good enough - we'll have to get Billy or somebody to find out."

Well, they couldn't. Neither Billy nor Sally could find out how long is Maria going to stay. Maria always evaded the question, she just talked around the subject. Billy said, "A little while in Latin America can be two months and you may have a house guest here for quite some time, and I can't come over here every day forever, either."

It reached the stage where Maria said to me: "I understand you have something like commissary privileges" -- that's what she meant -- "and I want to buy some things." I said:

"Like what?"

She said: "Like refrigerators," plural. Oh ho, I know what she's going to do. She's going to buy the damned things as household affairs, ship them in as hers, and I'm going to have my name attached to this monkey business. Somehow I'm just stupid enough to get caught in the middle. I don't know what I'm doing in this thing. So I said:

"I can't do that. You have to go down and make arrangements through the embassy, making purchases and doing these things."

She didn't say anything about not doing it but she didn't do it, either. So she asked everybody who came to our parties how to buy things, how to sell things. I don't know what success she had. She didn't get any help from us, but after about a week -- I don't know how long, maybe longer than that - Bob said:

"Somebody's got to tell her and I guess it's going to be me." So she did. She said:

"Maria, what time are you going to go?"

Well, Maria ducked the question but Bob said:

"I've got to know."

Maria didn't answer, so Bob said:

"I've got to go see your embassy then."

Well, Maria blew her top then. I don't know exactly what happened, but Bob did go down to see the embassy. Maria was in the opposition party, she had no intention of going anywhere near the embassy, so Bob told the embassy:

"You have to put her some place because I just can't do this any more. I can't take her. I don't know Spanish. I don't know what she wants. I don't know how long she's going to stay. I can't get answers to questions. I just don't know. So you have to help me."

They said, "No, we won't help. She's up here, she has a visa for New York, probably, we don't know anything about it. I'm so sorry."

Bob came back and said:

"Maria, you've got to go down to the embassy and check in."

Well, it came to where Bob said:

"You have to leave. You simply have to leave." Bob's very direct. She said, "You have to leave because

I cannot do it any more."

Well, of course, Maria got angry, not too angry. I was surprised that there wasn't any –

Q: With that much gall, I wouldn't think –

Adm. B.: Well, she didn't want to stay in Washington. I don't know whether she stayed here or not. I know she went to New York to finish her primary visit. She wrote a very nice letter that she enjoyed her visit. She could understand many of the inconveniences she had due to her lack of English. She thanked us for her few days there, she was so sorry that she, a poor widowed person, had had so much difficulty, she did not understand the jokes and things like that, she was awfully sorry that she had been asked to leave, but she was counting on doing that, anyway.

Q: She was counting on leaving, anyway?

Adm. B.: Yes, but she didn't say when, but she didn't know what the reason for that was, she couldn't understand that. She was getting to know New York and she was going to go home on some ship or other. She was making purchases, which was a dig at me for not helping her make her purchases. She thanked us for the parties and she enjoyed the language struggle that we had.

Q: Is that the last you ever heard of her?

Adm. B.: No. I wrote and thanked her and said I was sorry, too. No, we had several subsequent letters. She was laying the groundwork for coming back for more and we discouraged that right fast.

The reason that this is important is that I learned more from that experience probably, on the difficulty of understanding, with or without language, the differences in culture. This same thing happened later. I should have known better. An Ecuadorian did the same thing to us. This didn't cure me. It should have but it didn't. Later on, when I was CNO, I went down to Ecuador to help establish the Ecuadorian naval academy, and I got a call while I was there that a man from Manabo, Ecuador, had named his son for me and would I please be his godfather. Well, correspondence went on. Of course, the father, Simon Bolivar F--- was Catholic. I didn't know anything about being a godfather to a Catholic child. I didn't know whether I could be, so I went to a Catholic priest and asked if this was possible. He said only if they got dispensation, and not really a godfather but something similar to that in Latin America, you can be without being a Catholic. Every time I've been a godfather before I've been required to bring them up in the religion in which their father is or their mother, some specific Protestant religion, but I'd never been a Catholic godfather before!

Arleigh Falquez. He's now sixteen or seventeen, probably older than that, I guess he must be. This boy's older brother was named - it doesn't matter, for a famous Latin-American. The mother was an Indian, the father, Falquez, was of Spanish extraction, he may have been part Indian, but they said they were coming up here and I again said, "Stay with us," which they did with two kids. I think we were living here then. I think we'd moved here. I didn't know that she was Indian until she appeared. Now, she's a very nice person -

Q: They weren't accustomed to so many servants, were they?

Adm. B.: Yes.

Q: Were they!

Adm. B.: Yes, they expected a great deal. This girl, his wife, was sensible enough to change right quick. She was more sensitive than her husband. Her husband was not. They were going on to Europe. They had plenty of money. They stayed quite a while. Fortunately, it wasn't too long. I mean three or four days, but that's a long while -

Q: A family of four!

Adm. B.: Yes, a family of four in a foreign country.

I've had a lot of letters from them over the years. I don't answer some of them now because in one of the last letters the boy wanted a motorcycle from up here.

Q: From his godparent.

Adm. B.: From his godfather, yes. Well, he's got money enough to buy a motorcycle down there. He's got more money than I have, I'm sure. But this is a different custom. I should never have accepted that godfather business from a stranger. I asked the ambassador down there what I should do and he said I should do it and that sort of stuff, but I should never have done that. I was accepting a responsibility and I didn't know what it took to fulfill, so I misled the kid, or rather, his father. They later got a divorce or they separated or something like that. She came up afterwards by herself. Bob took care of her.

I've got a hell of a lot of other small subjects here, thirty or forty of them. Maybe we'd better do that next time.

Q: All right, Sir.

Interview #10 with Admiral Arleigh Burke, U.S. Navy
(Retired)

Place: His home in Bethesda, Maryland

Date: Thursday morning, 30 August 1979

By: John T. Mason, Jr.

Adm. B.: This Op-30 outfit was a very hard-working group of people.

Q: An exceptional group of people as well?

Adm. B.: They were. The only way you can keep an outfit like that really moving fast is to have comic relief every now and then, so they were great for practical jokes and little jokes. One of them sent up to me "Satchell's credo for use in Op-30." It was six rules for staying young: One is to avoid fried foods, which angry up the blood; two, if your stomach disputes you, lie down and pacify it with cool thoughts; three, keep the juices flowing by jangling around gently as you move; four, go very light on the vices such as carrying on in society, the social scramble ain't restful; five, avoid running at all times; six, don't look back, something might be catching up on you. It was the last one that this lad

Burke #10 -- 295

thought was the most important.

Q: And this, in summary, was a way to avoid ulcers?

Adm. B.: I don't know whether it avoids ulcers but it made them smaller, I guess!

Adm. B.: During this period in Op-30, I had a great deal to do with the Naval Institute. They asked me to come on the board in 1952 and I regretted because it was inadvisable to accept membership on the Board of Control when I was as busy as I was. I was too busy to really do a good job on the Institute's board, so Joe Taussig accepted that. Roy Horn then was the editor of the Institute Proceedings. He and I were very good friends, so I wrote to Roy one time suggesting that little by little naval officers were losing their salty, expressive language and the language of the sea, and were increasingly adopting the befuddled language of land-locked mentalities. What the navy needed was a book of vigorous, clear-cut nautical expressions of the sea for use in our planning business. He agreed with that and so he looked for a lot of books and we got quite a few of them, mostly British books which didn't quite apply. But there never has been that I have seen, there probably is now, but I hadn't seen a book of naval expressions and what they mean. There are quite a few books on pieces of equipment but not very many on naval expressions, or

I haven't seen any on naval expressions.

Q: Yes, we have one on terminology, which is largely pertaining to equipment and so on, naval terms.

Adm. B.: I didn't know that. The Naval Institute does?

Q: Yes.

Adm. B.: I'll have to get it.

Roy did have one problem. They were writing a ship-handling book in the Naval Institute. It was to be written by the staff of the Naval Institute, and Roy called me up one day and said that one of the members of the staff who knew about Naval Institute plans was writing his own book on the same subject. He had heard that I was going to write a foreword for this young man. Well, I knew the Naval Institute was writing a book but I agreed to write this foreword. I thought it was the same book. I knew the young author and he was very good, so I told Roy yes, I had agreed to write that foreword and, since I had agreed to it, I intended to do it, unless the Naval Institute objected to it, and that should go to the Board of Control because I didn't know anything about this problem and it should be settled down there. I wasn't going to make a decision on it.

Well, I wrote the foreword and eventually they

ironed the problem out. I think they published both books, but it was a very unfortunate event because Roy Horn was a very good editor and his staff was very good, including this lad who wrote the book. The trouble was not laying all the people's thoughts on the table when they were discussing the thing, I think it was. It's another instance of misunderstanding because people did not speak frankly at conferences.

Q: Interoffice communication broke down.

Adm. B.: Interoffice communication, and it wasn't cleared up until they got into irons on the thing, speaking of naval expressions!

I told Taussig, who finally got into this dummy book, that I didn't care whether I wrote any foreword or not and I thought it would be better if I didn't write a foreword for either book, but I think eventually I wrote a foreword for both books. I'm not sure of that, I don't remember. Anyway, I found the forewords down in my files.

One of the other things that Roy Horn asked me to do quite frequently was to review books, and I did once in a while, particularly books that pertained to the strategy of the United States or pertained to naval operations. This book that he asked me to review was <u>Korea 1950</u>, which was issued by the military history section in the Department of the Army. It was only a few pages of text and a lot of photographs, he sent the book up. It was a very good book and, surprisingly enough, it contained a philosophy that the navy had been preaching for a long time, in those few pages. It was a beautiful book. They asked me to review it and so I did.

This was an example of the army getting the word, army people who started originally, I think, not believing in what the navy thought was good warfare, and finally accepting it due to battle conditions, experiences in battle.

Q: A lot of that is reflected in that long letter you wrote on lessons of the war in Korea, which I hope to include as an appendix.

Adm. B.: That report put out by the army was readable and concise and had exactly the right philosophy in it. The nice part about it was that they gave a great deal of credit to the marines, where it belonged. It was a just book, and it was a very fine book for all the services. The final part of the book was excellent, too. The book and the war were both incomplete, but the book just stopped and the war was going on. The struggle against communism will go on until the communists become convinced that they cannot dominate the world, as they have avowed they will. It won't be easy to convince them, nor can it be done quickly. It may take several generations of struggle, of constant alertness, and perhaps many areas of combat to instill in them the knowledge that free men prefer to remain free. The communists recognize only force. Nothing else persuades them. The Free World knows that now, and to survive they must be able and willing to fight for their survival.

That's part of my review, but also it is the philosophy that's in that book, and that was good.

Q: I wish that final statement was universally accepted, that the Free World knows!

Adm. B.: We thought it had then but it isn't now because it's like any other evil, it's hard to kill completely. It grows again.

Q: Each succeeding generation has to be convinced all over again.

Adm. B.: It has to be convinced and it has to fight for its own freedom. The state of the world right now is an example of that because there's so much divisiveness that all countries are retrograded a little bit, India, Iran. I had a long conversation yesterday with a lad who wants me to help in Saudi Arabia. It doesn't have anything to do with that but we thought at the time that after the

Korean War had been fought for a couple of years people would recognize that we had to be able to resist communist aggression, that it was not going to stop just because we wished it to stop. We'd have to fight, we'd have to be prepared to fight, and it hasn't worked out that way.

There is one thing on this seamanship book. They asked me for examples and in a book that was put out by the Naval Institute they gave one example in manuscript - I don't know whether it was in there finally or not - and it was put in by Commander King, I'm sure, but I'm very proud of this little statement because I didn't write it and I'm sure he did. It said that "In 1948 the USS Huntington (CL-107) commanded by now Rear Admiral Arleigh Burke moored to a buoy at Taranto, Italy, to represent the United States Navy at the Italian Navy Day celebration. When the Huntington's departure time neared, it was obvious that all eyes of the Italian Navy present were on her. A bit of showmanship was definitely in order. A stiff wind of 25 to 30 knots was blowing and a moderate sea was running outside the breakwater. The breakwater entrance lay one or two points abaft the port beam. The engineroom was warned to stand by for 20-knot speed as soon as under way. As the ship guard left and the moor was slipped, the ship fell off rapidly to port and set down from the buoy. By the time the forecastle had all the gear on deck partially secured, the ship had turned 90 degrees left and was steaming with the wind now on her starboard beam and the breakwater entrance was sharp on the port bow, all engines ahead full, with the first bell ordered with steady as she goes. The ship rapidly gained way and sped through the entrance with only enough windset effect to require no course change at all. The Italian "well done" flew from the flagships. Was this an exhibit of foolish pride or recklessness? Definitely not." I was very glad to hear that Commander King felt this. "The entire plan was sound and well conceived. The wind was used, the delay did not detract from the maneuver and permitted the forecastle time to temporarily secure the gear and get clear before hitting the heavy seas outside. Later, speed was reduced and a down sea course taken until the security was completed and the breakwater was cleared, and although the breakwater was damaged, Admiral Burke was assured that his speed would embarrass no one outside of behind the breakwater. The speed was a safety factor, not a hazard, for the ship was responsive and well in hand by the time the entrance was reached. The speed eliminated the danger of a ship being set down by the wind. Self-confidence born of knowledge and experience is a requirement for all good shiphandlers."

Q: And would you identify Commander King for me?

Adm. B.: Commander King was operations officer in the <u>Huntington</u>. He also included an incident in the book when we were in Montevideo when I made a very stupid mistake. I had had command by that time of a great many small ships, I'd gone through the war handling ships, and I'd had command of a cruiser for several months. Montevideo has a very small harbor, and one cruiser in that harbor just about fills it. We had moored bow-away from the entrance to the harbor, so much meaneuvering was required to spring the ship's stern out and to twist her in her own water, on a dime, and put her through this narrow harbor entrance. I had twisted her clear of the dock nicely and I was swinging her very well and then I became careless. I was overly confident. I ordered the engines two-thirds ahead starboard and two-thirds astern port, when I should have done just the reverse. The mistake was noticed by a young bluejacket on the stern to give us the data on what the stern was doing, and he called out, "The stern's going the wrong way." He told us right away, so I reversed it and saved the ship from going on the rocks. This is how a man, no matter how experienced he is, can every once in a while have a period of stupidity and do the wrong thing.

King was very proper in including that remark, too.

Well, that's all of that.

Dr. E. B. Potter and I at that time had a great deal of correspondence. Dr. Potter had written a book on army and navy tactics and strategy, and it hadn't gone over very well at the Naval Academy. It had been published, put in the Naval Academy curriculum, and it hadn't gone over well, very well, and the reason for this primarily was because the midshipmen did not have enough background to understand the differences, to understand why there were differences in land warfare and warfare at sea.

Mr. Potter was then in the process of writing a new history restricting it solely to naval history until midshipmen had got that under the belt and then he would have another book, he hoped, on army history, so that he could compare the two later. I don't think he ever completed the second book, but I find that there's this voluminous correspondence between Dr. Potter and myself along about that time. I don't think I ought to include that here, but I will give you these papers, if you think there's any part of it that you would like to put in.

I notice also a rough draft here of a letter and a smooth draft of it. The rough draft is about five times as long as the smooth draft and contains a lot of information that I never gave Dr. Potter, which I recognize now I probably should have. I was trying to keep all letters short.

Now I'm coming to this list of very small subjects.

Q: That you dealt with in Op-30?

Adm. B.: In Op-30, yes.

The first one I have is the old studies on geography.

I think I mentioned this before, but everybody in that section soon got the idea that geography was a very important thing. I remember them looking, when they were studying Soviet geography, trying to find an analysis that Napoleon's staff must have given him on the weather and geography before the Napoleonic campaign that ended up so disastrously, but we never found it. We did find data on roads and their raw resources at that time, but no data on the weather expectations.

Q: But you had a strong assumption that it was provided?

Adm. B.: It must have been provided because they surely wouldn't fight a war without consideration of the weather in which they were going to fight.

Q: No, but they came to grief because of the weather, too.

Adm. B.: Because of the weather and because of the stubbornness of the Russians' fighting, but somebody just overlooked it. It's one of those things that, again, are so obvious that it wasn't done, and this happens right now. We look back on each sad happening and say, "How is it that this was done and no consideration was given to this factor?" It's done over and over again.

Frank O'Beirne, whom I met in the Archives on Tuesday when I went down there, is writing an article on his patrol squadron, VP-22, right at the beginning of the war. He went down to Australia with the patrol squadron right after Pearl Harbor and it was the first reinforcement that our forces got in Australia after the war started. Of course, as soon as he got down there, he reported to Admiral Hart, who had just arrived in Australia. Admiral Hart asked him about the damage to the U.S. fleet. This was about a month or six weeks after Pearl Harbor, and Frank said he couldn't believe that nobody had told Admiral Hart the damage. They just simply hadn't told him and he said, "How could such a thing be done? When I told Admiral Hart the extent of the damage, he was horrified and he called in all of his staff and had me give a briefing on this damage."

He said: "You can't be right. Are you sure you're right?" And Frank said:

"I was there, Admiral, I know it. The ships are sunk and it'll be months before most of them are ready for sea." He said, "I had the details. I knew that they would want to know some of the details, but I didn't have any idea that they had nothing at all. They had no knowledge at all except the most general knowledge that a lot of damage had been done."

Frank was upset about this and I tried to reassure him that these things happen all the time. It's not because anybody was deliberately trying to keep it from Admiral Hart because they were trying to keep it from the newspapers, and they just forgot.

Q: There was such turmoil.

Adm. B.: Such turmoil and they just forgot. This happens over and over again, and this was one of the reasons why this advice from Admiral Nomura to make sure you know the things that don't change because nobody's going to destroy a river.

The next subject has nothing to do with my duty as Op-30, but I had a friend whose son was killed in naval aviation right after he had passed his examination as a naval aviator.

Q: This was in Pensacola?

Adm. B.: In Pensacola. He wrote to me and asked would it be possible for him to get a posthumous commission and designation as a naval aviator for his son. His son had passed all the requirements, it was just that the paper work hadn't been completed. Well, I could see why he wanted that, so I went to BuPers and, sure enough, they said they could do it somehow. They checked up and found out that the report was correct, so they did give his son a commission and a designation as naval aviator on the day he died, which shows thoughtfulness in BuPers, which a lot of people don't think it has.

Q: Compassionate.

Adm. B.: Right.

Q: I know that there was a great deal of compassion exercised when Smeddy was over there.

Adm. B.: There always has been. I'm sure that's what Olga McNeil is finding out this morning. They help but a lot of times it doesn't seem so.

Another item is that at this time I was building a Japanese house. While I was in Japan I had made some oversize Japanese equipment like shoji doors and I had them shipped back. Equipment was very cheap in Japan, the shipping charges were more than the gear. I had a Japanese house designed but I couldn't get those designs approved here because they wouldn't stand up, they thought, but they stood up in worse climate in Japan.

Q: What was your overall plan, to build a Japanese-style house here in Washington?

Adm. B.: No, to build it out on a farm. I owned a little farm out near Great Falls on the Virginia side. I bought that farm when Roy Gano called me up one time when I was back here on duty. He'd just been out and looked at it but he said: "I don't have enough money and I don't want to put my money into it, but it's a hell of a good buy. Why don't you go take a loot at it."

I went out, and I didn't have enough money either, but I borrowed enough so that I could make the down payment and I bought the land, forty or fifty acres, outright on Difficult Run. So I was going to build a second house out there, a sort of summer house, and I chose a place where I could be down on Difficult Run high enough above the run so that high, high water –

Q: So that it wouldn't be flooded?

Adm. B.: It wouldn't be flooded, I thought, and low enough so that I couldn't see any other house from down there at all. Around in that area it was just like being out in the wilderness.

Q: I want to be alone!

Adm. B.: I want to be alone, and there was a beautiful little spot. Well, I finally built a log house out there in Japanese style and I had a great deal of difficulty in getting a rise on the corners of the roof. You know, they come up and to put those curves in that the Japanese put in their houses, but I had worked out a system to do that and the carpenters did a fairly good job, but I didn't have a regular builder do it.

Q: You didn't have an architect, either?

Adm. B.: Oh, yes, I had to have an architect because I had to have the plans modified so that they would pass specifications for a house in Virginia. The architect said, "If you put a fireplace in here, a stone fireplace, then it will be strong enough and will pass the examination." Well, stone fireplaces don't blow down and that would give it the strength. So he did that and I had an addition to what the Japanese had, a stone fireplace. It turned out to be right beautiful. But I was building that -

Q: This was when you were in Op-30?

Adm. B.: Yes. I think I was just completing it then. I don't know exactly, but it was in Op-30. I would go out and help however I could on the weekends sometimes, but since I didn't have most weekends off - but it turned out to be a fairly good house.

Later on, Goat Mendenhall, a classmate of mine, used to come out there for exercise, clear woods, do a lot of sawing and things. Goat would come out and help me and I said:

"Goat, what the hell do you come out here and do my work for?"

He said, "Well, do you mind selling me part of this land? And I said, "No. Measure off what you want and I'll sell it to you for the proportinate price that I paid for it."

He said, sure, but before he finished the deal I'd gone to sea. I've forgotten when that was but I think it was about - it was at the beginning of the Korean War. I'd gone to sea and so he wrote and I said, "You do all the paper work back there and leave me out of it because I don't have time to fiddle with that."

He went to a lawyer to get it all squared away, and the lawyer said, "We can't do this until we get approval." Goat said: "I've got approval." The lawyer said:

"Have you figured out the amount you're going to pay him? He's got to agree to that." He said: "Oh, he'll agree to it." And the lawyer said:

"No, it can't be done that way. This is the damnedest thing. It just can't be done that way."

He said, "Okay, you write a letter to him and get agreement." So I wrote back and said I didn't know the details at all but anything Admiral Mendenhall says is correct, I know that. He'll lean over a little bit backwards maybe, but it will be correct. The money, whatever he says, I approve.

Well, the lawyer thought that was a hell of a way to do business but they did.

About six or eight months later, while I was still in Korea, they found that they had done everything correctly except they forgot to have a road in to Goat's place!

Q: A right of way.

Adm. B.: A right of way. So this lawyer very shamefacedly wrote me a letter and said they'd forgotten about a right of way and they would like to have this right of way, and he sent me a plot, and I said again, "This still applies. What Admiral Mendenhall says is correct will be correct. If he wants to modify this in any way when he starts to put it in, have him modify it. He won't take more than he needs."

The lawyer was amazed and dismayed that business could be done that way, but it turned out all right.

Also, after the Korean War, we had a jeep. I bought a jeep from surplus some place in Washington and when I would go to sea I would sell the jeep to Goat for ten dollars. When I came back, he would sell it to me for ten dollars. So we sold that jeep back and forth so that the man who was left had title to it. Eventually, it got flooded out and it went down the river. I don't know what happened to it but it wasn't worth ten dollars by that time, although it ran very well.

Q: And may I ask, did your house get flooded out? You intimated –

Adm. B.: I sold the house quite a few years ago and it had not been flooded out. It had been broken into many times. That's why I sold it. There was no way I could keep - for example, I had a collection of arms used in the Korean War that had been captured. While I was out there I decided to get one weapon of each type, and a lot of them were homemade, handmade guns and equipment, and I had perhaps thirty of them. I had them all fixed so they couldn't fire in Japan before I left and I had them shipped back. The army really collected this for me. So I took all of these guns and put them out in a display on the side of this fireplace, and somebody broke in and stole the whole darned works. Those guns can't be fired. They're no good, but there were some very crude weapons there that I would like to have had. I found a couple of pieces down in the stream bed years later that somebody had thrown away as things that they didn't want. The same thing was true of Japanese lanterns. I had a couple of Japanese lanterns out there.

Q: The iron ones?

Adm. B.: No, they were stone.

Q: I see.

Adm. B.: They were thrown into the river and broken up. I got some of them back later on because some of those had been broken, and later on I went to Japan when I was CNO, and I told my marine aide:

"I want to get some lantern parts here and I won't have time to do it, so see if you can get lantern parts," and I gave him an approximate size and I said, "If you have any doubt, buy the damned thing because we won't have a second chance."

So, he did. Well, he thought maybe these parts won't be enough and maybe they won't fit right, so I'll buy him a stone lantern, too. So he did that, but the flag lieutenant who was with me had heard me talking to the marine and he went by a place one time and he saw some stone lanterns in a shop in a courtyard and he went in and thought he'd buy one just in case the marine didn't make it. So he bought some lanterns. They didn't tell one another about it and they didn't tell me, they didn't have time. When we were on the way back they told me about the stone lanterns, and that's why I have so many stone lanters stuck around this place! In spite of the fact that a couple of them had been broken up, I've got plenty of stone lanterns that the aides had bought me!

I sold that house because it had been broken into.

We made a profit on it - Goat sold his, we sold them together - and I went out to see it a few years ago. Water had come up about two feet above the house, the floor of the house, and had ruined it, but the thing had been vacant for a long time. It was a nice summer cottage, although people did live in it. After I finished it, somebody rented it, from the <u>Christian Science Monitor</u> as a matter of fact, a reporter rented it. He liked it, but he was a bachelor and so he enjoyed that.

There was another thing in these Op-30 files. I notice I signed a tremendous number of letters, not in my personal files but in official files. Those letters obviously I didn't originate, most of them. Most of the letters that I wrote then and when I was CNO were written by somebody else. I would correct and so it would be unfair for any historian to think that I originated all that stuff. I didn't. I'm sure they know that. Of course, I wouldn't have signed it if I didn't agree with it, but I had a little incident here with this biography. The lad who was writing it didn't quite understand that. You know, it was not something that I originated. Sometimes I did.

In Op-30 we had a terrific amount of paper and we resented when additional paper came into the mill. When a service submitted a plan or a paper to the Joint Chiefs of Staff, it was submitted on a yellow form, I think it was, but a colored form, colored paper, so that you'd know that that was a submission and was not an approved Joint Chiefs of Staff paper. The other services would comment on it, and they would comment on purple paper, that is comments on somebody else's paper. Of course, we were swamped with purples. The Joint Strategic Plans Committee, which was the planners of all the services, met together once a week, or twice a week I guess it was, and I objected. I said:

"We've got to do something to stop this tremendous load that we all have, of us all submitting a lot of papers." "What are you going to do about it? It won't do any good to put out an order." I said no, it won't, and eventually I suggested that we have an order of the purple, that every week we have a little two-minute ceremony in which we'd give the author of the most stupid paper, stupid purple, for the past week, we'd give that author the Order of the Purple.

Q: Did Proxmire get his current idea from you?

Adm. B.: No! But, you know, that reduced the paper work quite a bit, because all the services took that up very nicely and, of course, they ragged the hell out of the lad who got it, the Order of the Purple. But eventually it died out because after a while you don't get those real stupid papers and it's not fair to give somebody who's just low man on the totem pole the Order of the Purple.

But it is a way of reducing things sometimes.

In 1952, in late August, I went up to the Lincoln Laboratory for a conference on air defense of the continental United States.

Q: That's the Lincoln Laboratory?

Adm. B.: Yes, at MIT.

At that time Dan Gallery had been writing to me about air defense of the United States and that we could not possibly put up enough guns or enough missiles or enough radars around the periphery of the United States to avoid an attack, if somebody wanted to do it. They would find out where all of these fixed installations were and figure out a scheme to bypass them. We had quite a bit of correspondence on that you may have seen. Dan was quite vehement that why didn't I do something about it.

Well, I didn't want to take that up because it would have been an unending battle that required a lot of work and wasn't really very significant, I didn't think. But I went up to this conference at Lincoln Lab and Charlie Lauritson - I don't know whether you remember him or not?

Q: He was a scientist, wasn't he?

Adm. B.: He was a scientist. He was one of the greatest

physicists in this country and he was a very down-to-earth man.

Q: Southern Cal, wasn't he?

Adm. B.: Yes, and he had something to do with the Lawrence Laboratory in California. I don't know exactly what. Anyway, he was at this conference and he presented a paper that went right down the line of Dan Gallery's paper, except that it was in better English and better prepared. So I accused Charlie, whom I'd known for quite a while. I said:

"You took Dan Gallery's paper and presented it. It's a good thing. I haven't done that."

He said: "I don't even know, who's Dan Gallery."

So I came back and wrote to Dan Gallery and he said he'd never heard of Lauritson!

Those two papers had exactly the same ideas, which shows that lots of times things do generate from different people simultaneously.

Q: Yes, in various parts of the world.

Adm. B.: In various parts of the world.

This is a new subject. You mentioned that you thought that George Anderson had come into my shop and I said I didn't think so, into Op-30. Well, he did.

You were right.

On the 28th of September in '52 I got a letter from George saying that he'd heard rumors that he was coming. He did come for about a month and then when Admiral Radford came back he went up as chief of staff to Admiral Radford.

About the same time George wrote to me about another rumor. He was in France at that time. He said that he'd heard a rumor from one of his air force friends that they were going to get Burke to hell out of the planners' office of the navy in Washington because he was causing too much trouble for the air force. Of course, Anderson thought this was wonderful, so did I. I never heard anything more about that, but it is important to know what might happen, to have the data on what –

Q: You mean that that kind of pressure could be exerted within the naval service?

Adm. B.: Yes, it was exerted, too. Not at that time, at least I don't think so. But we did the same thing to the army. If some army man was a very hard man to deal with, we tried to get him to hell out of there. Usually you'd go down and say:

"Look, Colonel So and So is just – we can't get together with him."

He'd know that. You'd know it, too.

One of the most difficult problems that I never tried

to solve while I was in Op-30 was the problem of a letter from a Filipino. He wrote to me. He'd been one of my stewards at sea in Korea. He wrote to me and said that he was in a very difficult position. He had put in for shore duty and he couldn't get it in the Philippines. He wanted it very much. He said he'd had six years on sea duty. He wanted me to help him get back to his home because his wife was expecting a baby soon, and I never did find out how in six years at sea! I never asked him. He got his shore duty.

Q: That was a little too personal to ask him!

Adm. B.: Sometimes it's better not to know.

Also there's a letter in there from Colonel Drysdale, Lieutenant Colonel Drysdale. That letter is dated 15 September 1952. He was in the Royal Marines. I don't think I've mentioned this. I know we were discussing Korea. The Royal Marines sent a company of marines over to Japan and they insisted that they would be under naval control, like our own marines, and so they were. When they came to Japan we had a company to fit in some place. They were a commando unit. The Marine Corps were up on the battle line and they couldn't use commandos. The Royal Marines did not want to be put in an ordinary straight-line battle formation. They wanted to be used as commandos. So Drysdale had come around to see me and I said:

"Well, I don't know how the hell to use commandos. Have you got any ideas?"

He said no, so I said:

"Commandos are supposed to operate behind the enemy lines. We are not going to send a single surface ship on a raid. So we eventually figured out that maybe we could send a commando unit to the east side of the coast of Korea in submarines. I said to him, "Would you like that?" and he would, so we had some exercises. We got one of our submarines and stripped it down as much as we could without losing its combat capability, and we could take quite a few marines in a submarine for a very short trip. We got rubber rafts, rubber boats, and all the equipment they would need to land in the surf from the submarine. All that equipment had to be either destructible when they got on the beach or the submarine had to take it out, so that it had to be collapsible.

Well, they did a pretty good job. They landed several times and destroyed tunnels and destroyed railroads. It wasn't any spectacular thing, but it was annoying to the communists.

Later on the army tried to get Drysdale and we had a big difficulty in keeping his unit - but we did.

Q: They never did operate under the Royal Navy, however?

Adm. B.: No, they were operating under our navy, and that was the purpose of it because the Royal Navy had ships out there but they didn't have any outfit that had marines with them.

Drysdale and I got to be very good friends. So in 1952 he wrote to me saying that he was out in Coronado training in submarines. He had been assigned to the U.S. Marine Corps as a training officer for this kind of commando work, and he had gone to the marine base in San Diego. We had converted a couple of old submarines into SSPs, that is submarines, personnel, for commando use. We thought maybe that would be worthwhile trying. He was working then with PhibLant, and he gave me a report on these landings. They had usefulness under some conditions.

Q: Who would be paying for them at that time? The U.S. Navy?

Adm. B.: The U.S. Navy, because he was training officer for the U.S. Marines, the same thing, he was training our people.

About that same time I got a letter from a Major Averell in our Marine Corps saying he wanted SSP training. He'd read a little bit about it and he wanted SSP training right now. He had finished his combat service in the Marine Corps, he was a good combat officer, and there wasn't any combat left much. He was just about at the bitter end, he thought.

I wrote back and said he'd fight again some day if he'd just hang on. He was a good combat leader and he hadn't seen his last duty as a combat leader, and I tried to get him this SSP training, which he eventually got. That use of submarines doesn't have very many suitable occasions. You can use submarines for that sort of business, but not often, so they were cut out in a year or so. I don't know what ever happened to Major Averell.

On another subject, I find here a letter from a civilian, Mr. Hanson, who was out at the Naval Air Missile Test Center in Point Mugu. He had helped a great deal in the B-36 investigation because he was a technical expert. He was one of those brilliant people, very bright, very fast, very impatient, and gets exasperated quite easily. He was complaining that it took too long to get things done out at Mugu. People didn't pay any attention to his brilliant ideas and he couldn't get enough done.

I wrote and told him that I was familiar with the process of establishing an end result that they desired and then, after they'd established the result that they wanted and got that clear in their mind, then they would determine the reasons for having it. I said that's partially what you're doing, maybe. He got very angry at that! Impatience with getting things done has not been limited to that day.

Q: I recall you telling me years ago that you didn't have much patience and that your wife insisted that you construct a ship within a bottle in order to develop this patience! Was it effective?

Adm. B.: I don't know whether it's age or her instruction but I'm getting more patient, I hope! I've still got some ship models out there that haven't been completed yet.

Q: So you can still work on this problem!

Adm. B.: Models do teach you patience because you can't do it wrong. If you do it wrong, then you have to go back and undo all the things you'd done before for one stupid little hurried mistake.

Q: Needlepoint is like that, too!

Adm. B.: I guess so. I've never tried that. You know, Don Griffen is very good at needlepoint.

Q: I know he is, and rug-making and so forth.

Adm. B.: Rug-making, I guess it's rug-making.
    Here's another item about Carl Bendetzen. He was the assistant secretary of the army, and he had working

with him a Dr. Ralph Watkins. Watkins I knew pretty well and he used to come over and talk with me when I was on the B-36 investigation and also as a planner. Carl Bendetzen was a good friend of mine. I didn't agree with him sometimes, but he wrote a great big long paper that he distributed through the Army - that he sent up through channels, on the policies of the United States, and he sent me a copy of it before it had been widely distributed, asking what I thought of it. In that paper he had some very good remarks that I thoroughly agreed with.

This was during 1952 and '53, and he said:

"We are preparing for a war that will never be fought. We are losing the war that we are in, and that after two years of combat, not because we could not win it, not because we do not have the military potential, but because we have no strategy for winning, because we have blinded ourselves to the existence of unconventional wars, we are lacking a strategy. We are always on the defensive, both diplomatically and militarily. The time has come to change that and to face our problems realistically."

That was a very good paper, but he didn't have any more influence than the rest of us.

During this period, of course, there were a lot of exercises at sea that Op-30 had an interest in. We didn't have any direct responsibility but -

Q: Would you ask for reports on them afterwards?

Adm. B.: We got the reports on them, particularly reports of what did not turn out well. One of these was Mainbrace. Mainbrace was one of the biggest exercises that we had up to that time. It was a command exercise.

Q: Was this in NATO?

Adm. B.: Yes. It gave tactical training to the major commands that might come under NATO. It was a very good exercise but they found that a lot of things didn't work very well, particularly logistics –

Q: Communications, too?

Adm. B.: Communications, and the understanding of new ships joining the force. They were good ships operating in their own environment under their own customs, but you put them with a new group and they didn't quite understand and things got messed up, just like the ABDA forces in the early part of the war in Southeast Asia. We've never gotten over that yet. You can't assign ships to a force permanently, to a NATO command, for example, because you have got to change them and you've got other uses for those ships. But there is also need for enough training – either enough training so that all the ships can operate together at maximum efficiency, not just do it partially well, or to have enough forces of one nation to carry out one objective by themselves.

Q: A combined force, of course, runs into the difficulty, does it not, of cultural differences, customs, and so forth?

Adm. B.: Well, yes, that's true. When I was CNO, you know, this was a problem and I opposed going too far down in exchanging people because you can't exchange enough of them, only a few. Cultures are different, food is different. I guess it came from some other nation, I don't know where it came from, but a paper was submitted for us to have a few ships that were manned by multi-national crews.

Q: This was an idea that Ricketts had, wasn't it?

Adm. B.: Not that soon, I think. Ricketts had the idea all right, that ships of NATO nations had to work together so that each ship could be efficient, but this was an actual multi-national crew. It may have been his idea, I'm not sure.

Anyway, I said that this was approved providing that we always insisted that we had French cooks, Italian electricians, American commanders, and British communications, or something like that, because each nation is particularly good at some element. We sent people now - it's good to send a few because the word spread, but we can't do it enough. We can't even do it with other services in our own country.

Q: You have to remember the biblical lesson of the Tower of Babel, don't you?

Adm. B.: The Tower of Bable, that's right.

We had trouble when we brought Germans over here to train in this country, just our food. They wanted to put cooks in our galleys, and we agreed because they knew what they wanted, they could cook it any way they wanted to.

Q: Earlier we had difficulty in World War II, did we not, with our submarine personnel and supplies from Australia? Mutton!

Adm. B.: Yes.

Many people still don't like mutton. We got a lot of meat from them.

That brings up another point. There was a man named Harry Walker. He was out, I think, of the class of '21, but maybe '22, who had resigned from the navy, gone into the reserve, and was in the navy during World War

II. After the war, he wrote to me as a planner and said that in World War II he had not gotten the proper food and he had some ideas on aquaculture that he thought were very good, growing vegetables in faraway lands, and did the navy have any plans for doing that. I wrote back and said no and I didn't think we would have, so we got into quite a correspondence about it and he insisted that we should have, otherwise we'd get caught just like we were before, and he had something there.

So I checked with the other services and found that the army did have a great big installation in Chofu in Japan for hydroponics and that even the navy had one, which I didn't know, down in Trinidad. We grew a tremendous number of vegetables in Trinidad, hydroponics. As a matter of fact, they grew all the fresh vegetables down there that were required by stations and the ships coming in. But I never could satisfy Harry Walker. He wanted to see some sort of an installation in the United States and to get some real plans out, but I bet you a nickel that the next war we don't have it.

I think I told you that I was forbidden to speak when I became Op-30?

Q: Yes, you did.

Adm. B.: Except to war colleges and to service organizations. Well, they loaded me. I made a lot of speeches to various war colleges. I went up to the Naval War College on their global strategy seminar and I made a lot of speeches there –

Q: But your remarks were unreported in the press?

Adm. B.: They were not in the press, no, thank goodness.

I went out to the Air War College, too, and I always had a lot of fun there because both the army and the air force knew about my B-36 investigation activities –

Q: Who didn't!

Adm. B.: Who didn't! They gave me a workover every time, but it was a lot of fun. They were very good about it.

Did I ever tell you about the time that I went out to Fort Leavenworth? This was when I was a captain and in Op-23. I was asked to go out there and make a speech to their staff college at Fort Leavenworth.

Q: The army?

Adm. B.: Army. I went out and they had a reception the night before where I was to meet a lot of people. It wasn't a big reception. I think it was really a reception for something else, but anyway I met a lot of people there and there was a group of young women that came up.

They were very polite and very attentive and asked me questions. They knew quite a bit and they worked me over. They asked intelligent questions about the navy's position on various things. I thought they were remarkably intelligent women.

Well, it wasn't until I met the husband oe one of them, who was the aide to the commanding general out there, and it was after I had given my speech - I mean the speech and then the question period -

Q: This was in the general assembly that the women were asking the questions?

Adm. B.: No, they asked me the questions at a reception, a social reception the night before.

It wasn't until afterwards that I found out that they had had a course that these young wives could go to before each speaker, and they surrounded the speaker and got him to talk. They'd find out for their husbands what good questions to get in, what will be his answer, how can you upset him. It was very well done, and I never forgot that.

Q: They had to surround him the night before?

Adm. B.: Yes, at the reception. This young captain, then he was, in the army set that up for me. I wasn't the only one who had that happen to him, but I got fooled very thoroughly.

Q: Slightly subversive, wasn't it?

Adm. B.: Oh, it was subversive as hell! I tried to do that in the navy afterwards, but it didn't work. Navy wives didn't - well, it never worked.

Q: You're not casting aspersions on navy wives, are you?

Adm. B.: No, I know better than that.

One of the problems that I had wasn't really a strategic problem but it was with the code of conduct that everybody always has trouble with, all nations, all times, and this is gifts from foreigners particularly, but gifts in general. What should people do? You can't say, "Well, the U.S. officer won't accept any gifts," as they're doing now, so that you can't have lunch with somebody or something like that. That's silly. We went back to the old rule that if you could eat it or drink it, it was fine, that's all right, or if it costs less than ten dollars or a small amount, it's all right. But anything that's expensive, don't take it.

This brought back a problem when I was down in the Navy Yard before the war. I'd been brought up by some pretty tough people, and Jack Hawley, who owned Northern

Ordnance, sent Bob and me two or three great big turkeys for Christmas. Well, that was the beginning of the war and that was too much, so I sent them back and, of course, they spoiled. I got an awful lot of running from Hawley that he'd wasted his money, I wasted the turkeys, and he was right. I was wrong.

Q: He was somewhat irked?

Adm. B.: Of course, he was irked and I don't blame him because this was a rude, stupid action on my part.

On the other hand, years later, I guess after I'd retired, I had another good friend, Jack Bergen — I had arthritis very badly and was taking exercises — and he said, "Did you ever see one of these exercise tables?" I said no, so we went down someplace, I guess to his club, in New York and they had an exercise table there. Well, it jiggles, it does a lot of things and it was helpful. So I got on this thing and said:

"This is just marvelous."

I got the name of it and everything, but about two weeks later in comes a great big exercise table to our house. Well, it had a price tag on it some place that he had forgotten. That thing ran nearly $200.

Q: Was he head of the Navy League at that point?

Adm. B.: No, this was after that. But he just sent it to me because he thought I probably couldn't get it down here and it was very thoughtful of him. Well, I didn't want to send that damned thing back and I wanted the table, so I sent him a check, and we had a terrible time with that. That was too much, but you couldn't make Jack see that. He finally accepted it, but he got hurt, too.

This thing of gifts from people can be very bad. We know that some people, a shopkeeper out in Hong Kong, say, would give somebody a little piece of ivory. If it's cheap, okay. Sometimes it was expensive ivory and the receiver paid for that somehow.

Q: That's always the assumption, that through your official position you're going to pay somehow.

Adm. B.: Yes, that's right.

There's a story here about Paul Guthrie. Paul Guthrie was an army officer that I went to Michigan with.

Q: What was his rank?

Adm. B.: He was a major then or a captain, I've forgotten which.

Later on, he was in Persia, a colonel in the Corps of Engineers. He was a good construction man and he helped build a railroad from Basra up to the Soviets. Did I tell you the story of his drivers, his Arab drivers? Well, I won't repeat that, but I got a lot of letters when I was Op-30 from Paul Guthrie, who was in Denver at the time and still remembered his times in Michigan.

I didn't know Admiral Ruge of the German Navy at this time but I did help Admiral Ruge in a six-week course in the Naval War College.

Q: Up in Newport?

Adm. B.: Up in Newport. Although he spoke English very well, this was to get him acquainted with and spread the word in Germany, which he did and helped us a good many years later. That was the origin of this idea of mine when I was CNO of establishing a regular course for foreigners. He was the first one.

I have told you about Hersig, who went to Michigan with me. He was a metallurgist and we had a good many courses together in Michigan. When I was a planner, he was the chief research man for Climax Molybdenum, and that was the time when he developed a process for producing pure molybdenum. At this time I got a letter from him saying that "three years ago, when you came up to visit me in the lab, you suggested sintering this stuff. Now we can make pure molybdenum, but we have trouble with people understanding what molybdenum is good for." We helped him give some lectures to various organizations that the navy had in the steel business. It was very good for armorplate and things like that, but we don't use armorplate any more.

Q: It's a rather esoteric metal, isn't it?

Adm. B.: No, it isn't. It's a metal that makes steel very, very hard. Their big mines are up in Climax, Colorado, very high altitude, but they use it quite a bit now. I think they have for quite some years.

Tommy Robbins had the Naval War College at the end of this tour of mine and he wanted to start a war game using electronics at the Naval War College, and he put in an installation. I thought it was a good idea, too. So did a lot of people. He probably had the first electronic maneuver-board system in the United States. It's been redeveloped many times since then but this saved a lot of seagoing and it gave a lot more people instruction.

During Op-30, too, we had a tremendous number of base negotiations, for bases in Spain, Turkey, Greece, sometimes big bases like Rota and sometimes just harbor facilities, a little bit of an agreement, small agreements for the use of their present facilities.

Q: Did that come under Op-30?

Adm. B.: It didn't come under it, but we had a great deal to do with it. It usually came under Op-04 but we had a great deal of input to go into it, to see whether we would really need them or not from a strategic point of view in time of war, and we had to know about it. That's why I've got it down here under "small items" because it wasn't really an Op-30 problem, it was a problem that we dealt with.

Q: In the case of Rota, now, those original negotiations were very protracted, weren't they, and very difficult?

Adm. B.: Oh, yes.

Q: John Lodge was on the other end of it, wasn't he?

Adm. B.: Yes. Did you know about John Lodge?

Q: No.

Adm. B.: Well, he was ambassador to Spain and he was promoted to captain in the reserve force. I was over there with the Sixth Fleet and I gave him a box or something like that to "Captain-Ambassador." He was very proud of that title.

Q: Captain-Ambassador, hyphenated!

Adm. B.: Yes, Captain-Ambassador, he thought that was pretty good.

Also, during this period, I went down to Marine Corps bases to give speeches to some of the officers. One time I went down and Frank Good, one of my classmates, had the Second Division. I went down and inspected his whole division with all their equipment and that takes up darned near three-quarters of a day.

Q: Makes you sort of dizzy, too?

Adm. B.: Makes you sort of dizzy.

Q: How many thousands of men are involved?

Adm. B.: I think actually about twelve thousand. Of course, that doesn't count the tail!

There was a great big wood sign that I had made in Japan, in oak, it's about two or three inches thick and maybe six or eight feet long and two and a half feet wide, and it's engraved with "Op-23 on Difficult Run." That's what I had named my little house out in Virginia. I thought it would remind me. That I've given to the Naval Museum now. If you ever see it, that's where that came from.

One of the things that we had to do in Op-30 was —

and they still do, I suppose - to put a murder board on every paper, to try to tear your own papers to pieces. To do that, you have to have people with a good knowledge of what the other services particularly are going to ask, what they object to. We kept a list of questions that could be asked by the army or the air force or anybody, and then sometimes a little description of why they were asked, why they would ask this question, this particular question.

We had a tremendous packet of questions on various subjects. We tried to codify them by subjects in general so that when a paper came through, you could go back and crank this paper through that mill, and it would be helpful in finding out whether or not that paper was complete enough to answer the questions before they could be asked.

Q: Interesting, indeed, and it seems to me that the people who asked the questions would have to have some of the characteristics of a hatchet man.

Adm. B.: They do have. All the services are very good at that!

To put a group of people to try to destroy your own papers is not a bad idea. It gets so that you've got the answers before you let the paper go forward or you've got a better answer in it.

I mentioned this last time, I think. In the last period of my duty in Op-30 I got a suggestion from a naval officer in NATO why not commit forces that we knew very well we could not really commit, but commit them on paper, and, of course, I blew my top at that time, and I ran across this letter to him, saying we cannot commit paper ships and we must never commit to anybody forces that we may not be able really to commit, particularly that we know we can't commit. We have to restrict those forces to the forces that we have and not the forces that we hope we may have sometime. We have to lean over backwards to be absolutely honest in that.

Q: What was his theory?

Adm. B.: If we committed on paper a few more forces than we actually had, they could depend on those more and they would ask for more and more and it would generate forces. It would be a scheme of generating requests for more forces.

Q: Certainly idealistic!

Adm. B.: It works. The air force did this with their B-36. They pretended to have more forces available than they actually did have and Symington, I think, said the air force will never refer to the B-36 except that it has a range of 10,000 miles at 10,000 feet and 400 knots and can carry a load of such and such.

Q: That's its stated capability, huh?

Adm. B.: Its stated capability.

Each one of those can be done separately, but they could not be done concurrently. In other words, if you carried the load, you didn't have the range, and that sort of thing.

This can be a very dangerous thing in planning.

Q: Pretty deceptive, I would think.

Adm. B.: Deceptive, and the worst of it is it's not so bad to deceive an enemy or to deceive even one of your friends, if you think he needs it, but when you start deceiving yourself - that's where that thing can lead you.

Q: That idea wasn't ever adopted, was it?

Adm. B.: No, but it's used sometimes without knowing really what they're doing, without really purposely lying, people do lie, and it's a very bad thing. It's marginal some places sometimes, and you have to lean over backwards to make sure that you're a little bit more austere with yourself, or with your outfit, than you really believe to be true, just to make sure you're on the safe side.

Along about early 1954, or maybe the late summer of 1953, I started looking for a relief for me and I found Dennison. I did not put the finger on Dennison but he never believed it. I think he had a cruiser division down in Norfolk. I'm not sure. Anyway, he didn't want to come.

Q: It's the sort of job he excels in, however.

Adm. B.: Well, he should have, he should have wanted to come but he didn't want to and he fought like hell. Then he started saying he wasn't qualified and lots of stuff like that, so we said:

"Well, what do you need to become qualified?"

He wanted to go round the world, talk to all the people in the world. We started to arrange that, found he couldn't go all that way, but we sent him to the Pacific. I notice here a fifth schedule for Dennison was made out, four of them were knocked down because either they took too long -- the first one, I think, took about six months! But the fifth one, he did to to the Pacific and talked to the people out there and got their plans. Before he went, though, he had to know what he was talking about, so we set up briefings for him and we spent just about as much time in the last month or so training my relief as on anything else.

Q: You simply wouldn't let him off the hook?

Adm. B.: No, I wasn't going to let him off the hook. I didn't put him on the hook but I was awfully glad he was there. He finally took the job over. At the same time, I was assigned as Commander, Cruiser Division 6, which Dick Stout had at that time and I was trying to get the dope on that, but I couldn't find out when I was to be relieved until Dennison relieved me, and I wanted to take a little leave. I did afterwards. I spent a week down in Fiddler's Green and Avery Island, at Ringle's.

Q: In Louisiana?

Adm. B.: Down in Louisiana. He was probably my best friend, but even then, after we'd made all the arrangements to go fishing and all the other things that we were going to do, he said:

"You've got to stop in New Orleans, anyway. You've got to shift planes there, and if you get in here at four o'clock you'll have plenty of time. I've arranged for a speech for you that night."

It was before some international society down there. I made the speech but I wanted to go fishing.

I was detached on the 19th of March 1954 and then went fishing.

Appendix

TO ALL MEN TO WHOM THESE PRESENTS MAY COME,

GREETINGS, KNOW YE THAT,

ADMIRAL ARLEIGH BURKE

Global Gladiator Extraordinary, Strategic Schemer Maximus Wielder of the Green and Defender of the True Concept,

Having, by Skillful and Judicious use of the Principles of War, the Justinian Code, Corpus Juris Segundum, Jiu-Jitsu, the Evil Eye, and Other Lawful, Legitimate and Legal Precedents, Ruses, Plans and Plots, Both Christian and Machiavellian, Over a Long and Trying Period of Time While Serving as

DIRECTOR, STRATEGIC PLANS DIVISION

Contributed, as No Man Before Him, to the Status Quo Ante Bellum and to the Greater Glory of the Mystic Realm Where Neptune Is GOD, Mahan His Prophet and There Is No True Faith But the United States Navy, and said

ADMIRAL ARLEIGH BURKE

in Addition to the AboveMentioned Acts and Accomplishments, was Despite Strong and Valid Pleas, Motions, Petitions and Briefs, both in Law and at Equity, and with Malice Toward All, and Charity Toward None, Successful in Inventing and Conducting Exhausive Tests, Said Tests Having Made Many of His Servants and or Agents Sick, Sore, Lame and Disabled, on What Has Become Known to All Men as

"THE BURKE DAY"

To Wit

"TWENTY FIVE HOURS AT THIRTY ONE KNOTS"

Therefore, in Testimony of the Above Mentioned Acts and Accomplisments on the Part of the Aforesaid

ADMIRAL ARLEIGH BURKE

the Membership of the Strategic Plans Division, in Executive Session, Assembled, It Then Being After Regular Approved Working Hours in the Office of the Chief of Naval Operations, but Well Within the Working Hours As Related to "THE BURKE DAY", Do, By These Presents and in Recognition of the Aforementioned Acts and Accomplishments of the Said,

ADMIRAL ARLEIGH BURKE

Wish Him All Happiness in the Future and Particularly, as

COMMANDER CRUISER DIVISION SIX

Signed by 72 Members of OP-30

4 June 1948

MEMORANDUM TO THE SECRETARY

The following is submitted for information only, and concerns a current Navy General Board project.

A few months ago, the General Board was given the task of preparing a "Study of Nature of Warfare within the next ten years, and Navy contributions in support of National Security."

Although the General Board has not yet presented the study formally to the Secretary of the Navy, they have sought advice and recommendation from a wide range of prominent persons, both civilian and military, so the subject might be brought to your attention some time.

In attempting to define the problem and plan a course of attack, the General Board selected two alternatives: First, it could proceed on a limited study based on the Navy's "functions," as recently defined, without attempting to tie in the policies, plans and programs of the other Services; or, Second, it could attempt the more ambitious task of compiling an estimate of a national plan of action for the security of the United States, and deducing from that plan the Navy's most effective contributions.

The Board decided on the second alternative. They did so with the full realization that it would be a practically impossible task for a small group, such as the General Board, representing only one service, to prepare a complete and accurate national plan of action in a short enough space of time to be useful. They decided, however, to tackle the job, and at least to set up a framework that might appeal to our National planners as a needed and useful working tool of reference.

A glance at the tentative table of contents, TAB I, will show the completeness of the over-all coverage contemplated for this study.

The study, in outline form, with stimulating questions on the various topics to be covered, was then sent out to a sizable group of prominent civilians, as well as Naval officers, requesting criticism, comments and actual assistance in preparing write-ups on some of the topics with which certain individuals were particulary familiar.

The Board has had generous support, and most of the topics have been written up, with the final first draft to be completed late in June.

A glance at the tentative preface to the study, TAB II, will show that the track taken by the General Board is a broad and objective one. Instead of trying to fit the Navy's capabilities into its assigned roles and missions, their approach is first to build a national plan of action upon the firm foundation of our national resources, economy and interests, and then tie the over-all military responsibilities to this, which in turn would lead to the logical solution of where Naval capabilities can contribute the most.

If the General Board's conclusion is correct, i.e. - "a coordinated over-all plan of action for national security should be prepared, kept up to date, and made available to all working planners of Departments and Agencies," the question is "who should do it, and keep it up to date?" The General Board's product will probably be sketchy on some of the components involved in such a broad coverage, and, of course, will represent the basic work of only one of the Services. In this respect, however, the thinking of the other two Services has been incorporated, and some of the preliminary drafts of the topics present most objective and realistic solutions. Sample attached, Tab III - "Middle East"

The study will at least be a framework upon which to build. Captain Arleigh Burke has been, I feel, the prime mover on this project, and it is his hope that the other Services as well as other Departments in the Government, will recognize the need for such an integrated compilation; and that a commission or board could be created by the Secretary of Defense, or the President, to keep such a national plan of action up to date and available to all who have a hand in planning our national policies and security.

It would be a prodigious job to keep such a plan up to date. I doubt if the Joint Staff, with their many day-to-day problems to solve, could do it, or any other agency that I know of. If the idea has merit, it raises the question of the advisability of an independent advisory or "general" board, such as has been considered, from time to time, for your office. At the same time, it strikes me that a good bit of work being done by the Navy General Board on this project is duplicating that being done by the Joint Staff, the Security Council, and other activities.

Perhaps the hope for a national plan of action containing all substantiating data on our economy and resources, with facts and estimates on capabilities of possible allies and enemies, together with probable intentions and courses of actions of the latter, and finally containing approved decisions as to U. S. courses of actions -- is too much to hope for. It comprehends a written correlation of matters dealt with by such an array of Departments and Agencies as, State, Military Establishment, Munitions Board, R & D Board, National Resources Board, Security Council, Civil Defense, Joint Staff -- with an over-all plan for national action flowing therefrom.

In any event, the General Board deserves credit for long-range thinking and initiative; and the paper should be stimulating and productive of thought.

What the Secretary of the Navy will do when he gets the General Board's study, I don't know. In preliminary conversations, at lower echelons, I have advised that it should be presented to the other two services because a plan for national action must contain the viewpoints of all contributing services.

Finally, my evaluation is that, if such a comprehensive study is deemed worthwhile, as a common foundation of reference for all National Planners - and as a check on progress in evolving plans - it would have to be kept up to date by a separate, detached board or group, which might report to the President, through the Security Council, or yourself through the Joint Staff.

Respectfully,

C. A. Buchanan

CAB:sdh

This copy of letter from Admiral Burke to Captain Alexander McDill, USN (in the office of the Secretary of the Navy) covers Burke's ideas on the lessons to be learned from the Korean War and the U. S. participation therein.

PERSONAL FILE

ADMIRAL ARLEIGH A. BURKE, U. S. NAVY

PERIOD: September and October, 1950

DUTY: STAFF COMNAVFE

COMMANDER NAVAL FORCES, FAR EAST

NAVY NO. 1165

FPO, SAN FRANCISCO, CALIFORNIA

9 October 1950

Dear Alex:

Your interesting letter, with its implication was most gratefully received. I hope that I'll be able to present to you some ideas which would be worthwhile in the article which you proposed. It is just the question of finding the time to dictate when I'm not pooped.

The most welcomed lesson of the war to date has been the strategic enlightenment of many fine career officers in the Army and Air Force on the Navy's true role in National Defense; the expensive and somewhat painful discovery that Naval power is an absolute necessity for successful projection of our military power across the seas. They have discovered that our own military forces in Japan could not have moved, except by sea, the short distance to Korea; that none of the supporting stateside ground elements, neither Army nor Marine Corps could have come to South Korea's rescue without an ocean highway and naval transport; that our troops could not have been landed without the Navy's amphibians; that these same troops, once ashore, could have been neither protected nor supported without the tactical support of the Naval Air Arm with its carriers standing off-shore as it had previously promised, to deliver the bullets and bombs when they were needed, where they were needed; that the Navy's seagoing artillery, its destroyers, cruisers and battleship were conveniently maneuvered off-shore to turn the enemy's flank, disrupt his behind-the-lines communications destroy his tanks and artillery and diminish his will to resist. The Navy was able to do these things with a minimum force and with practically no casualties.

Another lesson of equal importance has come from the North Koreans themselves. On a battleground of smaller scale, but significantly similar to Europe's western peninsula, the Red troops were able to march 200 miles against overwhelming odds to within an unpleasant range of our last outpost, Pusan, before being stopped.

Against them were an angry populace conducting vicious guerilla warfare against them was geography; rugged mountains, many rivers, narrow rough roads funneling through points vulnerable to both air and sea attack. Against them were countless strategic bombers hitting at their supplies and industrial potential, tactical planes, although proportionately fewer in number, effectively spreading napalm, shooting rockets and bullets, all with deadly accuracy. Besides all this, they were confronted with the omnipresent and omnipotent military problem of maintaining, with each day of advance, a longer and more tortuous line of communications. They had to support a large body of troops in a large area far from their source of supply. They had to bring up tanks and artillery to oppose our heavy supporting forces. They had virtually no sea force, no air force, little anti-aircraft protection, and still they came.

They brought up tanks, trucks, field pieces, plus the necessary food, clothing and ammunition for thirteen full divisions against a completely superior air force only a short haul from its home base in Japan.

Although it is regrettable that some of our own strategists had to learn the hard way that an army can advance against an overwhelmingly superior Air Force, it is even more regrettable that the Soviet leaders learned in advance the easy way. They were able to learn without sacrifice and at our expense, a valuable lesson in the projection of military power.

There has been sufficient evidence in the Far Eastern Theater of Operations to convince many, but not nearly all military strategists that a balanced, flexible, mobile Navy is a must in any global conflict. Men like Army Generals Hickey and Wright, Air Force Generals Weyland and Craigie are exceptionally well-qualified to conduct joint planning and operations. They are intelligent, sincere, cooperative and self reliant. Men of their calibre do not feel that they, and they alone, have the capability for conducting every military operation whether it be air, ground or naval. They are not grasping for power nor trying to build an empire.

As an example of the opposite, as much as I regret it, the Japan Logistics command self-righteously feels it should run the Navy's ships. The Transportation Corps, short on experience but long on ambition, tries to mother MSTS and other elements of the Navy. Occasionally an Army Ground commander shanghais an LST and tries to his everlasting sorrow to conduct an amphibious operation. His mistakes, usually elemental, were made by the Navy years ago. He may forget to check the weather, the tide, the charts or one of a hundred bits of information essential to an amphibious commander before shoving off. A considerable loss of life has resulted recently in the Far East from those zealous, if not blundering, attempts to travel the ocean highway without proper experience and training.

Slowly the senior Army and Air Force officers in this theater are realising there is more to naval power than is apparent to the casual yachtsman, that the sea is a hard mistress to be treated with diffidence and respect. These officers seem to fear the sea, want no part of it, and yet, deep down in their hearts, they think they would like to command seaborne operations.

We cannot hope for an overnight awakening. The principal of centralized control, issuing orders to the field commanders with no prior consultation, is almost sacred. Since the General Staff delegates no authority to its own organization, it cannot easily accustom itself to delegating authority to a subordinate naval command.

All naval officers must constantly be on the alert to demonstrate their competency and ability to control the sea. This attitude in the Navy, plus a few more inevitable mistakes by those not qualified and the sea will be given back to the Navy. After all, there might never have been a Navy Department if James McHenry, our First Secretary of War, hadn't used green timber in his ship construction program.

To maintain our present skills, naval officers must anticipate and actively seek a vigorous seagoing life. The service has no room for a man searching for a lush life in a soft billet. But, on the other hand, it has ample space for the individual seeking intellectual growth and attainment.

Knowledge of the sea must be carefully nurtured, and conscientiously checked periodically to see that its growth is not stunted, that it is in step with a man's age and capability, that it is supplemented by military habits which seniors will admire and subordinates follow.

The Navy's fine tradition developed over the years by courageous leaders searching and experiencing the scientific truths must neither be allowed to languish nor tarnish. It must be at least maintained and, if possible, improved.

The shocking admission which follows is most embarrassing, but one which can better be faced with embarrassment now than tragedy later.

It is an inescapable fact that some naval officers are looking for the easy way. They are leaning on their colleagues to do their thinking and their work, content to live in the past and enjoy the present.

This trend, although not yet serious, if allowed to continue could become an epidemic, making us all weak in character and selfish in spirits. This mental lethargy must be checked in its early stages, for God help us if we should come down with it.

Although the Navy was mentioned first, this same disease has hit the Army and the Air Force as well, and, I fear, perhaps with greater impact.

It is a fact that, against a strong, virile aggressive opponent, our Army ground units were unable to advance while our Marine Corps, against the same kind of opposition, forced the enemy to take to his heels in full retreat.

The explanation cannot be traced to heredity or civilian training and background for both forces come from the same cities, many times from the same families.

What then brings the big change for these young Americans in such a short period of time? The answer must be found in their indoctrination and training, training from the bottom up as well as from the top down, facing the issue squarely that combat forces must be trained for combat, that strat gists are helpless without winning tacticians.

Distressing as it is, we must admit that many of our ground troops were inadequately trained or equipped for combat.

A combatant force must be just that, confident, willing, fearless and effective.

Training from the bottom up is fundamental to success. Close air support, an issue that will be batted around ad infinitum, is a good example of what I mean. The Marine concept of close air support begins with the leatherneck carrying the rifle. What can the airplane do to facilitate his swift movement against the enemy? Who knows best what he needs to advance? Who knows best when he needs it? The leatherneck on the ground, of course.

The Marine Corps places a control unit near this leatherneck on the ground, sometimes on company level so the ideas from the man on the ground can be instantly relayed to the pilot overhead; so the pilot, in turn, can reciprocate immediately before the target has disappeared or his colleagues on the ground have been killed. This system builds confidence and teamwork.

Can you imagine the effectiveness of a football team if the blockers depended on the coach for downfield blocking instructions after the ball is snapped? Yet, this system is used by the Army and Air Force. The front line control unit is told by the troops of a nearby target. This control unit relays the request for air support to a rear echelon, who supplies the plane which attacks the targets. Meanwhile the target may have advanced, retreated, or have been bypassed. This difference of operational control may seem technical and inconsequential to the staff in rear echelon, but it's most important to the man on the firing line.

The Navy's and Marine Corps' superior air support reflect no discredit on young Air Force pilots who are equally as valiant and willing. It does reflect unfavorably on the doctrine of centralized control, for it is apparent that the system works from the top down. The end results eventually deprive the front line troops of on-the-spot tactical control. The weakness of this system magnifies when these same front line infantrymen have no voice in the development of suitable aircraft and armament.

When the responsibility of troop support and protection are given to a comparatively young and still growing organization, whose avowed primary mission is strategic air warfare, it's only logical that tactical aircraft, which is of secondary importance anyway, will not be given the careful consideration from the man whose success may hinge on it.

Air strikes behind the enemy's lines are important, but close air support is invaluable.

If close tactical support is not precise, it can do more harm than good. It is sure to destroy the confidence of the troops if it doesn't destroy the troops themselves.

If we have learned nothing else from Korea, we know now that pouring all our resources into one type of warfare is unsound, whether the single type be inter-continental bombing or amphibious warfare.

We were fairly well prepared for strategic air warfare, but when a little bit of a country decided to fight another type of war, they not only scared us to death, but literally kicked the hell out of us. Sure, this little country was furnished materials by China and Russia, but it supplied its own Troops.

An old cliche becomes increasingly appropriate - We need a balanced force.

If any unbalance is to be maintained, it should be in the direction of the most probable type of warfare, rather than the one we would like the enemy to pursue.

The present war has been more primitive in many respects than World War I. It was the type of war the enemy chose to fight. We must surely know, by now, our civilian population as well as our military leaders, that the aggressor chooses the time, the place, and the type of war. Unless we abandon our ideals, and we too, become an aggressor, we shall necessarily be forced to counter the enemy's attack.

Proper intelligence can warn us in advance and it had better do so. For Russia is a big country with tremendous industrial and manpower resource Supporting her also is the incalculable Army of Communist China. We cannot match Russia man for man on the battlefield. To compensate, we must concentrate on lethal tactical weapons combined with an unprecedented psychologica warfare. We can, if we try hard enough, convince the Russians that their life would be better if they overthrew the present regime.

One point we must remember, Asiatics do not subdue easily. Japan prove that; Korea has demonstrated it again. The fear of death will not, in itsel force an Asiatic country to surrender. It is no different from America in that respect.

One of the things that caused some difficulty (but not nearly as much a if the enemy had had all types of weapons) was identification. This is the bugaboo of every war and sometimes in this one. Somehow, there must be developed a method of distinguishing friend from foe. This is important as between aircraft. Modern high-speed aircraft have relative speeds so high that visual identification can no longer be relied upon to provide time for the decision to identify and pull the trigger. The identification of aircraft by ships and ground forces is equally important. If we go to war with an enemy who has a large number of planes flying around too, we are going to shoot at a lot of our aircraft. Many of our own aircraft will be shot down by enemy aircraft which our lads thought were friendly. The same sort of identification problem arises between the ground forces and the air. This has resulted, at times, in killing our own troops. Aircraft have difficulty in identifying our ships and sometimes have attacked our ships. Positive identification must be provided somehow. Even though nobody is killed, as a result of lack of identification, there has been much delay and wasted effort caused by not being able to identify friends. Our fleet unloading at Inchon frequently knocked off unloading and prepared for combat upon the appearance of planes which later turned out to be friendly. Time is one commodity over which we have no control, and wasted time, in war, is usually serious.

Perhaps one of the greatest and most striking aspects of this war is the elephantine logistic effort required to supply our forces. It is striki because the ROK forces, against the same type of enemy, supply themselves much easier and with much less equipment than do we. Long truck columns, wh no attention to the sign on each truck "keep 25 foot distance," are impressi but they are expensive. They are expensive in money, of course, but they ar more expensive because they require men who should be in the front line troo It takes equipment and lots of men to supply our small combat force. It would be interesting to compute the number of men on the combat line compare to the number of men required for support. Any analysis comparing only service troops vs. combat troops won't tell the whole story. Integrated within the combat divisions themselves, there are large numbers of people who are, in effect, service troops. If we fight a big war, there is not going to be enough equipment nor enough men even to supply the luxurious logistic support with which we have now been blessed.

One of the big decifiencies in our Army, and perhaps in the Marine Corps too, to a lesser extent, is the small number of riflemen in a divison. One of the reasons for incorporating ROK troops in our divisions was to obtain an adequate number of riflemen. There are other advantages, in addition to this one, such as training of ROK troops and the combat ability of the ROKs. There should be a complete and thorough analysis of all our armed forces, including the Navy, to make certain that we put the maximum number of people in combat, adequately supported, but not too generously supported.

In connection with this logistic support, the contention of the Navy has been demonstrated again. Most of the logistic support had to come by sea with just a trickle by air. That trickle was noisy and important and well-published, but, after all, it was only a very small part of the total support. The support by sea was furnished with peacetime regularity and with just about peacetime hazards. Had we found it necessary to protect our sea lanes against an enemy with any kind of a Navy, especially against submarines and sir, the logistic support of our forces might have become most critical. For example, even under those ideal conditions, the supply of aviation gasoline to the place where it was needed was, at times, a most serious limiting factor. We didn't quite run out, but we came very close to it at times. A few ships sunk would have caused delay, and the Air Force would have had planes grounded for lack of fuel. The Air Force air lifts were wonderful. They fill in a gap that had to be filled. The Air Force Cargo Command has done a remarkable job. But, as forcibly as anybody knows how to present it, there should be brought out that air transport is one of the most expensive methods of transportation there is, and it is limited in its capacity. It is limited by the air fields we must use, if nothing else. Air transport will always be necessary, but a good deal of the stuff that was carried by air during this war had to be carried by air because of the improper planning.

That brings up another subject. This subject of planning. It is amazing to see the difference between this war and the last one. Our plans in the last war were sometimes hurriedly conceived, but they were thorough. It was not necessary to continuously change plans as conditions changed, for all possible variables were considred in drawing up the plans, and all alternatives were discussed in the plans. As a result, frequent changes of plans were not necessary. Or, if they were, they were changed in a preconceived orderly manner.

There are a good many reasons for the difference between this war and the last one insofar as planning is concerned. In the last war, the Navy operated with its own plans, at least in the Pacific. They understood such things as radio silence. They realized that amphibious operations require ships to start moving many days before D day. They understood that plans had to be complete before the first ship commenced to land. They knew that the reason for this was the precise time and coordination necessary on D day and subsequent days. This timing could effected only if plans were prepared well in advance and if plans were complete.

In this war, the Navy has been, in effect, under Army command. The Army Staff has had an unusually fine group of people, but they are used to handling Armies. They have a tendency, which was natural enough, to handle the Navy the same way. They shove their own battalions around each morning. They evaluate the situation each day and they change their plans to fit the most recent evaluation. They have difficulty in understanding that such things cannot be done in any Navy. As a result, there had to be continual representation, all on a very friendly basis, to convince an Army Staff that naval warfare is different from land warfare. This might have turned out to have been extremely serious had naval forces been directly under the control of an Army Staff. As it turned out, in this war, it was exasperati but, because of the calibre of the Army officers, it did not reach serious proportions. There is an old proverb, which you underlined, that applies to this situation. Ben Franklin said "Let everyone ascertain his special business calling and then stick to it, if he would be successful."

If the Navy wishes to survive, it must beware of the kindly efforts of our friendly sister services to force us to operate in the manner which is efficient for an Army but would be deadly for a Navy. This is quite difficult when you are dealing with courteous Army officers who desire nava support so very much and yet, do not understand that they can obtain better naval support by telling the Navy what they need and letting an able Navy do it. Even this much gets dangerous at times, for there has been a tendency for Army commanders to treat the fleet as the water-borne corps of the Army. They slop over and tell us how to do our business frequently. They do the same things among themselves, so it isn't that they are treatin the Navy any differently than they would treat their own organizations.

I can attest to one very good lesson myself. I flew all over North Korea in a reconnaissance B-29, which took off from Johnson Air Force Base near Tokyo. It was a 15-hour flight. We had to fly, and fly, and fly, before we arrived over North Korea. Then we had a long trip back to our base after leaving North Korea. When you sit in the bombadier's seat for 15 hours, you have an aching realization of the Desirability of bases close to your combat area. The Air Force has really done a superb job in trying to give air support to the Army. They were not equipped for this. They were not psychologically prepared for it, but they have done their best to accomplish it. One of the biggest difficulties in their way was the need to fly long distances before they could be effective. A study of the relative amount of time spent over the target by naval aircraft and by Air Force aircraft should reveal some startling statistics. This statistic would not be in existence if they always operated from bases near the enemy This question also ties up with logistics. There is a large amount of gasoline burned because of the distance of our bases from the combat area. The Air Force planes, because of this need for range, had also to sacrifice weight of armament. Even when they were over the target, they did not have available the guns, the bombs, or the rockets which they could have had had their base been close to the enemy. The Air Force realizes this now and I expect they will try to correct it. It's a lesson that the Navy should neve permit itself to forget.

Carriers did provide bases comparatively close to the enemy lines and they could move these bases to fight the enemy lines. This was because Korea is a peninsula and the same favorable conditions will not apply in many areas of possible warfare. Nevertheless, Navy planes operating from carriers close by the operating areas were able to support their brothers on the ground with more effective ammunition loads than did the hardworking Air Force. Even in the design of aircraft, the Air Force planes were designed to carry loads over a long distance and so, weight for weight, Navy aircraft types were able to carry much heavier loads, depending on carrier mobility to keep their bases close to the target.

Another statistic, which is interesting, is the number of sorties per plane per day which is also a factor of distance of bases from their operating areas.

This base story can be applied equally well to the surface Navy too. Naval Operating Bases are expensive to maintain, but they are less expensive in the Far East than they are in the political atmosphere of the harbor cities of our own country. Even if this were not true, it's important to keep bases near a possible area of war. I hope that we shall be able to retain Yokosuka as a full-fledged operating base, capable of supporting a fleet. It could be operated in a reduced status or even a very reduced status, if necessary. A war in the Far East would prove its value. That little sideline is an important lesson, and it isn't the least one.

When this war started, the Navy had no intelligence organization here. It depended upon getting it intelligence from G-3 of the Army. G-3, along with all the other intelligence organizations made an improper evaluation of the situation before the war. Maybe this is too broad a statement, maybe I am including too many intelligence organizations in it, but I don't think so. The point is there was only one intelligence organization here and that intelligence organization did make an improper evaluation. If the lack of duplication ever showed an ugly side to it, that was the incident. Had we had our own intelligence organization, it's possible that our evaluation would have been different. It might even have been correct and we might have been a little better prepared. When we have only one viewpoint, we have harmony and tranquility, but we also have the danger of a single viewpoint. The biggest danger is that the viewpoint will be wrong. There is a surprising tendency within the Army and, in the Air Force to try to give the boss the answer his subordinates think he wants. As you know, Navy subordinates are apt to present a different viewpoint from their boss just to show they are thinking for themselves. The Navy habit requires the boss just to settle many arguments, although he is usually acquainted with more than one aspect of the problem.

Intelligence is evaluated by fitting together many fragments of conflicting information. These fragments sometimes form a pattern. The trick is to know which fragments to use and which to discard. Most any preconceived pattern can be supported if only selected bits of information are used.

Unconsciously and unknowingly, the head man will give an off-hand opinion based upon unevaluated data. This pattern then becomes the form into which the fragments, which will fit, are placed, and all other fragments are thrown to one side. The mosaic presented is one possible picture and is the one on which reliance is placed. The other possible pictures are not presented. The pattern brought out is frequently correct because the off-hand opinion of an experienced man is pretty good. Nevertheless, it is not always correct and when other possible solutions are not brought out, there may be a rather fullgrown fiasco as a result.

Elimination of duplication is good at times but when ideas or possibilities are eliminated under that guise, trouble is ahead. It is most desirable that different viewpoints, on intelligence matters especially, be laid out so that the top people can have the benefit of all the possibilities and act accordingly. The Navy or the nation should not again place complete reliance upon any single intelligence evaluation. It is one field in which much checking may provide better answers.

Perhaps another interesting lesson is the variation among services in the handling of men. Many surprising things happen and one of them is the seemingly callous attitude of complacency as long as the replacements equal or better the casualties. One of the reasons for high morale in the Navy and Marines is the old Navy requirement that men shall be considered as individuals, not numbers only. It is a good characteristic for a Service to have, may we always keep it.

Tied up with this is the necessary provision for handling casualties. Planning must always be done early to take this factor into account. C.G. Army 9 made accurate predictions on his casualty rates, but hospital facilities were woefully inadequate. It has been known for generations that the chances of recovery for a wounded man are in inverse ration to the time required to get him to proper medical facilities (not just first aid). The morale of the Navy and Marines is influenced by the careful provisions made by the Navy to handle its wounded promptly. The Army has a more difficult problem. Nevertheless, the Army has been thankful for the Navy planning and execution of these plans for hospitals and assistance ashore, to say nothing about the magnificent work of the hospital ships, to which were assigned the most critical cases (on our request). The Army has been grateful to the Navy for its support (less perhaps the Transportation Corps who would like to take over the Hospital Ships).

There were many minor lessons available for learning too. They are details - but some of them may turn out to be the mail, the loss of which makes a grand epitaph.

One such thing is the Navy's inability to supply trained teams for jobs which are bound to come up in war. We are-or will-start to prepare a manual similar to a "Gub" Manual for staffs, so that a Commander who is faced with a rapid expansion problem can say "Send me Staff 7X with two additional M-3 Units" and get people, equipment, etc, in one package, or, at least, the people back home would know what he wanted. We may be able to get a rough draft of a "Sears-Roebuck Staff Catalog" after this thing is over. The catalog, however, is only part of the solution. The other part is to provide small nucleus teams who do some training and know what is needed. Warm bodies are not enough. Warm, intelligent bodies are not enough either. Warm, intelligent, trained bodies are required. Small intelligence teams, small operational, planning, PIO, maintenance, logistics, personnel and all other activities which you can think of would help. They could work in Navy Department or in some more pleasant spot, at normal tasks related to their team work during those short periods of no combat. When combat came along, they could put on their fire suits and come help put out the fire without the hurly-burly of confused frantic cries of exasperation and impotence while new people learn a complicated job. Of course, this idea could be carried to extremes.

Teams of evaluators, technical specialists, do-gooders, USO shows, MACTUs, sightseers, shoppers, and maybe even special combat units could be well utilized too. There are quite a few now. An examination might reveal that more could be profitable. The trained teams always do good work. Sometimes enthusiastic, well-meaning individuals require more effort to support them than they can accomplish.

Communications, the ever present naval problem child, since the days of the galleys, is still with us. Our increase in communication facilities does not keep us with demands placed upon them. The increase required for Joint actions is colossal - and I mean - it's a right big increase. The other two services, with their point-by-point communication systems, and no necessity for coding and decoding, write long pages of OP Orders, summaries and the like. Some of the data contained in them are necessary for the Navy. Any attempt to place them all on the communications system would cause the system to collapse at once. Yet, our own Commanders need some of the data, so we brief it. Such things as bomb lines, target data, other combat actions are all interesting to our fleet commanders. If they don't get it, they ask for it. More than this I d though, is the two-way communication necessary because of the coordination which is essential. When the very considerable load of prospective changes in plans and suggestions to assist the other services is added to this, the volume of traffic is startling. When operating with other forces, especially under the general command of another service, naval communication load is increased, possibly as much as twice the normal wartime load, to get matters settled. Should the fleets have to maintain radio silence under such conditions, there would be a lot of consternation among the other services. A partial answer to this perplexing problem is education of ourselves and the other services. That's a slow process in which we are now engaged. More research on communications is necessary though. The problem must be attacked from both sides at once, i.e., to cut down the amount of traffic necessary and to increase our capability for handling more traffic.

There are other major lessons, such as; the value of ship gunfire support; the effectiveness of naval carrier task forces; the technical aspects of new weapons, such as bazookas the need for early Evaluation of combat Actions and, the necessity for a Navy to conduct amphibious operations (others lose the ships).

Cautions: Be most careful about drawing too positive conclusions from this war. Lessons must be carefully evaluated against the background of this type of warfare. The enemy had a very small navy and air force. Many variables of warfare were not present. This may have been done purposely by the enemy to permit a careful testing of their theories of the use of one variable, i.e., the Army, under controlled conditions. This could have been an experimental war, like Spain, and if so, Russia was conducting the experiment, while we, as laboratory assistant, contributed, and, if we are wise, will learn just as much.

Air had a field day. No air opposition, poor enemy anti-aircraft, and poor radar. If we draw too firm conclusions, based on these conditions, the boys may have very unpleasant surprises when heavy opposition comes along.

The same thing applies to naval operations. Our amphibious landings were well conducted, but the INCHON landing was hazardous to the point where any one of several enemy possible courses of action might have meant disaster. I'll take those points up in the order of their probability.

a. The enemy could have concealed their artillery until the landing was underway, and have a good chance of sinking transports and enfilading our boat waves. Fortunately, they had had no experience in repelling amphibious assaults. Maybe they have gained experience now.

b. There was a delay in mining the approaches, which would have caused trouble, lots of trouble. The Russians know that now too.

c. Air and submarine attacks were absent.

d. The beach line was not heavily defended, which is different from the proper use of the defenses they did have available.

Many Army officers now believe amphibious assaults can be accomplished easily. They do not recognize the detailed planning, the careful training and the many factors which must be considered to effect a successful landing against heavy skillful opposition. Consequently, I foresee that the newly made converts will be too loud in their praise and have too much faith in our ability to produce success under all conditions. There will be a tendency to treat an amphibious assault as a simple water lift, and, if it isn't quite that simple, the Navy will be able to overcome all obstacles as it has in the past. There is, at the present time, more adequate knowledge of what a Navy can do when there is no Navy to fight, just like there is more knowledge of what aircraft can do when there are no aircraft to fight. But, naval officers, themselves, may mislead themselves. Bombardment against enemy strongholds, who have passive defense of mines, is a different sort of a game than trying it against air and naval opposition. We know that, but instincts of people result from experience, and our instinct must be well conditioned. I don't mean to imply we should be super cautious (we've had enough of that), but we should be careful to consider the many factors which effect naval warfare and not overbalance the scales with our most recent experience.

The Air Force has a point along the same lines too, although, I believe (many in the Air Force do not), that the effectiveness of strategic bombing on an enemy's capacity to conduct war has been grossly oversold. It does have an affect, but the effect is not immediate; it is not total; it is not the answer by itself; but, it is expensive.

This letter is long enough.

Regards,

Arleigh Burke
RADM, USN

Captain Alexander McDill, U. S. Navy
Office of the Secretary
Department of the Navy
The Pentagon
Washington, 25, D.C.

Index to

Series of Taped Interviews

with

Admiral Arleigh Burke, USN (Ret.)

Volume II (Special Series)

ADVISORY BOARDS: Burke comments on merits of such board, p. 13 ff;

AFGHANISTAN AND IRAN: Burke's concern (1952) that these countries might become hot spots, p. 171-2;

ALLAH: Burke's story of his friend, Paul Guthrie, and the Iranian truck driver, p. 262-4;

ANDERSON, Admiral George: p. 317-8;

ATOMIC WEAPONS - use of: p. 135; p. 142;

BELGIAN NAVY: p. 265-6;

BERGEN, Jack: p. 332-3;

BLACK SEA: p. 151; p. 258-9;

BLANDY, Admiral William H.: order to become CincLant after death of Adm. Mitscher, p. 5; p. 7; p. 25; p. 42;

BROOKINGS INSTITUTE: Burke joins the Institute for study of governmental policy and strategy, p. 54; p. 56;

BUCHANAN, RADM Charles A.: p. 72; p. 93;

BURKE, Admiral Arleigh: ordered to General Board (March 1947 - July 1948) 1 ff; back injury in the Caribbean, p. 6-9; advised by Smedberg immediately after leaving General Board (July 1, 1948) that he should get out of the country at once,--the saga of his departure to join his cruiser in the Mediterranean, p. 86 ff; his interest in Estate Management because of predicament of Mrs. Mitscher after the Admiral's death - Burke writes pamphlet on estate management, p. 57-8; gets Adm. Parsons to talk to General Board about nuclear energy - out of that came data Burke used later with development of POLARIS, p. 59; Burke's comments on the hundreds of studies made in government - and general lack of implementation, p. 73-5;
his story of Randy Lewisohn who worked with him at outset of WW II in coverting certain plants to war production - Lewishon's proposal that Burke go into partnership with him in post war era, p. 184-6; Burke's arguments with President Eisenhower over Eisenhower's contention that JCS should arrive at a single opinion on an issue and then present it to him, p. 245-7; Burke's farm in Virginia and the

Japanese house, p. 307-14; Burke attends conference at MIT (Lincoln Lab) on fixed air defenses in the U. S., p. 316; interest of Op. 30 in foreign bases, p. 335-6; Dennison comes in as relief for Burke and Burke detached on March 19, 1954, p. 341;

CARNEY, Admiral Robert B.: p. 139; had command of U. S. Naval Forces in Eastern Atlantic and the Mediterranean - then appointed CincSouth, p. 250-1;

CHICOMS (Chinese Communists); see entries under Op. 30; also - their use of air power, p. 132; p. 156-7; p. 170;

CINC EUR: (Cinc US Forces Central Europe) set up with responsibility for supply lines - close cooperation with Sac Eur, p. 249; p. 257;

CINC NELM: a U. S. Command - to support NATO - but actually to command U. S. Naval Forces in Europe, p. 250; main problem under Adm. Wright was its relationship with Sac Eur, Cinc South, p. 254; takes over Middle East Command, p. 256; attempt to get several ships in the Black Sea, p. 258-9;

CINC SOUTH: p. 138; p. 144; p. 249-50;

COLE, The Hon. Sterling: Member of Congress from New York state - his efforts with Secretary Forrestal on the right of naval officers to express their opinions before the Congress, p. 23 ff; Burke has correspondence with Cole over the disagreement between Cole and Forrestal, p. 28 ff;

CYPRUS: p. 141

DENNISON, Admiral Robert L.: p. 241; relief for Burke in Op.30, p. 341;

DOMINICAN REPUBLIC: p. 135;

ECUADOR: Burke helps to establish the Naval Academy in Ecuador - his Ecuadorian godson, p. 291-3;

EISENHOWER, The Hon. Dwight David: p. 61; p. 133; p. 241; his feeling that the Joint Chiefs should settle their differences and make a single recommendation to him as President, p. 245;

ERITREA: p. 136;

FAST CARRIERS: p. 142;

FECHTELER, Admiral Wm. Morrow: Burke reports to him upon his return from Korea, p. 115; asks JCS to hear Burke on Korea, p. 116; approves of Burke doing a series of TV appearances on Korea - later the series is cancelled, p. 119-20; p. 174; p. 212; Burke accompanies him to London for coronation of Queen Elizabeth II, p. 279 ff;

FORMOSA (Taiwan) - Defense of: study in Op.30, p. 141;

FORRESTAL, The Hon. James: Secretary of the Navy - his correspondence with Sterling Cole on right of naval officers to express opinions before Congressional Committees, p. 24 ff; p. 27; Burke stimulates interest in Forrestal for the General Board study, p. 30; Secretary impressed with Burke study on the Middle East - takes it to the President, p. 72-3; p. 93-4;

GALLERY, RADM DAniel V.: his opinion on over centralization in the military, p. 209; on fixed installations - air defense, p. 316-7;

GATCH, VADM Thomas L.: Acting CincLant during last illness of Adm. Mitscher, p. 4;

GENERAL BOARD: Burke's tour of duty (March 1947-July 1948), p. 1 ff; Board is assigned a survey of the shore establishment, p. 10 ff; lack of status for the General Board after WW II, p. 14; members of Board realized this was a sensitive issue - shore establishments - because of possible loss of jobs, p. 17 ff; Burke finds Establishment study impossible without some idea of a policy for government; what are the goals, etc. p. 20-2; reaching out to other departments p. 29 ff; study on morale and efficiency, p. 42-45; BuShips, p. 46-7; merchant ships and increased speed, p. 47 ff; problems with merchant marine unions in WW II, p. 53; Burke's interest in overall governmental policy and strategy, p. 54 ff; Panama Canal study, p. 55-6; Burke asks that General Board be briefed by Adm. Parsons on atomic energy and the navy, p. 58-9; Burke asks that General Board be briefed on the United Nations, p. 59-60; Burke's interest - stockpiling of strategic materials, energy, etc. p. 62-3; also p. 76-83; WAVE uniforms, p. 63-4; Burke's interest in the naval academy and motivation of midshipmen, p. 64-7;

Burke given job of coordinating and writing paper on U. S. National Security in Ten Years ahead, p. 70 ff; a component part of the paper - one on the Middle East, p. 71-2; results - in the National Security Council, p. 73;

GERMAN NAVY: p. 255; p. 273-4;

GOVERNMENT STUDIES: Burke's comments on the hundreds of special studies inaugurated by government bureaus - and the general lack of implementation of the results, p. 73-5;

GREECE - TURKEY: and NATO, p. 133;

GREEK NAVY: p. 148;

GRIFFIN, Admiral C. D.: p. 96-7;

GUZOWSKI, Chief Yeoman George: Burke's story of the Chief's tour of duty with Burke at Munsan-ni in Korea, p. 187-9;

HALSEY, Flt. Admiral Wm. F. Jr.: his comments on the LIFE Magazine article called BULL'S RUN, p. 61-2;

HART, Admiral Thomas C.: p. 305-6;

HODES, General Henry Irving (Hank): army counterpart of Burke on the negotiating team in Korea, p. 100-1; p. 103; p. 189;

HONG KONG: possible evacuation of, p. 149-50;

USS HUNTINGTON: Burke takes command in Mediterranean after duty on the General Board, p. 87 ff; p. 282; p. 300-1;

INDO-CHINA: p. 149; p. 156-7;

INDONESIA: p. 148;

ISRAEL: a unifying factor for the Arab world, p. 261-2;

ITALIAN NAVY: p. 142;

JAPANESE NAVY: p. 267 ff;

J. C. S.: p. 124-5; p. 130-2; responsibilities in connection with covert operations and guerrilla warfare, p. 133; duties of Op.30 for JCS, p. 243-4;

JOY, Admiral Charles Turner: p. 109-111;

KOREAN ARMISTICE: Burke serves on the Armistice delegation - Munsan-Ni is headquarters - p. 95 ff; Burke on the necessity to use power in negotiating with the communists, p. 97; Adm. Hill asks him to write an article on Korea for Proceedings, p. 100; one of the most important negotiating points - where is the line to be that separates the two forces, p. 101-2; an illustration, p. 102-3; Gen. Hodes and Burke learn about the communist tricks, p. 104-8; JCS orders negotiators to accept present battle line as final line of demarcation, p. 109 ff; Burke, back in Washington - talks to JCS, CNO and President Truman, p. 114 ff;
Burke's speaking tour is de-railed, p. 120-22; p. 173-5; the paper Burke wrote for Adm. Fechteler on what we should do in Korea, p. 173-8; the story of Chief Yeoman George Guzowski at Munsan-ni, p. 187-9; use of methods of psychological warfare, p. 259-60; Burke's review of the Army's book - KOREA, 1950, p. 297-8; the use made of Colonel Drysdale and his Royal Marines, a commando unit, p. 319-20; p. 324; see appendix for Burke paper on Korea - also pages 173-4;

LATIN AMERICA: p. 147;

LAURITSON, Dr. Charles: physicist, p. 316-7;

LEBANON: JCS plan for Lebanon, p. 247;

LEWISOHN, Randy: the story of his work with Burke at outset of WWII in converting plants to war production - his postwar attempt to get Burke to go into partnership with him, p. 184-6;

LOVESTONE, Jay: present at the Brookings Institute foreign policy seminar in Dartmouth (1949), p. 277;

U. S. MARINES - in the Mediterranean: p. 133;

McMORRIS, VADM Charles H.: p. 10; p. 12; p. 14; p. 70;

McNAMARA, Robert S.: Secretary of Defense, p. 207-8;

MIDDLE EAST: feasibility of U. S. holding area - study in Op.30, p. 140; p. 147;

MINE WARFARE: p. 137-8;

MITSCHER, Admiral Marc: Towers asks Mitscher to release Burke for duty on the General Board, p. 3 ff;

NAFAC (Naval Academy Foreign Affairs Conference): Burke expresses opinion on policy of NAFAC, p. 67-9;

NATO; p. 137-8; NATO forces vs. U. S. Forces, p. 143-4; p. 163-4; NATO staffs were expanding in 1952-3 - need for additional naval officers to represent navy point of view, p. 215-18; NATO commands not very desirous of receiving naval personnel, p. 219-20; Op.30 much concerned by failure of top NATO people to use naval officers on their staffs, p. 221-2; geographic limits of NATO, p. 255-6;

NAVAL AVIATORS; Blandy asks General Board to investigate feelings of naval flyers who thought of switching to the Air Force, p. 25 ff;

U. S. NAVAL INSTITUTE: Burke's relations with Institute while on duty in Op.30, p. 295;

NAVY LINE OFFICERS - vs SPECIALISTS: p. 32-34; p. 36-38;

NAVY - MORALE AND EFFICIENCY: Admiral Blandy instigates a study by General Board on morale and efficiency in the navy, p. 42-45;

NAVY REGULATIONS: p. 38-40;

NOMURA, Admiral Kichisaburo: Japanes Admiral - friend of Burke - sees him off from Tokyo airport on departure from Korea, p. 114-5; p. 170; Burkes entertain Admiral's son, Tadashi, and his wife during Easter vacation (1952), p. 180 ff; Nomura writes for Naval Institute (1951-2), p. 267-8;

N. S. C. (National Security Council), p. 196-7;

OP 30 (Strategic Plans Division); p. 96; p. 98-99; Burke takes over office in Dec. 1951, p. 131 ff; mission of the office, p. 131; Burke lists a multitude of problems Op-30 was charged with studying, p. 132-151; the Monday morning sessions, p. 153-4; the personnel share Burke's thesis on the exercise of power, p. 159-160; p. 163; methods by which staff tackled problems, p. 161-168; thinking process in navy planning, p. 191-3; differences in Army and Navy planning, p. 203-5; attempt at safeguards with establishment of DOD, p. 204-5; illustration of centralized control in OKW of German army, p. 206; the Japanese war machine, p. 207-9; Dan Gallery on over-centralization in the military, p. 209; Op-30 begins to question master plans, p. 211-12; concern in Op-30 about failure of NATO staff to use naval personnel in planning, p. 221-2; Burke's comments on plans that are never realized, p. 225-6; Burke makes effort to find good men for NATO staffs, p. 227-32; necessity for security in personal correspondence on plans, p. 233-4;

Burke's system of correspondence - to let people know what was being considered and to take take steps for contingencies before plans were completed, p. 235-9; a major duty in Op-30 was handling JCS papers, p. 242-3; the efforts to build up foreign navies, p. 264 ff; Burke on outright gifts of ships, arms, etc., p. 266-7; the Belgian navy, p. 265-6; the Japanese navy, p. 267 ff; the ROK navy, p. 270 ff; the German navy, p. 273-4; comic relief in Op-30, p. 294; interest in studies on geography, p. 303-4; letters signed by Burke in Op-30 and as CNO, p. 314; the Order of the Purple, p. 315;

O'REGAN, VADM Wm. Vincent (Micky): Burke relieves his classmate as head of Op-30 - Strategic Plans Division, p. 96; p. 98-99; p. 152;

PANMUNJOM: place of negotiations with the North Koreans, p. 102;

PARSONS, RADM W. S. (Deke): Burke has him invited to General Board to talk about atomic energy and the navy, p. 58;

PETROLEUM: Burke's interest in subject - and report on petroleum and mineral resources, p. 62-3; p. 76-83;

USS POCONO: flagship of CincLant, p. 4-7;

POLOARIS: p. 59;

PORT LYAUTEY: Burke's flight to Lyautey, p. 90-3;

POTTER, Professor E. B.: p. 202-3;

PROPAGANDA - use of: p. 145-6;

QUEEN ELIZABETH II: Burke accompanies Admiral Fechteler (CNO) to her coronation, p. 279 ff;

RIDGWAY, General Matthew: p. 109-110; p. 118; p. 247; p. 279;

RILEY, VADM Herbert D.: p. 190;

ROK NAVY: p. 270 ff; Burke's visit to their naval academy at Chinhoe, p. 271-2;

ROOSEVELT, President F. D.: example of administrative skill, p. 168-9;

RUGE, Admiral R. (German Navy): Burke works through him in trying to help the German Navy rebuild, p. 273-4; the commissioning of the DD CHARLES AUSBORNE, p. 275-6;

SAC EUR: p. 134-5; p. 144; p. 215; p. 223; Vosseller with SacEur, p. 247-8; Eisenhower as SacEur, p. 247-9; CincSouth - the southern component commander of SacEur, p. 250;

SALT II: Burke on the proposed treaty, p. 124 ff;

SANTILLAN, Senora Maria Ema de Aignasse: Burke's story of her hospitality in Buenos Aires and the resultant visit to Washington, p. 282 ff;

SMEDBERG, VADM Wm. R. III: aide to Secretary Forrestal - warned Burke of impending assignment - tells him to join his cruiser in the Mediterranean without delay, p. 86 ff; what was the crisis? p. 93-4;

SPAIN - Military bases: p. 148;

U. S. STATE DEPARTMENT: p. 122; Burke on the policy of State to shun use of power, p. 122-4;

SUEZ: p. 146;

TAYLOR MODEL BASIN: p. 41-2;

TOWERS, Admiral John: p. 3; p. 12-14; p. 58-59; p. 61; p. 70;

TOWNER, VADM George Crosby: he maintained that Israel was the one country that held the Arabs together, p. 261-2;

TRUMAN, The Hon. Harry S.:   p. 72-3; p. 80; Burke's session with the President on subject of Korean negotiations, p. 116 ff; p. 121; p. 173; p. 176; p. 241;

UNIFICATION: p. 27;

UNIFIED COMMANDER: question of how much control, p. 150;

VIETNAM WAR: p. 128-9; p. 208;

VOSSELLER, VADM Aurelius B. (Abe.) on staff of SacEur, p. 223-4; Burke's method of corresponding with him on SacEur staff, p. 235; p. 251; p. 253; p. 279;

www.ingramcontent.com/pod-product-compliance
Lightning Source LLC
Chambersburg PA
CBHW081521220426
43209CB00102B/1479